THE FAITH IN THE LAST DAYS

To Bro. Jim & Sis Julie

From Bro Clive

Suggest you might
like to start at section 4
The Tree Of Life

With love in the LORD

10/11 Coctober 2015

THE FAITH

IN THE

LAST DAYS

A Selection from the Writings of
JOHN THOMAS, M.D.

With an Introduction on his life and work
by
JOHN CARTER

THE CHRISTADELPHIAN
404 SHAFTMOOR LANE
BIRMINGHAM B28 8SZ

First printed 1949

Reprinted 1965, 1982, 2005

ISBN 0 85189 028 8

Printed and bound in England by

THE CROMWELL PRESS
TROWBRIDGE
WILTSHIRE
BA14 0XB

2005

CONTENTS

INTRODUCTION

A SELECTION FROM THE WRITINGS
OF JOHN THOMAS, MD.

Originally published in *Herald of the Future Age* (1845-8) and *Herald of the Kingdom and Age to Come* (1851-61). Source dates and page numbers are given in *italics* below.

PREFACE

THE year 1848 was a landmark in European history. It was also an important year for thousands of people who have rejoiced in an understanding of God's Word. In that year Dr. Thomas visited England to lecture on the purpose of God revealed in the Scriptures, and to set forth the light that Bible prophecy shed on the events then current, events which disturbed and alarmed many people. Dr. Thomas's stay extended throughout the year 1849.

The Committee of the Christadelphian Publishing Office thought appropriate recognition of the centenary of this visit to Britain could be made by publishing a selection of the writings of Dr. Thomas which appeared in the magazines he edited. It was also decided to include a short introduction giving a brief outline of the life of Dr. Thomas, and of the revival of the witnessing to Gospel Truth, with an assessment of his work. The undersigned was commissioned to prepare the Introduction and select suitable articles. The order of the articles as printed is not the order in which they were written. Chapters 2, 3 and 4 belong to an early period. The writing of chapter 12, as explained in the Introduction, led Dr. Thomas to recognize that his immersion by Walter Scott was not the One Baptism of Scripture ; chapter 28 is the Declaration of what he had found to be Bible Truth after many years of earnest reading of the Scriptures.

May, 1949.   JOHN CARTER.

PART I

INTRODUCTION

INTRODUCTION

(1) THE TRUTH IN THE LAST DAYS

THE purpose of God at the present time is to take out of the Gentiles a people for His name (Acts 15 : 14). The separating process indicated by the " taking out " is achieved by the preaching of the gospel. " Go into all the world ", Jesus commanded the apostles before ascending into heaven, " and preach the gospel to every creature ; he that believeth and is baptized shall be saved ". Thus commissioned and empowered by the Holy Spirit which was poured upon them at Pentecost, the apostles preached Christ and salvation in his name among the Jews. The response was immediate, and the number of believers grew quickly. But persecution arose, testing the sincerity of those who believed, but also, by scattering them abroad, enlarging the spheres of their labours.

The preaching in the first generation was supported by a divine witness in the bestowal of Spirit gifts. These varied in form and consequently in purpose, but Paul taught that those gifts were most important which enabled the brethren who received them to build up the ecclesia by doctrine and exhortation. During this period the books of the New Testament were written and given to the ecclesias, so that when the spirit gifts were withdrawn the New Testament was completed, and with the Old Testament, formed the authoritative revelation of God's purpose.

The preaching of the apostles, though guided by the Spirit, nevertheless largely consisted of reasoning out of the scriptures. They appealed to the Old Testament for the evidence of God's purpose as summarized in the phrase " the gospel of the Kingdom of God and the name of Jesus Christ ". The New Testament was a complement to the Old Testament, and together they formed the source of any knowledge available of God's will. From the end of the first century the saving truth of God's purpose continued to be set forth by the diligent application of men and women to God's word written, and by their earnest contention for the faith once for all given to the saints.

If we had no information we might think that those who knew God's purpose revealed in His word would so value it that it would be preserved without corruption. But such a view ignores all the history of man's response to God's revelation. The Old Testament is a divine record of repeated human failure, and of degeneration. Again and again God made fresh beginnings—at the Flood, in the call of Abraham, and repeatedly in Israel's history—but always decline followed. We might therefore expect that history would repeat itself in the present dispensation. This expectation becomes a certainty when we look at the predictions of the apostles concerning the course of events after their death.

The apostles were urgent in pressing upon believers their duty to maintain sound doctrine. Warning was given of declension when fables would be substituted for truth, and when men would believe a lie. By a law of life this was inevitable ; men turn from truth, and the lie becomes a power that blinds them concerning its true nature. Paul puts it plainly : because they received not the love of the truth God would send them a strong delusion that they should believe a lie.

The context of this prophecy in the epistles to the Thessalonians is more particular than other references in setting forth the way the apostasy would develop. The day of Christ would not come until there had been a falling away, and " a man of sin " revealed who would claim divine honours. But this " man of sin " was hindered in his development in apostolic days and for some time afterwards. " He that hindereth will hinder until he be taken out of the way." That which hindered was the rule of pagan Caesars ; and when they passed and Christianity became the State religion in the days of Constantine, by common consent of historians, if it could be said that paganism had become Christianized, Christianity had also become paganized.

The history of the " man of sin " is revealed in two books in the Bible which are distinguished by the form in which prophecy is given. Both record chronological prophecy— Daniel in the Old and the Apocalypse in the New Testament. The simplest form of chronological prophecy is in the image seen by Nebuchadnezzar in his dream. The same theme is revealed in greater detail, and therefore with more complexity, in the vision of the four beasts seen by Daniel. The fourth beast— the Roman—covers the Christian era : and the details of its horns foretell the uprise of many kingdoms when the Roman Empire was broken up. One of the horns was conspicuous among the other horns. Its character, its arrogance, its blasphemy, its duration are all revealed. It would be a persecutor of God's saints for 1,260 years, a record covering the last half of the appointed times of the Gentiles. The loss of power would come at the time of the end ; and the establishment of God's kingdom is associated in the prophecy with its fall. So closely connected do these events appear that the expectation of the Lord's return at the time when its predicted duration would close appeared a reasonable conclusion. The little horn was identified with the Papacy, and this lost its power at the expected time, but the idea that the Lord would return at that time proved to be premature. Looking back from the present time we see that other events had to transpire before the advent, but the fall of the Papacy as a temporal power with ability to persecute those it describes as heretics, at the time students of prophecy expected, is a well established landmark of the time of the end.

The fourth beast with its horns, and particularly " the little horn ", are the basis of the symbolism in the Lord's last message. Here we find the fuller details of the conflicts between the upholders of truth and the apostasy during Christian times. We are given the same period of time when God's people would be subject to persecution as in Daniel's prophecy ; but we read also of a period when the witnesses were slain.

Taking a broad view of the history of Christianity with all the divisions, heresies, and conflicts that have arisen, it is pertinent to ask whether anything is revealed which indicates that truth would survive ? An examination of the prophecy shows that there are reasons for believing a revival of witnessing of gospel truth would take place prior to the end of the age.

We have first the prediction that the witnesses would be revived in Rev. 11. Looking at the work of the witnesses and what is written concerning the " slaying " of them, we see that the term covers all who opposed Romish blasphemy. Some resisted by the sword ; some by the word of God's testimony ; but all at the time when the witnesses were slain sealed their witness with their lives. The revival took place in the French Revolution when forces were liberated which have done much to restrain the Roman Church, and which have entered largely into the shaping of the events of the last 150 years. But coincident with the uprise of the political witnesses a revival also of the true witnesses might be expected. Such a view indeed receives specific endorsement from a warning of Jesus which is connected with his reappearance on the earth. " Behold, I come as a thief: blessed is he that watcheth, and keepeth his garments, lest he walk naked, and they see his shame." Such a prophecy requires that there shall be living at the second advent some who are waiting and looking for Christ, who know God's way of salvation and have been " clothed " with God's righteousness. The above is but the briefest of outlines of the prophecies that deal with the subject : a fuller treatment with a reasoned exposition may be found in *Eureka*, an exposition in three volumes of the Apocalypse, and in *Elpis Israel*.

The articles reprinted in this volume are a contribution to the evidence that the testimony concerning God's great salvation is again heard in the earth, and that for a century the truth of the second coming, the Kingdom of God, the promise of everlasting life, as revealed in God's word, have been faithfully proclaimed.

(II)   THE PREACHER

WE have seen that the prophecies of Scripture require that at the Lord's advent a people should be watching for him. A work then must develop during the closing period of Gentile times in preparing a people for the Lord. Such a work must take the form of preaching the gospel, a knowledge of which can only be obtained by careful and diligent study of the word of God. " The Scriptures are able to make us wise unto salvation ", and therefore Timothy was enjoined to " Preach the Word ". There must then be a preacher, for as Paul said, " How shall they hear without a preacher ? " Hearing there must be, for faith comes by hearing, and a preacher then must be raised up.

Since the Spirit-gifts were withdrawn God has overruled the affairs of His people without visible indication of His power. But the hand of God has nevertheless been present, ruling in the Kingdoms of men, and controlling " all things " that they " work together for good " for those who earnestly seek to know His ways. We might expect, then, that for the revival of His truth God would so overrule the affairs of suitable men that their minds were directed to the study of His word ; and so doing, they would acquire a correct knowledge of that gospel which is God's power unto salvation. This book itself is evidence that the gospel has been revived : and to all who, through the work of the writer of these reprinted articles, rejoice in an understanding of God's revealed purpose, information concerning the man is of more than passing interest. A short outline of his life will therefore be given first, and then consideration of the circumstances and influences which fostered his study of the Bible which resulted in the gradual unfolding of the One Hope.

John Thomas was born in London on April 12, 1805. He died on March 5, 1871. More than half of the 66 years of his life were spent in diligent study of God's word, in preaching and writing about the message of that Word. It was not an arrangement that was planned before ; editing a religious journal and discoursing on religious subjects formed no part at all of his aims in life. While his father was trained as a minister of religion, he did not follow a settled life ; for periods he was a clerk to the East India Company ; he also kept a boarding school, and between the two he served as a preacher with Independent congregations in London, in Scotland for a year, and afterwards at Chorley in Lancashire. While in Chorley, John Thomas began medical studies with a private surgeon ; and when his father left Chorley, he remained for some months to continue his studies. He then returned to London and studied for two years with a general practitioner ; after which he became a student at St. Thomas's hospital, attending lectures for three years, when he took his diploma. Then followed a year as companion to a physician for whom he wrote a course of lectures on obstetrics ; after which he practised as a physician on his own behalf for three years. This was in Hackney ; and Dr. Thomas began to write a history of the parish which was so disapproved by the authorities that the unfinished manuscript was purchased and suppressed. During this period articles were contributed to the medical journal, *The Lancet*.

By training and education the natural qualities of his mind were developed. He had great powers of both perception and reflection, with earnestness and a capacity for application to study, with independence, and a courage to hold to conviction reached by careful study. The early life was a preparation for later developments.

The circumstances which changed the course of Dr. Thomas' life were arresting enough. His father, who had in the meantime joined the Baptists, decided to go to America, where many were at the time emigrating. This was in 1832. It was decided that the son, John, should go first to investigate conditions there. He therefore secured a post as surgeon on a passenger ship of about 500 tons carrying about ninety people in all. The whole voyage was stormy, and quite early a considerable amount of damage was done to the ship, to the alarm of the passengers. Nearing the American side the ship grounded, sprung a leak as the result of the beating with the waves, and for ten days the pumps had to be kept at work, until at the end of eight weeks from leaving England the ship reached New York. Several times the passengers were in a state of panic and fear of drowning. Dr. Thomas was much exercised by the experience ; he realized that he had made no study of religion ; and, faced with the possibility of death, his sense of uncertainty was so borne upon him that he resolved that if he reached land safely he would not rest until he had found out the truth about what lay beyond death.

The resolve was soon tested. A letter of introduction to a Baptist preacher was presented, and in the conversation the preacher asked the destination of his visitor. On being informed that he was going to Cincinnati, the Minister remarked on the hospitality of the people, but said they were much influenced by " the reformation ". The reference was to the movement known today by the name " Disciples of Christ " in America and as " Churches of Christ " in Great Britain ; but sometimes described as Campbellism from the important part played in the early history of the body by Alexander Campbell. This was the first intimation he had of the " reformation ", but his life during many years became closely bound up with it.

Within a few days of arriving at Cincinnati Dr. Thomas had been immersed and become associated with the " reformation ". It came about in this way. Invited to the house of a Major Gano, who had espoused the teaching of Campbell with great earnestness, the subject of baptism was discussed, the Major pressing upon his visitor a pamphlet by Campbell. On another visit within an interval of few days, he was given a further pamphlet by Walter Scott, who was an important leader of the new movement particularly in formulating its teaching. Scott was due to preach on the following Sunday, and Gano invited him and the Doctor to his house. In the conversation during the evening, Scott pressed the need for baptism, and Dr. Thomas replied that if evidence could be produced from the New Testament of baptism being at once administered after belief he would no longer resist. The very challenge, as the Doctor later declared, only revealed his ignorance ; for Scott at once pointed to Acts 8 : 27. The citation proved the point, as Dr. Thomas immediately perceived ; a decision was made and immersion in the canal that passed the house took place at 10 o'clock by the light of the moon.

An introduction soon followed with Alexander Campbell, who pressed Dr. Thomas into speaking duties. As his services were more called for, so his studies of the Bible increased. But a greater impetus sprang from the decision to edit a small monthly magazine devoted to the extension of " the reformation ". The work and study of preparing this magazine led to a progressive grasp of God's purpose, and as each point was perceived it was faithfully accepted.

The magazine was called the *Apostolic Advocate*, and the first issue appeared in May, 1834. The sixth number contained an article which may be regarded as the beginning of the troubles which led finally to the break with Campbellism. Discussion followed, provoking closer application to the Scriptures on the part of Dr. Thomas who in consequence published in December, 1835, thirty-four questions under the heading " Information Wanted ". In this way the question of the nature of man was raised. While these questions were formulated to secure information, unfriendly critics regarded them as statements of opinions already held by their author.

The opposition caused Dr. Thomas to determine that he would seek to comprehend the Bible teaching on the questions raised ; and his fearless acceptance of truth when perceived and its courageous advocacy broadened the breach with Alexander Campbell. Several times Campbell in scurrilous language attacked Dr. Thomas, who replied in a spirited manner. In 1839 the *Advocate* was suspended.

Efforts to earn a living by farming followed without much success, and in 1842 Dr. Thomas returned to literary work, publishing a weekly newspaper for a very short time, when the enterprise was disposed of ; then a successor to the *Advocate* entitled *The Investigator* was begun which only reached one or possibly two volumes.

In 1844 Dr. Thomas started a new magazine, the title of which indicates the progress of his understanding in God's purpose. It was called the *Herald of the Future Age*. Its preparation intensified the study in which he had for years been engaged—a study which quickly bore fruit. In 1847 a critical reference to some of the points of his teaching about the reign of Christ on David's throne and related doctrines, led to the penning of an article reproduced in this volume on "The Hope of the world and the Hope of Israel". While reasoning that any hope, to be of value, must be established on divine promises, he perceived that when he was baptized he was ignorant of the true hope of the Gospel. His baptism therefore was invalid. He at once published a "Confession and Declaration", and was baptized into the true Gospel Hope.

The next stage in development of the witness was connected with a visit to England in 1848. This year was one of great unrest throughout Europe, so important that during the centenary of it in 1948 practically all leading journals have recalled the remarkable events that then occurred. The most important development for those who rejoice in a knowledge of God's truth was the production of a book entitled *Elpis Israel*. Dr. Thomas lectured in Britain and Scotland to thousands of people, the current events leading to great interest in his lectures on prophecy. Following earnest requests to prolong his stay and put in writing what he had said in his addresses, he went to London, and in four months had written the book.

When he left U.S.A. copy for the *Herald* was left with friends who continued its publication to the ninth issue, but the volume was not completed until Dr. Thomas returned in 1850. The *Herald* dated 1848 thus contains the prospectus for *Elpis Israel* which was published at the beginning of 1850.

The publication of the *Herald* was resumed under the altered title of *The Herald of the Kingdom and Age to Come*, and this continued for eleven years during which expositional articles were poured out with amazing regularity. The selection in this volume is drawn largely from the work of this period. The difficulties created by the American Civil War led to the suspension of the *Herald*, and another visit was made to Britain in 1862. In 1864 a magazine, *The Ambassador*, was started in this country, approved by Dr. Thomas, and under the changed title which he suggested for it, continues still as *The Christadelphian*, and this took the place of the *Herald* as the medium of Dr. Thomas's communications.

The first volume of *Eureka, an exposition of the Apocalypse*, was published in 1862, and the second and third volumes occupied the time of Dr. Thomas from his return to U.S.A. in 1863. In 1865 the name "Christadelphian" was adopted in order that representation for exemption from military service could be made, the authorities requiring some distinctive appellation by which the community could be known. The third volume of *Eureka* being completed at the close of 1868, in the next year another trip was made to Great Britain, visits being made to many towns where communities of believers were established.

A decision was reached at this time that Dr. Thomas would settle in this country, but this was not to be. He returned to America to settle up his affairs. He visited fellow believers in places in the States and Canada, fell sick and never fully recovered. He never left home again, and he died in the early months of 1871.

(III) THE TRUTH RE-DISCOVERED

REFERENCE has been made to the early contacts with the " Reformation " on Dr. Thomas's arrival in America. He had intended to keep free from any sectarian association, but contrary to inclination he found himself not only linked up with a religious movement but within two years involved in a controversy which continued for many years.

The " Reformation " had its roots in Scotch Presbyterianism. John Glas (1695-1773) was a minister who made an effort to return to New Testament principles, and was deposed in 1730 for opposing alliance with the State. His son-in-law, Robert Sandeman (1723-1771), espoused his views, and established a weekly breaking of bread, emphasized intellect as against emotion, and established a simple form of government for each church in which the work of teaching was extended to others outside the official ministry. Michael Faraday was a member of the Glasites.

The Baptist movement in Britain early in the sixteenth century sprang from the Anabaptists in Germany. In the early periods the Baptists had a hard struggle for religious freedom, and one Roger Williams left England for America where he founded the State of Rhode Island and established the first Baptist Church in America. A member of the Glasite churches in Scotland, Archibald McLean (1733-1812), renounced the practice of infant sprinkling, and in 1765 was immersed. McLean had considerable influence, the Scotch

Baptist Churches having their origin in his work. His influence extended to England and Wales. In Wales the uncle and foster-father of Mr. Lloyd George was an elder of a McLean Church, and thus a Prime Minister of Britain in early life was associated with that fellowship. William Jones, who became a minister of a Scotch Baptist Church in London, was also influenced by McLean ; he later published two volumes of the *Millennial Harbinger* (1835-6) in which Alexander Campbell's writings were made familiar to English readers. As Campbell's views were modified Jones published a criticism of them. Another McLean Baptist was James Wallis, who founded a church in Nottingham and was associated with the publication of the *Christian Messenger*, which ran for 12 years (1835-47), and which was followed by the *British Millennial Harbinger* at first edited by Wallis. Both these magazines were designed to introduce the teaching of Alexander Campbell in this country. When Dr. Thomas visited Britain in 1848 Wallis strongly opposed him.

Thomas Campbell, the father of Alexander, was born in Ireland, but was educated at Glasgow University for the Presbyterian Ministry. He became a minister of a section of the Presbyterian Church which had sprung from the Seceders. The Seceders had withdrawn from the Presbyterian State Church because they claimed the right for each congregation to choose its own ministers. The Seceders later divided on the question of taking an oath which bound to certain beliefs and practices. The section which would not take the oath were known as Anti-Burghers ; to this section Thomas Campbell belonged. Although much strife and bitterness followed these divisions, Campbell, deeply grieved by the bigotry manifested, tried to bring about reunion in Ireland, but failed. In 1807 he went to America, followed two years later by his son.

The Campbells were both opposed to divisions arising out of doctrinal difference ; yet through an effort by the father to overcome these differences by inviting people of all sections of the Presbyterians to partake of communion together, still another sect came into being. Opposition to his policy was so strong that he was compelled to withdraw from the Presbyterians ; people of different denominations followed him, and in 1809 an association was formed for which Campbell drew up the " Declaration and Address ". This " Declaration " renounced all systems of theology as tests of fellowship, and this has remained a feature until today of the Churches founded by Campbell. Another revival movement similar in aim to that led by the Campbells was proceeding during this time in America under the leadership of Barton W. Stone. He also was forced out of the Presbyterian Church ; he then founded churches known as " Christian ", and in 1833 the followers of Stone and Campbell united to form one fellowship. Before this, in 1812, the Campbells were convinced that infant baptism was not scriptural, and both were then immersed on a public confession of the Lord Jesus. For a short time they found a home with the Baptists—an association which was not happy and which was finally broken in 1832, when a separate organization was formed.

Walter Scott joined the Campbells in 1820. He had been educated in Edinburgh for the Presbyterian Ministry but emigrated. In 1827 he was chosen to be an evangelist, by his labours winning many converts. He appears to have had a logical method of preaching, and presented " the terms of salvation in their Biblical order ". These terms were considered to be " Faith, repentance, confession, baptism, remission of sins, and the Holy Spirit ", and in the words of the writer quoted : " Thomas and Alexander Campbell both gave him credit for restoring these to the church in a practical way "

In 1823 Alexander Campbell started the *Christian Baptist*, which ran into seven volumes, and in these Campbell's theology is worked out. In 1830 the *Millennial Harbinger* followed, and in this journal the contention with Dr. Thomas was waged. The movement started by Scott and Campbell has grown extensively. It is still marked by abhorrence of sectarianism, and an avoidance of a creed (although in general doctrines it in no way differs from other churches of Christendom). It claims to be a return to the faith and practice of early Christianity in the observance of adult baptism and breaking of bread. Its followers are called " Disciples of Christ " in America and number today about one and a half millions ; in Britain the assemblies are called " Churches of Christ ", and have about 13,000 members. Throughout the world there are two million adherents. These " Churches of Christ " are represented at the Conferences convened by the Protestant Churches ; and the historian of the Baptist Churches, Dr. A. C. Underwood, writing in 1947, says[1]: " Quite recently conversations have taken place between representatives of the ' Churches of Christ ' and the Baptist Union, with a view to closer relations, not excluding the possibility of union "

We must add to this outline of the Campbellite movement a reference to the fact that the early decades of last century were marked by general relig is confusion, mixed with wild enthusiasm. Sects abounded in America, with bitterness and hatred rife, with fantastic notions based on weird interpretations of a few texts. Claims to Holy Spirit guidance were often made ; wild scenes at such revivalist meetings, not free from immorality, were common. Religious discussion at that time was marked by blunt invective, and a harshness of speech was common, and must not be judged by present standards.

Against this background we will now briefly trace the development of Dr. Thomas's understanding of the Scriptures.

We have seen how Dr. Thomas was convinced by Walter Scott that he should be immersed ; and also have noted the influence of Scott on the method of presenting the doctrine of the " Reformation " : " Faith, repentance, confession, baptism ". We have also noted the close connection of the " Reformation " and the Baptist Churches, a connection which led to many Baptists becoming associated with the new movement. They were accepted without any further immersion. In No. 6 of the *Apostolic Advocate* Dr. Thomas published an article entitled "Anabaptism ". In it he points out that the word which signifies " baptized again " is wrongly used of those who were immersed who had previously only been sprinkled, and that while the term is to be deprecated, there are cases where re-immersion was necessary. He discusses the meaning of the word *baptize*, tracing its use by dyers. Only when there has been a change of colour of the article dipped would it be called baptism. To dip an infidel would avail nothing for salvation, the prerequisite faith, repentance, and confession being lacking. Quoting the process of salvation as set out by Walter Scott, but without mentioning his name, Dr. Thomas argued that an immersion of a Baptist or of a member of any other sect was lacking in understanding and was therefore invalid. The argument is logical and applies Campbell's own principles in a way that should have been approved by Campbell. The movement " began with a stressing of intellectual values " as Dr. William Robinson, the leading scholar of the " Churches of Christ ", admits. In this emphasis it followed the method of McLean who was a reasoner on metaphysical lines. But the Baptist members of the " Reformation " resented the implications of Dr. Thomas's article, and Campbell himself was not pleased, as he saw it would hinder the numerical advance of the movement.

Discussion followed in which Dr. Thomas quoted in support of his position an earlier writing of Alexander Campbell. Dr. Thomas then addressed four letters to Campbell, published monthly in the *Advocate*. They are marked by close reasoning, and a courage to uphold what the writer saw to be truth. He concludes. "And now, brother Campbell, I have brought to a close my views upon this matter. You and my readers can judge whether the Word of God is for or against me. I write not for applause but for truth. An eternity of weal or woe is staked upon our uprightness or demerits here. In view of this, I have not calculated on the approbation or displeasure that may accrue to me for the position I have maintained. I cannot but express my confidence that you will meet what has been said fairly in the *Harbinger*. You certainly owe me reparation for the unintentional misrepresentation of my practices, which you have published to the four winds of heaven."

In 1835 the series of 34 questions already mentioned were printed in the *Advocate* under the heading " Information Wanted ". They concerned the nature of man, the purpose of God with the earth, the fulfilment of the promises to the fathers in an everlasting inheritance of the earth. Of the response to the request for information, Dr. Thomas, twelve months afterwards, wrote : " Instead, however, of some one condescending to instruct him, and to impart the information sought, he was forthwith beset on every side. A correspondent wrote putting certain questions to him. The letter containing these obliged him to investigate the subject alluded to more closely, and, unlike the course adopted towards him, he honestly and frankly replied to said querist, according to the light he had. Then began the din of war. The artillery of ' the present reformation ', began to play from the heights of Bethany . . . His Christian character was traduced ; he was classed with ' the wits and the wags, the Paines, and the Voltaires, and all that herd '. Discharges of small arms were levelled at him from divers points ; and discontinuances came in from various quarters, because he had the presumption to ask for information few had the courage to give him. But notwithstanding this fusilading he still lives at the service of his friends and readers."

All the clamour and denunciations and attacks on his character, as he declared later, failed in the desired effects.

" Instead of intimidating us and putting us to silence it only roused our determination to comprehend the subject ; if wrong, to get right ; and when righted to defend the right, maintain the right, and overthrow the wrong or perish in the attempt."

In 1837 Dr. Thomas engaged in a debate with a Presbyterian clergyman on the immortality of the soul, the summary of it being published in a large pamphlet, *The Apostasy Unveiled*. In it Dr. Thomas shows the Bible teaching concerning the nature of man and the true hope of life by resurrection. The effect was virtually a bull of excommunication from Campbell, since Campbell disclaimed all fellowship with him unless he renounced the offending doctrines.

It would appear that the Churches of the " Reformation " were much exercised about Dr. Thomas. This is evident from the fact that the church in Virginia of which Dr. Thomas was a member issued a report about him following a suggestion made in the *Harbinger* that the church he attended should investigate his teaching. The report condemns as high handed the attitude of Campbell, indicates that some of the members regarded Dr. Thomas's views as speculative, but speaks highly of him as a man. "Although we may hazard the loss of fellowship with many, yet we feel bound to risk the loss rather than sever from our communion one whose walk is so exemplary, and whose devotion to truth is so ardent as that of Dr. Thomas." Another church in Virginia published to all churches a defence of Dr. Thomas personally while dissenting from his views. " We have seen him in private and in public, and we have seen nothing but the exemplary Christian ; his morals unexceptional, his life rigidly self denying."

Efforts were made by friends of the two disputants to effect a reconciliation, which closed the breach for a time, but only for a time. Reopened again, no further effort was made to bridge it. Owing to Dr. Thomas's removal to another state the *Advocate* was suspended in 1839.

The next short period, spent on the *Investigator*, can be passed over as it contributes no information on the development of Dr. Thomas's understanding of the Word. In 1844, however, we reach another stage in the work of reviving the Truth. In that year the first number of the *Herald of the Future Age* was published. During the first year of the magazine Dr. Thomas removed to Richmond, Va., and stayed with a friend named Malone. Together they visited a Campbellite church in a neighbouring town, with which the Doctor's friend was in fellowship. Dr. Thomas was known to the people and was invited to speak, to which he responded. There was objection to this which led to the expulsion of the Doctor's friend, and this in turn led to a few beginning to hold meetings independently of the Campbellite assemblies. Editing the *Herald* led to intensified study of God's Word, with a growing perception of its teaching. The progress may be seen from a published summary of " Things Elaborated from the Word during Ten Discourses at New York in 1846 ". The elaboration of these " things " would give to the New York listeners a good understanding of the first principles of the Truth. But up to this point it had not occurred to the Doctor that the increased understanding of God's purpose made applicable to himself the argument he had used against Baptists being received into fellowship without reimmersion,—an argument which had begun the course of investigation now nearing its close.

A criticism of the New York lectures concerning Christ the heir to David's throne and the coming restoration of the Jews led to an enquiry on the value of these things as part of the divine revelation. Was any part of divine revelation of no value ? He began an article on " The Hope of Israel and the Hope of the World ". After his manner he examined passages dealing with hope, and found Paul said " We are saved by the Hope ". What was this hope ? A number of passages crowded into his mind, and with these scriptures came also a realization that when he was immersed by Walter Scott he was ignorant of this Hope that saves. His immersion then was of no avail ; it was not an obedience to the form of doctrine which had been delivered by the apostles. At the time of his baptism he was ignorant of God's promises by which we might become partakers of the divine nature. The Campbellite claim to have restored " the ancient gospel " was not correct : all they had done was to restore the ordinances of apostolic times in their simplicity. With this recognition his duty became clear, and as throughout the controversy he had followed faithfully where the instruction of God's word led, so now he did not hesitate. He wrote a confession and abjuration, in which he reviewed briefly his early life and his contacts with Walter Scott ; he gave reasons why he should " abjure the whole transaction, in which we once firmly thought we had believed and obeyed the one only true and apostolic gospel of Jesus Christ ". The Confession was followed by a " Declaration " in which he set out what he now saw was the teaching of the Scriptures, and what therefore must be believed for a complete return to apostolic faith and practice.

With the outbreak of revolution in Europe in 1848, Dr. Thomas decided to visit Britain. The visit had important results, which must be noted in this short survey of the revival of Bible Truth. Dr. Thomas at once made contact with the Campbellites in this country, some of whom bitterly opposed him ; understandably so, the more firmly they adhered to the teaching of Alexander Campbell. But a much wider hearing was secured than the Campbell assemblies. This was particularly so in Glasgow where several thousands attended a series of lectures in the City Hall. At a *soirée* held at the close it was suggested that Dr. Thomas should write the substance of his lectures so that those who had heard them could continue their studies after his return to America. This proposal was approved ; Dr. Thomas decided to prolong his stay in this country, went to London, and wrote *Elpis Israel*. His own account of how he wrote the book must be here reproduced. He is speaking of 1849, and says, " By the beginning of the new year I was enabled to commence the composition of *Elpis Israel*. I did not allow the grass to grow ; but worked while it was called today, and much of the night also. For six weeks the world without was a mere blank, except through a daily perusal of the London *Times* ; for during that period I had no use for hat, boots, or shoes, oscillating, as it were, like a pendulum between two points—the couch above, and the desk below. In about four months the manuscript was completed."

The publication of this volume might be regarded as the end of the journey begun 15 years before. The book is comprehensive, and its sufficiency to enlighten men and women concerning the great salvation is evident from the fact that it has been the means of very many being led to the Truth. For many years it was the one book which was available to introduce the Gospel. A few years later the same truths, in the form of chapters on items of the Faith, were made available in the book *Twelve Lectures*, later entitled *Christendom Astray*, by Robert Roberts, but *Elpis Israel* opens up a wide and comprehensive view of the whole Scriptures. The first two sections of the three into which the book is divided, will in the writer's judgment never be surpassed. Of the third, dealing with prophecy, some things made necessary by passing time will be said on another page. The lectures by Dr. Thomas in Britain, and the book *Elpis Israel*, which was the outcome, led to the formation of ecclesias ; and the work of preparing a people to be ready for the Lord has gone on for the last hundred years. The preaching of the coming of Jesus Christ to set up God's Kingdom on the earth, the restoration of the Jews, the Millennial reign and its purpose, the offer of everlasting life in Christ by resurrection at his coming, the unity of God and the divine sonship of Jesus, are doctrines which others during the last hundred years have taken up, but it belongs to the work of Dr. Thomas that all parts of the Truth were brought together into a complete presentation of God's purpose.

(IV)   THE WORKER

DR. THOMAS had a remarkable capacity for applying his powers to any matter in hand. All his work is marked by intensity and earnestness. This is seen in the energetic way in which he investigated the Scriptures from the first association with the " Reformation ". It is seen in the self-denying labours on behalf of the gospel in extensive travelling that he undertook. It is seen in the industry with which he plied his pen.

With his abilities he could doubtless have secured for himself a very comfortable if not a lucrative practice as a physician. Instead, he accepted toil and sacrifice in order that he might have time to devote himself to the work of the gospel. Repeatedly in the magazines he edited, circumstances caused Dr. Thomas to make references to personal affairs of a nature which would hardly be expected in a journal today. Nevertheless, looking back they afford a glimpse of the sincerity and self-sacrificing spirit he displayed. Explaining a delay in publishing an issue of the *Advocate* in 1837 he says : " The *Advocate* is not issued as early as we could wish. It is not our private affairs which cause this delay. We have devoted ourselves for life, at least as long as we possess health and means, to the dissemination of what we believe the Scriptures teach. We consider this the business of our life ; our domestic affairs merely subordinate to it. Absence from home on the things of the Kingdom and a fracture of the rod by which the platen or impression plate of our press is suspended, are the cause of the late issue of our paper. Another cause of its late arrival at its destination is owing to the irregularity and tardiness of the mails. The *Advocate* remains about a fortnight in the post office here before it can get a fair start on its journey outwards. Ours being only a one horse mail, it requires several ladings before its monthly editions can get into their several routes." On one occasion when asked how he lived he replied that he reduced all his wants to bare necessities and then exercised every economy. When, before the final separation from the "Reformation" it was suggested that he became a regular minister of a community of believers, he answered: "With many thanks to our brother for his kind disposition, we answer emphatically No! We cannot afford to sell our independence for a mess of pottage. How could we teach the rich faithfully the unpalatable doctrine of Christ concerning the proper use of the mammon of unrighteousness, and be dependent upon them for the perishable pittance of a few hundreds per annum? We must be free if we would be faithful to the truth. We object not to receive contributions in aid of the cause we advocate; but they must be spontaneous, not extorted. We cannot preach for hire."

From the very early days of his connection with the Campbellites he appears to have been in demand as a speaker. When he was Editor of the *Apostolic Advocate* he undertook tours of churches involving frequent and lengthy addresses. He began with a definite disinclination for the work, and at any time he was only concerned with placing before his hearers the message of God's word, and had no interest in rhetorical effects. At the same time his style must have had a compelling interest or his audiences would not have grown night after night as often happened.

A brief recapitulation of a few of his journeys will give us some idea of his labours as a preacher. In the *Herald* for 1851, he describes the personal difficulties overcome in keeping an appointment and is led to make some reflections on the duty of all in spreading the Gospel. He had been ill, and in a week from getting up he left home against the advice of friends for a twenty-five mile journey to keep appointments, the first of which was a three day meeting. Others were expected to be there to take part, but did not arrive on the day expected. The Doctor thus speaks:

"We expected to meet two or three brethren at the meetings who would take upon themselves the labour of formally addressing the people, while we should have nothing else to do but to prove by our presence our willingness to speak to them, but our inability from extreme weakness to do it. Our dismay was considerable, however, when we found that they had not arrived, and that the work of faith and labour of love must be performed by us alone. Our principle is that difficulties which cannot be avoided must be met and overcome. It is bad policy to make appointments and not fulfil them. We therefore determined to do what we could, and to try to discourse even if we had to come to an abrupt and speedy conclusion. The first appointment was a three days meeting at Acquinton. A brother who accompanied us from Richmond attended to the preliminaries, after which, we, following the example of Jesus (not being able to stand) sat down and taught the people. At first our friends did not think we should be able to hold out fifteen minutes ; but though weak in body the subject was itself an inspiration, and to our own surprise we spoke with comparative ease on the Representative Men of the prophetic word for upwards of two hours.

" Encouraged by our success in this effort we did not doubt but we should be able to get along from day to day as the appointed times came round. We were strengthened by the consideration that sufficient to the day is the evil thereof ; so that it was quite unnecessary to assume the evil of many days and lay it all upon one. We experienced, however, some relief from the fact that one of the brethren announced to take part in the meetings arrived at Acquinton on Lord's day ; so that had we proved unable to occupy the time there was help at hand to supply our place and to make up our deficiencies. He remained with us all the week, and was no little assistance to us in conducting the worship, and leaving us only the pleasant labour of persuading the things concerning the kingdom of God, and of declaring all His counsel to the people. We spoke at Acquinton on three successive days ; two days after at a school house ; and on Saturday and Sunday at the old state-church house called West Point. At all these meetings put together we spoke about twelve hours and a half on things pertaining to the kingdom of God and the name of Jesus Christ ; and instead of increasing our debility, we recruited our physical energy every day. In our own person then we have proved that the truth is an inspiration which gives health to the soul, through which it operates nothing but good to the outward man."

Many of his yearly lecturing tours extended over weeks and involved very great inconvenience in travel. It was not unusual for two addresses, each of two or two and a half hours's duration, to be given on a Sunday, with addresses equally long night after night during the week. The extent of his work in building up small ecclesias and in preaching on these journeys can be best appreciated by a few short extracts from the accounts he published year by year in the *Herald*. When he was not travelling he practised his profession (although regular periods of absence would not help to build up a practice) and engaged in writing for the *Herald*, and gave frequent addresses to the meeting in the city where he lived.

Of the summer of 1846 he wrote : " During the season now numbered with the days bygone we have not consumed the bread of idleness nor of the hireling. From the early part of May to the end of August we have travelled between 950 and 1,000 miles in the Old Dominion and addressed the people forty-seven times on ' The things of the Kingdom of God and the Name of Jesus Christ ', to say nothing of the time and labour bestowed upon the little flock in this idolatrous city ".

The difficulty of travelling, much of it by river steamer since that was the means of transport which had been opened up the most in the '40s of last century, can be illustrated from the following statement : " Though assured by the skipper of the boat that it would leave the wharf at 10 a.m. we did not leave our mooring till 5.0 p.m. Cursing, lying and cheating are the boat characteristics of the Ohio and Mississippi. They will say anything for money. I have learned to discern the truth in the diametrics of their declarations. He knew well that we could not possibly get off at the time stated ; for there were four steamers in the shallow ditch they call a canal, that connects Louisville with Portland below the Falls. But he lied to prevent us from leaving his boat and seeking another beyond the canal. If I could have come to a knowledge of the truth in the case, I might have spent some pleasant hours with some old friends in the City of the Falls ; as it was, I was obliged to confine myself to the boat, not knowing when it might be off ".

During this same tour he was fifty-seven hours on board a steam boat which had taken his passage money, the boat being jammed in by others at the landing, while cholera was rampant in the town, two hundred people dying each day.

He was absent in all six weeks and travelled 3,500 miles. On arriving home he found a large mail awaiting him with orders for three hundred copies of the book *Anatolia*, after-wards re-named *Exposition of Daniel*. " These ", he says, " I despatched with all expedition ".

Of a journey to the South in 1854 he says, " Thus then was brought to a close my visit to the South for 1854 after an absence of six weeks. I addressed the people some twenty-five times, and when I arrived in New York concluded my journey-ings for the year, having travelled since the 1st June a distance of 5,500 miles ".

In 1855 he visited Kentucky, and the following detail illustrates what travelling involved. He says, " We decided to return to New York city, issue the July and August numbers of the *Herald*, and then depart for Richmond. Accordingly we made two or three attempts to leave Henderson by steamer ; but the boats passed without attending to our signals. Not knowing how long we might be detained thus, we determined to go by land, and cross the Ohio to Evansville. Our friend very obligingly procured a buggy and sent us thither, with the expectation that we should take the cars at two o'clock. But on arriving there we found that they did not leave till six in the morning. It was now about twelve ; so that there were eighteen hours for the exercise of patience. Evansville is a thriving town of 12,000 inhabitants on the right bank of the Ohio ; but of no particular interest to a stranger having no business or other connections with it. We were glad, therefore, when we found ourselves in the car rushing onwards to Terre Haute with Evansville increasingly in the rear. At 8 p.m. we were at Dayton, Ohio, via Indianapolis ; in the morning we arrived at Cleveland on Lake Erie, where we breakfasted. All that day we travelled the Lake Shore and New York and Erie railroads, and the following night also, after which we arrived, without accident, at New York city about 11 a.m., having run 1,100 miles in 53 hours, stoppages included, a rate equal to the Parliamentary trains, the slowest in the British Isles ; but fast enough at present for comparative safety."

We have referred to the work that he did in the town where he lived, in addition to these travels. In the *Herald* for 1853, in response to a request from a correspondent that he should give his readers some account of his journeyings, he reviewed his activities during the year. He explained that he had been busy writing articles to get a sufficient store to keep the printers busy while he was on his next journey. From December until June he had spoken sixty times in New York.

When he arrived in December there were seven or eight people meeting in a private house but making no public effort. Led by the Doctor, lectures had been given, and he gives a short account of their experiences in the various ways they had employed in trying to interest people. In addition to this work in New York he had undertaken journeys of about 3,000 miles and in all had given 130 addresses. These references are but a bald narration of figures, but the record involved days of travelling and often nights also with not a little discomfort, and many journeys of upwards of 20 miles to the homes of the brethren after lectures had been given. As the imagination tries to fill in the details, one is struck by the Herculean efforts put out on behalf of the truth. There were giants in the earth in those days !

A reference to the lecturing work during his visit to Britain in 1848-9 throws light on the resources of Biblical knowledge the Doctor possessed and also his ability to present it in reasoned and logical form. This reference also shows that much of the time when not formally lecturing was spent in talking privately about the things of the Kingdom and in explaining difficulties : " Our audiences were drawn neither from the high nor low, but from the odds and ends of Edinburgh, who in every city are the most independent and Berean of the population. We addressed them some ten or a dozen times, mostly at the Waterloo Assembly Room in Princes Street, a spacious and elegant apartment, and capable of seating some thousand to fifteen hundred people. The impression made upon them was strong and, for the time, caused many to rejoice that providence had ever directed our steps to Edinburgh. Our expositions of the sure word of prophecy interested them greatly, causing our company to be sought for at the domestic hearth incessantly, to hear us talk of the things of the kingdom and name of Jesus, and to solve whatever doubts and difficulties previous in-doctrination might originate in regard to the things we teach. Our new friends had but little mercy upon us in their demands upon our time. They seemed to think that premeditation was unnecessary ; and that we had nothing to do but to open our mouth, and out would fly a speech ! Of our two hundred and fifty addresses in Britain, all were extemporized as delivered. There was no help for it, seeing we had to go oftener than otherwise from parlour conversation to the work before us in the lecture-room. Indeed, our nervous system was so wearied by unrest that we could not have studied a discourse. Present necessity was indispensable to set our brain to work. Certain subjects were advertised and had to be expounded. We knew, therefore, what was to be treated of ; and happily understanding the Word of the Kingdom, we had but to tell the people what it taught, and to sustain it by reason and testimony. In this way we got along independently of stationery and sermon-studying, which would have broke us down completely, and would have absorbed more time than our friends allowed us ".

This ability to extemporize addresses is evidence of the remarkable knowledge of the Bible stored away in Dr. Thomas's mind. It also shows that he had a good memory of his general reading. Reference is made in the preceding chapter to his writing *Elpis Israel* in four months. The mechanical writing of the book was heavy labour in so short a period, but what an amazing understanding of God's Word is revealed ! There was no library at hand, no well marked reference books ; out of the wealth of mature understanding he wrote the book.

There is a little sidelight on a practical matter which may be mentioned. The Doctor was mindful of any method by which the Gospel could be introduced to men. The following occurs in the context of his reference to the writing of *Elpis Israel*. " With the exception of two discourses at Camden Town, and two at a small lecture room near my residence, and an opposition speech at a Peace-Society meeting, I made no effort among the Londoners to gain their ears. I distributed printed bills, indeed ; but a few hundreds or thousands of these among upwards of two millions of people, were but as the drops of a passing cloud to the ocean."

It is difficult to assess the amount of writing undertaken from 1834 to 1871. For at least twenty years he was editor of a magazine. Apart from the routine editorial work of reading manuscripts, proof reading and make-up, and attending to correspondence, a considerable proportion of what he printed was written by himself. Many articles are the fruit of much reading in history ; all expository articles witness to constant study of the word of God. However great a man's native ability may be, to produce these articles much time and application must have been given. The output was not limited to an occasional article, or of one series even. It was constant for the whole period, and while some of it was essentially topical and related to the controversies in which he was involved, much is of a very high quality. Some of the contributions to the *Herald,* written as part of a monthly output, have been reprinted as pamphlets many times. Of these, *What is Truth ?, How to Search the Scriptures,* and *The Revealed Mystery,* may be particularly mentioned. In addition, occasional pamphlets were produced as well as those which had first appeared as articles in the magazine. Some dealt with current events in relation to prophecy ; one written near the end of his life, entitled *Anastasis,* was a consideration of disputed points connected with resurrection ; another was the outcome of a conversation in a train journey at the time of the Gorham controversy in this country during his visit in 1848—a controversy not quite dead, for an echo of it was recently heard in the ecclesiastical courts. This pamphlet was racily written but with the characteristic grasp of Scripture teaching.

Besides the regular work for the periodicals he edited, Dr. Thomas wrote three books which are still in active circulation : *Elpis Israel, Exposition of Daniel,* and *Eureka, an exposition of the Apocalypse* in three volumes of nearly 2,000 pages. The last two volumes of *Eureka* were fruit of the later years of his life, volume I appearing while he was still publishing the *Herald.*

If we put together the work of speaking and writing we see what an amazing amount of work was accomplished. Sixty addresses in one place in six months involves a wide range of topics and a corresponding ability on the part of the speaker. Long periods of travel, sometimes under difficult conditions, were a tax on both the mental and the physical man. But in addition, the numerous addresses and private talks undertaken on these journeys indicate both remarkable resources and a willing expenditure of them. Two hours appears to have been quite the normal time to be taken up in an address. Audiences as well as speakers of those days reveal either a stamina or a perseverance which are not manifest in present times.

The writing of books is usually accomplished by a man isolating himself and so devoting his powers to the work. Even so the production of three volumes the size of *Eureka* would be no mean achievement for most writers. By this standard we may judge the work of writing undertaken by Dr. Thomas. From 1862 he was not editing a magazine but from that date unto 1869 the second and third volumes of *Eureka* were written.

For something comparable in toil and in devotion to the gospel we look back to apostolic days. Then a full-hearted expenditure of heart, mind and strength on the part of the apostles carried the gospel throughout the Roman world. The work was divinely commanded and was visibly endorsed by miracles. The revival of the truth was a lesser work, but one nevertheless that called for similar courage, perseverance, and labour. By the test of work performed, gratitude and respect is due to the man through whom in God's providence the gospel of the Kingdom was again proclaimed.

(v) THE EXPOSITOR

WE have traced the process which had its origin in the activities connected with " reformation " in America, by which Dr. Thomas reached a knowledge of God's saving purpose revealed in the Scriptures. We have mentioned the chaotic condition of the religious world, the welter of religious opinion prevailing one hundred years ago, out of which emerged the self-styled " Reformation ". There is also another feature in the background which should be mentioned to get a complete picture. It is a less evident feature but nevertheless important ; it concerns the interpretation of prophecy.

There are three schools of interpretation of the prophecies of The Revelation ; Preterists, Futurists, and what has been called the Continuous Historic. The first puts all the Apocalypse in the past, generally interpreting its symbols of the fall of Jerusalem. The second regards the whole Apocalypse as a prophecy of the future—no part having been fulfilled. The last method of interpretation finds a correspondence between the " signs " of the Lord's last message and the outstanding events connected with the Mediterranean world from the day when the revelation was given unto the second advent, with information concerning events connected with the setting up of God's Kingdom, and a glimpse of beyond. The Apocalypse is seen as a sequel to Daniel's prophecies, being an expansion of matters connected with the fourth beast of Daniel chapter seven. This method of interpretation involves a number of things.

First the understanding of the prophecy must be pro-gressive. A believer of the early centuries could have only a dim understanding, if any, of much of the Lord's last message. He might see that a long history lay between the first and second advents ; that during this intervening period the affairs of God's truth would have varied fortunes—its adherents being always in the minority, persecuted and oppressed bitterly at times, but through it all God's purpose would be worked out ; and that at last God's Kingdom would prevail and righteousness triumph. But as the centuries went by the student would be able to trace out where the prophecy had been fulfilled : outstanding landmarks would fix the progress made along the chart : but always the unfulfilled portion would present problems, and interpretation would be marked by uncertainty. So it has been. During the centuries the understanding of the signs has become ever easier, and the analogy of the fulfilled has helped in a better interpretation of the unfulfilled part.

With the Revival of Learning in Europe which followed the taking of Constantinople, and the breaking of papal domination in Protestant Countries by the Reformation in which Luther played so conspicuous a part, the study of the Apocalypse progressed rapidly. Outstanding names of the early period are Mede, Jurieu, who saw that in the events of his own day the " witnesses " were slain, Vitringa, Daubuz, Sir Isaac Newton, Whiston (the translator of Josephus, and the successor of Newton as Professor of Mathematics at Cambridge), and Bishop Newton who was writing in the middle of the eighteenth century. Then followed, to mention the more important, Galloway, Bicheno, Faber, Cunninghame and Frere, Bickersteth, Habershon and Birks. During the early years of the nineteenth century Faber and Cunninghame with others engaged in warm controversy on some of the details of the Apocalypse. An Anglican magazine, *The Christian Observer*, founded in 1802, opened its columns to the controversialists and for 20 years articles appeared on the interpretation of the Revelation. An American edition was published in Boston month by month exactly corresponding to the English edition. William Jones, who edited the *British Millennial Harbinger*, previously mentioned, published *Lectures on the Apocalypse* in 1830. Miller in America and Irving in Britain about the same time were attracting attention to Bible chronology, the end of the Age, and the Coming Millennium. In 1831 and for five years a prophetic journal called *The Investigator* was devoted to exposition of prophecy. Many of these already named contributed, also Wolff, a missionary who travelled widely, mentioned by Dr. Thomas. Keith, in the past famous for his book on fulfilled prophecy, wrote an exposition of the Apocalypse under the title *Signs of the Times*.

Gaussen, well known as the author of *Theopneustia*, wrote more than one book on the prophecies. The year 1844 saw the publication of Elliott's *Horæ Apocalypticæ*. The above sketch leaves unmentioned a great many who in the first four decades of the nineteenth century wrote books or tracts dealing with prophecy, the second advent and the Millennium.

A student of prophecy of the Continuous Historic school sees that the prophecy leads on to a great divine intervention in human affairs. Usually such a student tends to believe also in the Millennium. Another tendency is to link up a resurrection with the second advent, and some writers who studied other parts of scripture as well as prophecy held mortalist views. Whiston, for example, was a believer in conditional immortality. But this was not an invariable rule. Prophetic interpreters have held strange and curious beliefs that seemed to be incongruous with a reasonable attempt to interpret the chronological prophecies.

The object of this review is to show that the subject of prophecy was " in the air " during the time when Dr. Thomas was unearthing the Truth and then preaching it. How many of the works of the authors mentioned were known to him we are not aware. That some of them were is evident from references either to writers or to topics. But of greater importance is the fact that Dr. Thomas himself was a patient student of prophecy ; many of his addresses touched upon prophecy and current events, and in this way attracted those who shared the interest which existed among many religious people at that time. It is interesting to note that on the first occasion he had to give a public address in connection with " the Reformation ", being impressed into the service without much warning by Campbell himself, Dr. Thomas recalled reading about the four empires in Rollin's *Ancient History*, and for half an hour he spoke on Nebuchadnezzar's image. From the beginning of his literary work this interest in prophecy is found. The first issue of the *Apostolic Advocate* has an article on Rev. 17, and throughout the five volumes expositions of the Apocalypse appear. In fact Campbell made a cheap gibe at the Doctor's interest in the Apocalypse, evidently forgetting that it is the one book that contains a specific reference to a blessing on the one who " hears " the message. Throughout the volumes of the *Herald* also frequent expositions of particular " signs " occur, but in articles generally in which the interpretation forms part of a discussion on current events.

It has been affirmed by unfriendly critics that *Eureka*, Dr. Thomas's exposition of the Apocalypse, was largely indebted to Elliott. That the author of *Eureka* had read Elliott is evident ; in his writings Dr. Thomas both commends and criticizes Elliott. But long before Elliott's *Horæ* was published in 1844, in his magazines Dr. Thomas had considered most of the points which have been the subject of discussion by students. From the first issue of the *Advocate* it is evident that Dr. Thomas had a good knowledge of history. On several occasions he gives lists of important dates with summaries of the associated events. When discussing current affairs and tracing the light which prophecy throws upon events, he is seen to be well informed and accurate.

We may attempt briefly to assess the value of Dr. Thomas's contribution to Apocalyptic interpretation and to the exposition of other prophecies. Obviously every student in this field is the creature of his own day, and could not be otherwise. Writers contemporary with Napoleon gave him a larger place in their interpretations than later writers to whom passing time had given a clearer perspective. But one detail of interpretation powerfully influenced not only Dr. Thomas but all others who held the same view. There were many who expected that 1866-70 would see remarkable happenings in connection with the Papacy ; the appointed period of its ascendancy was then due to end. Some confirmation was rightly found for this view in the fact that there had been a preliminary fulfilment of a time period connected with the Papacy, also expected before it came to pass, at the French Revolution. But prophecy seemed to indicate that the period 1866-70 would not only see the loss of temporal power by the Papacy, but would witness also the Lord's appearing on the earth again. Although it appeared a reasonable view, it was mistaken—not as concerns the fortunes of the Papacy, but in the then expected second advent. But this view influenced other interpretations. In 1848 only twenty years were to run to the expiring of the time, and in looking ahead in the interpretation of prophecy unfulfilled, everything had to be crushed within the twenty years. Actually much longer has been necessary for the fulfilment of many prophecies which were correctly interpreted, and the fulfilment of which was essential to produce the political situation which will bring the final clash of world forces divided into two camps.

Does the evident failure in the particular named so vitiate the Doctor's interpretation that its value is seriously impaired ? We believe not. Dr. Thomas had a sound grasp of principles, and the study of his principles of interpretation enables, for example, the third part of *Elpis Israel* which is concerned with prophecy and the time of the end, to be read with both discernment and profit. Many things he expected have come to pass. Of outstanding importance may be mentioned Jewish restoration, Britain's connection with Jewish affairs and the near East, Britain's interest in Egypt : and the ascendancy of Russia and the part she will yet play are faithfully indicated. The events connected with the Papacy have been mentioned earlier.

When we turn from prophecy to the general exposition of Scripture very little reservation has been found necessary by the most careful Bible students. The most important proof may be found in the fact that a careful reader who checks Dr. Thomas's exposition by an examination of the Scriptures themselves, finds he has the key that opens up the Bible. Experience shows that such an one will continue through life reading the scriptures only to be more and more confirmed that he has rightly understood them. With this general experience may be contrasted the statement of Pastor Russell of *Millennial Dawn* that a man could understand the Bible only through reading his books ; that if he then read only the Bible he would lose the meaning ; but reading only Russell's writings he would retain the teaching of the Bible. Dr. Thomas's writings make his readers into Bible students, who while retaining a lively sense of indebtedness to him find confirmation in their own independent study.

How came Dr. Thomas to acquire such an understanding that has stood the test of a century ? A few considerations will answer this question.

In a dialogue, in which one of the characters is only a thinly veiled representation of himself, and which in part is biographical, he writes : "As for my other friend of the *Advocate*, he has never been cursed (shall I say ?) with the poison of a theological education. His early years were spent in a private boarding school in England, and from his seventeenth to his twenty-fifth year among physic bottles, lecture rooms, and dead bodies. He knew, and he counted it his happiness to know, nothing about the writings of popular divines ; nor did he ever trouble himself much about ' divinity ' of any kind, till about 1832, three years and a half ago, when he obeyed the gospel of our Divine Master. Since that time, he has addicted himself to the incessant study of the Scriptures. Not having his mind perverted by human tradition, it just takes whatever impression the word may make upon it ; like a blank sheet the impression of the printer's types. This is the true cause of the difference between them—the teacher of the one is the word of God alone ; the teacher of the other is compounded of popular divines and the word. You need not marvel then that they come to such different conclusions."

His educational and professional training combined to give him keen perception. His natural qualities of fearlessness and steadfastness led him to hold fast that which he perceived to be the Truth. Like Paul the apostle, he had one consuming purpose, to respond to God's commands. Such a strong motive is a unifying force in life, and it gave zest to the study of the Oracles, earnestness in preaching, endurance in opposition, courage in disappointment ; it enabled him to put aside worldly gain, and to toil in bringing God's truth to others.

So fearless and outspoken a writer inevitably was charged with ambition for leadership. Dr. Thomas was not unaware of the charges : on one occasion he made the following reply : "A few brave hearts who understand, love, and practise the simplicity that is in Christ, are more desirable and efficient than a multitude who have a name to live while really dead in trespasses and sins. Our enterprise is not a pecuniary speculation, therefore numbers for lucrous purposes are not our aim. Our enterprise is to develop the truth formatively, that the truth as the incorruptible seed of God, may generate such a people for the Lord as he will not be ashamed of at his appearing. Our platform is this, and upon it there is no room for the old Adam and his traditions."

His whole aim in his work might be expressed in one of the last numbers of the *Apostolic Advocate*. " The work to be done now is not so much ' to convert the world ' as to induce the people of God to come out of Babylon, and to prepare a people for the Lord to receive him at his appearing. . . . But how are ' the people of God ', whether immersed or unimmersed professors of Christianity, to come out of Babylon ? If this question were put to me, I should reply by returning to primitive institutions ; by becoming obedient ; and by obtaining the knowledge of salvation in the remission of sins. And, it may be asked, how is this to be done ? To which I would reply, if you believe the gospel preached by the Apostles, be baptized in the name of Jesus Christ for the remission of sins ; observe the ' all things ' enjoined in relation to the New Institution in the apostolic writings ; deny yourselves of all ungodliness and worldly lusts ; live soberly, and righteously, and religiously in this age ; looking for the appearing of Messiah, who is our hope and our life. Let the people of God do this, and they are a prepared people ; let such a sect be found on earth, and it will be the subject of the rejoicings and exultations of those who give glory to the Omnipotent because the Lamb's wife has prepared herself ; and to whom it is given to be clothed in fine linen, pure and resplendent ; which is the righteous actions of the saints. This is the reformation I have sought, but in no one instance have I found it in community as yet ; but my confidence is that it will appear as the consummation of the present agitation in the religious world."

(VI) THE MAN

WE would like to get a glimpse of the man, but this is more difficult than finding out the external facts which reveal the expositor and the worker. What was the man himself ? Only two or three are still alive who saw Dr. Thomas, and any impressions they have must necessarily be the impressions a child receives. The writings do not help very much—in fact they may mislead in some particulars. The contributions to the *Herald* are either essentially expositional or controversial. The first only enables us to know the mind, the second, from one with the directness of speech that marked Dr. Thomas, can create an impression of a man who was merely a controversialist, and upon whose character the truth had left little impress.

We miss in the *Herald* the exhortational element which has been a regular feature in the *Christadelphian* almost from its beginning. Doubtless circumstances governed this; Dr. Thomas's work was that of a pioneer and the work of setting forth the true teaching of scripture predominated. When the *Christadelphian* took the place of the *Herald* more ecclesias had been established, a more regular form of memorial service adopted, and therefore the feature generally spoken of as " Sunday Morning " naturally found its place.

All the Doctor's writings, however, reveal a keen awareness of the need for living in harmony with God's commandments. Many pages of *Elpis Israel* can be cited as an example. There are occasional references in his travel records which show that he looked for the " fruits " among the brethren which should be produced when the truth is known. When his own character was slandered by his opponents, brethren and communities who knew him well were quick to declare the facts as they knew him—that he was a man of integrity who displayed the Christian graces in everyday life. From a man in love as he was with the Word of God such traits of character would be a natural result. The fact is, the very vigour of his advocacy for doctrine as taught in the Scriptures, together with pungency of style on occasion, has obscured the finer and gentler side.

Three quotations may be made bearing upon the spirit of the man. Many other extracts could be gathered up from scattered allusions, but these suffice. The first is the humble reference to his errors when he made his " confession and objuration " :

" We admit, that we have not accepted the slanders and reproaches bestowed upon us with that gratitude the word inculcates. Born and educated in a country where character is more precious than gold, we have, in time past, felt like Ephraim unaccustomed to the yoke, when suffering under the galling imputations of reckless assailants. Experience, however, has taught us, that in this country, slander is the people's broadsword with which they seek to slay the reputations of all who aim to serve them otherwise than in subservience to their passions, in the things of time or eternity. But, blessed be our foes in their basket and store. We thank them for their persecution, and opposition with which they have encountered us. But for these, we should have been, perhaps, like them, ' in the gall of bitterness and bond of iniquity '. Their course has compelled us to study more diligently than we might have done the Holy Scriptures, that we might be better able to give an answer to every one that should ask a reason of the Hope that is in us. Had they let us alone, it is probable we should have been in good repute indeed with them and their leaders : and might even have been teaching the same fables ; which, however, would have deprived us of the pleasure of confessing our errors and mistakes, and of thus publicly renouncing and bidding them adieu."

When he had been the subject of some very hostile comments he penned the following prayer :

"O Lord God in heaven above, merciful and gracious Father, what can we render to Thee for Thy goodness ? Thou hast appointed a day in which Thou wilt judge the world in righteousness by Jesus Christ ! Blessed be Thy holy name. We shall all be judged before his tribunal and not man's. Then the hidden things of men shall be brought to light, and their secret thought shall be unveiled, to their justification or reproof ! Thou God seest us all, for all hearts are open before Thee ! If Thou beholdest any thing in me displeasing in Thy sight, let me fall into Thy hands, and not into the hands of those who thirst for my destruction ! Grant me patience to endure their unrighteousness, and by fidelity and perseverance to overcome the iniquity of their doings ; and may the word of the truth concerning the hope of the glorious gospel of Jesus be established in these countries ; and may those who now oppose it, in ignorance and unbelief, find mercy of Thee, repenting of their waywardness, and purifying their hearts by faith, that they may be accepted when the Lord comes ! ' Forgive them, for they know not what they do ' ; and may we all at length find an abundant entrance into the kingdom of the future age, to the glory of the great Immanuel's name ! Amen ! Amen ! "

Our third quotation is from the pen of bro. R. Roberts, with whom Dr. Thomas found a home when he visited Huddersfield during 1862, and on his last visit near the end of his life, when bro. Roberts had removed to Birmingham. Bro. Roberts, meeting his guest at the station, says :

"At last a quiet, firmly-set, square-shouldered, literary looking gentleman, in frock coat and chimney-pot hat, with ruddy countenance and white beard, emerged from one of the carriages, and began to pick his way in the crowd, with one valise in his hand. I was quite timid about saluting him, because it might not be Dr. Thomas after all. After following him a little, I said to him with a palpitating heart, ' Mr. Thomas ? ' He said, ' Yes '. We then exchanged greetings, and I led him out of the station to a cab, and conveyed him to our apartments (by that time changed to 25, Albion Street, the house of brother Rhodes) where my sister companion awaited him in a state of excitement, which soon changed to comfort and joy, in the presence of the cordial and social dignity of a mature and venerable man whom we found so much more interested, if possible, than ourselves in the sublime matters that had engaged our efforts and attention for some years . . . It is impossible to exaggerate the charm of Dr. Thomas's company under our own roof (though it was but a lodging house roof). He was a totally different man from what his writings prepared us to expect. These writings were so pungent, so vigorous, so satirical, and had such a sledge-hammer force of argument and denunciation that we looked for a regular Boanerges—a thunder-dealer, a man not only of robust intellect, but of a combative, energetic, self-assertive turn, whose converse would be largely spiced with explosive vocables.

" Instead of this, he was quiet, gentle, courteous, well-mannered, modest, absolutely devoid of affectation or trace of self-importance. His calm, lofty, cordial reverence for the Scriptures was very edifying to us, after several weary years of contact with drivellers and blasphemers ; and his interest in all circumstances pertaining to the fortunes of the truth of which we had to tell him was very refreshing after a toilsome course of solitary labour in a cause that all our neighbours pitied us as fools for taking up. It was so gratifying and so strengthening, too, to have his fireside answers to the various scriptural questions we had to propound. ' Let me see ', he would say, ' where is that passage ? ' and would turn it up, and then proceed in his dignified and incisive way to ' open to us the Scriptures '. Household matters and business shrunk into their proper smallness in his company. It was truly a ' little heaven below ', the like of which we have rarely since experienced in the rugged journey of probation."

The following concerns the later visit, when Dr. Thomas was accompanied by his daughter :

" When the train drew up at the New Street platform, a white-bearded, military-looking gentleman, accompanied by a slim lady in black, became visible among the crowd that stepped out of the carriages. I quickly saluted Dr. Thomas, who was playfully disappointed. He said he had thought of going aside to an hotel, and not letting us know till he walked into the meeting on Sunday—which he hoped he might do, unrecognized as a listener ! I told him he had no idea of the state of feeling among the brethren, or he would never have dreamt of such a thing . . . The Doctor stayed in Birmingham about four weeks. They were weeks of pure enjoyment to all the friends of the truth—especially to those of us who had the privilege of intimate association with him. His lectures were interesting and powerful ; in private he reminded us of Christ by a gravity of deportment that was mixed with urbanity, and a dignity that was sweetened by unfeigned humility, a quiet penetrating depth of intelligence, unweakened by the least approach to frivolity ; a cordial interest that was free and natural in all things connected with the truth. It was a great change to us to have one in our midst who was, if possible, more interested in all our arrangements than we ourselves.

" The first meeting for the breaking of bread was a thrilling interest. We were meeting at the time at the Athenaeum Hall, at the corner of Temple Street and Temple Row West, a place capable of holding about 300. None of the brethren had seen the Doctor. They were in full muster to the number of 120 or thereabouts. None were late that morning except the Doctor himself, who came in after they had been all seated for about ten minutes. As he quietly walked in and was led forward to a front seat, there was a deep hush of attention. The meeting that followed was of the sort that goes deep into the memory. After hearty singing and preliminary exercises, the Doctor was called upon, and ascending the platform addressed the assembly. He made no personal allusions of the kind that are common with public speakers. He did not say how pleased he was to be there ; how gratifying to his feelings for such interest to be taken in his work, nor how deeply moved he was by the appreciation that had been manifested, etc. He simply said, in dignified and sonorous voice, ' It is written in the prophets ' (and proceeded to call our attention to the truth). I was a shorthand writer, but I was too deeply moved by the words of the speaker to take them down, and I am not aware that anyone else took notes of them. They were words of weight and power, such as we probably shall not hear again till we meet in the kingdom of God."

JOHN CARTER.

PART II

A SELECTION FROM THE WRITINGS OF JOHN THOMAS, M.D.

A SELECTION FROM THE WRITINGS
OF JOHN THOMAS, M.D.

I

GOD'S DESIGN IN THE CREATION OF THE WORLD

A WISE master Builder never begins to build without a design. This he drafts after a scale of so much to the foot. This is the extension, or time, so to speak, of the building to be erected. Having well considered the whole, he concludes, that it is the best possible plan that can be devised in harmony with the principles of architecture. It then becomes his purpose, his foreordination, predetermination, or design. All subsequent arrangements are made to conform to this recorded purpose, because it is the very best his most deliberate wisdom and ingenuity could devise.

The next thing he does is to collect together all the necessary materials, whether of brick, stone, lime, sand, wood or aught else that may be needed. If a spectator desired to know what all these crude matters were heaped up together in one place for—the Architect would reveal to him his purpose by submitting the draft of his plan in all its lines, circles, angles, etc. ; and he would describe to him such an arrangement of the materials as would impress the spectator's mind with an image of the edifice, though it would fall infinitely short of the reality when perfected.

If we suppose the mansion to be now finished, the Architect would then order the materials which were left, as unfit to work into the building, and therefore worthless—such as broken bricks, split boards, sand, and so forth, to be cast out as rubbish to be trodden under foot, or to burn. Thus the edifice is built out of the accumulated materials, according to the outline of the draft, or purpose of the Builder ; and the work is done.

Now, the Great Builder of the Heavens and the Earth is God. He either made all things at random, or He did not. Who will say that the Creator permitted chance to elaborate the terrestrial system ? The scripture declares that every thing was measured, meted out, and weighed, and that the Spirit of the Lord executed His work without any to counsel or instruct

Him. As it is written, " Who has measured the waters in the hollow of his hand, and meted out heaven with a span, and comprehended the dust of the earth in a measure, and weighed the mountains in scales, and the hills in a balance ? Who hath directed the spirit of the Lord, or being his counsellor hath taught him ? With whom took he counsel, and who instructed him, and taught him in the path of judgment, and taught him knowledge, and showed to him the way of understanding ? " (Isa. 40 : 12).

God then, had in His own mind a pattern, or design, of all the work that was before Him, before He uttered a word or His spirit began to move. This design, or archetype, which placed the beginning and the end of all things before Him in one panoramic view, was constructed in harmony with the principles—the eternal principles of His unbounded realm ; which coincide with the immutable attributes of His character. The work He was about to execute was for His own pleasure ; for, says the scripture : " Thou hast created all things, and for thy pleasure they are, and were created ". *But when the work is finished, which for His own pleasure God labours to elaborate, what will it consist in ?* This inquiry we make as spectators of the wonders of creation, providence, and redemption. We behold the materials of these departments of Eternal Wisdom, and we ask to what are they all tending ? What temple, or edifice, is the Divine Architect raising for His own pleasure or glory ? If we turn our thoughts within us, there is no voice there which unfolds the philosophy of His doings ; if we soar into the heavens, or descend into the sea ; if we search through the high places of the earth—we find no answer ; for " Who hath known the mind of the Lord, who hath been his counsellor, or who hath instructed him ? " No ; if we would ascertain what God designs to elaborate out of the past, the present and the future, we must be content to assume the attitude of listeners, that He may reveal to us from His own lips what He intends to evolve in the consummation of His plans.

God has caused a Book to be written for our information upon His design—His ultimate purpose in the works of creation, providence, and redemption ; which are the three grand divisions of His labour, and are all tending to the development of one great and glorious consummation. This book is termed THE BIBLE.

If we take up a book, how would we proceed to ascertain the end the author had in writing his book ? We should read it through carefully, and thus having made ourselves acquainted with its contents we should be prepared to answer the question intelligently and accurately. Why do we not do so with the Bible ? God is the Author ; Moses, the Prophets, and the Apostles are but the amanuenses of the whole. If then the question be put, what end had God in view in the six days' work of the creation ; in His subsequent providential arrangements in relation to man and nations ; and in the propitiatory sacrifice of the Lamb of God ; we proceed in the same way with the Bible in which He tells His own story, and answer accordingly to the light we have acquired.

Now the Book of God is peculiar in this—it narrates the past, the present, and the future all in one volume. We learn from the accuracy of its details in relation to the past and the present, to put unbounded confidence in its declarations concerning the future. In ascertaining, therefore, the ultimate design of Eternal Wisdom in the creation of all things, we turn to the end of the Bible to see what God has said shall be as the consummation of what has gone before ; for what He has said *shall be the permanent order of creation, must be the end He originally designed before ever the foundations of the earth were laid.*

Turn we then, to the last two chapters of the Book of God. What do we learn from these ? We learn that there is to be a great physical and moral renovation of the earth ; that every curse is to cease from off the earth ; and that it is to be peopled with men who will be deathless, and free from all evil ; that they will then all be the sons of God, a community of glorious, honourable, and incorruptible beings, who will constitute the dwelling place of the Lord God Almighty and the Lamb, the glory of whose presence will give a brilliancy to the globe surpassing the splendour of the sun. The globe a glorious dwelling place, and its inhabitants an immortal and glorious people, with the presence of the Eternal Himself—is the sum of the consummation which God reveals as the answer to the question concerning His ultimate design. The following testimonies will prove it.

" The inheritance of the saints in light " (Col. 1 : 12) ; "An inheritance incorruptible, and undefiled, and that fadeth not away, reserved in heaven " (1 Pet. 1 : 4) ; " I saw a new heaven and a new earth . . . and there was no more sea. And I saw the holy city, new Jerusalem, coming down from God out of heaven, prepared as a bride adorned for her husband. And I heard a great voice out of heaven, saying, Behold, the tabernacle of God is with men, and he will dwell with them, and they shall be his people, and he himself will be with them, their God. And God shall wipe away all tears from their eyes ; and there shall be no more death, neither sorrow, nor crying, neither shall there be any more pain : for the former things (or " Heaven and Earth " in which they existed) are passed away. And he that sat upon the throne said, Behold, I make all things new. And he said unto me, Write : for these words are true and faithful. And he said unto me, It is done. I am Alpha and Omega, the beginning and the end. I will give unto him that is athirst of the fountain of water of life freely. He that overcometh shall inherit all things ; and I will be his God, and he shall be my son " (Apoc. 21 : 1-7). "And there shall be no more curse " (22 : 3).

Now the creating of all things new implies that the constitution of things that preceded the New Creation was an old system, which had answered the end for which it was arranged in the first instance. This old system, termed by John " the former Heaven and the former Earth ", is manifestly the system of the World, based upon the six days' creation ; for the " former things ", which had passed away in the vision, were the sea, death, sorrow, sin, the curse and all their correlatives. This Old Creation with its constitution of time, then, is but a grand system of means to a still grander and inconceivably more magnificent Creation, which will be of an unchangeable and eternal constitution. The old Mosaic Heavens and Earth are to the New Creation, as the accumulated materials of a building are to the edifice about to be built : and hold the same relation to the New Heavens, as the animal system does to the spiritual. We repeat, then, that the creation of the Six Days, which we have termed Mosaic, because Moses records their generations, was not the end but the beginning, when God commenced the execution of His purpose which He had arranged ; the ultimatum of which was, to elaborate by truth and judgment as His instrumentality, a world of intelligent beings, who should become the glorious and immortal population of the globe under an immutable and eternal constitution of things.

We come now to a very interesting, and indeed, immensely important inquiry, namely, upon what principle, or principles, did God propose to carry out this ultimate design in relation to the peopling of the Spiritual or Eternal World ? Was it upon a purely intellectual, or purely moral, or purely physical principle, or was it upon all these three conjoined? For example, He peopled the present animal world by creating a human pair, and placing them under the natural, or physical laws ; will He people the spiritual world by physical generation and physical regeneration, or upon some other principle revealed in His word? To these questions we shall endeavour to reply.

As the doings of the Almighty are all for His own glory, we would ask this question : Would it have been to the glory of God, if He had made man a mere machine?—had He made inexorable necessity the law of His nature, which he must yield to, as the tides to the moon, or the earth to the sun? Who will affirm it? The principle laid down in the scripture is, that man honours God in obeying His laws ; but this honour consists, not in a mechanical obedience, such as matter yields to the natural laws, but in a voluntary obedience, while the individual possesses the power not to obey, if he thinks best. There is no honour, or glory to God, in the fall of a stone to the centre of the earth ; the stone obeys the law of gravitation involuntarily : the obedience of man would have been similar had God created and placed him under a physical law, which should have necessitated his motions, as gravitation doth of the stone.

Does a man feel honoured, or glorified, by the forced obedience of a slave? Certainly not ; and for the simple reason, that it is involuntary, or compulsory. But let a man, by his excellencies, command the willing service of free men—of men who can do their own will and pleasure, yet voluntarily obey him, and if he required it, are prepared to sacrifice their lives, fortunes, and estates, and all for the love they bear him ;— would not such a man esteem himself honoured and glorified to the highest degree by such signal conformity to his will? Unquestionably ! and such is the honour and glory which God requires of men. Had He designed a mere physical obedience, He would have secured His purpose effectually by at once filling the earth with a population of immortal adults, so intellectually organized as to be incapable of a will adverse to His own—who should have obeyed Him as the piston rod and wheels do the steam by which they are moved . . .

The following testimonies will show the principle upon which God designs to people the Spiritual World. " I will give unto him that is athirst of the fountain of the water of life freely ; and he that overcometh shall inherit all things " ;

" Blessed are they that do his commandments, that they may have right to the Tree of Life, and that they may enter through the gates into the city " ; " To him that overcometh will I give to eat of the Tree of Life which is in the midst of the Paradise of God " ; " He shall not be hurt by the second death " ; " To him that overcometh, and keepeth my works to the end, I will give power over all nations : and he shall rule them with a rod of iron " ; " If thou doest well, O Cain, shalt thou not be accepted ? " " These things are written that ye may believe, and that believing ye may have life through his name "—not a miracle ; "As many as received him, to them gave he the power to become sons of God, to them that believe on his name ; which were born not of blood, nor of the will of the flesh, nor of the will of man, but were born of God " ; " He that believes the gospel and is baptized shall be saved " ; " God will render to every man according to his deeds ; to them who by patient continuance in well doing seek for glory, honour, immortality—eternal life " ; but of testimonies there is no end. The law of the Lord is perfect and without a single exception. There are no " perhapses ", or " maybes " ; it is not " yea and nay, but amen—so let it be—in Christ Jesus ". The only way to the Spiritual World is in the path of obedience to the law of God.

Now from these testimonies it is plain that to attain the rank of sons of God in the Eternal World—where indeed all are sons without exception—human beings without respect to age, sex or condition, must believe and obey the truth ; for " without faith it is impossible to please God " ; it does not except infants, idiots, and pagans ; but it declares the principle without qualification. If faith then be required, it is manifest that God designed to move men *by motive*, not by necessity— *but by intellectual and moral considerations*.

Behold, then, the conclusion of the matter. There are two Systems, or Worlds, in the purpose of God ; the one, the Animal, the other, the Spiritual. Out of the animal, as the aggregate of buildings materials, God designs to elaborate the Spiritual World, as a new palace in His empire. This new dwelling place for the Divine Majesty is to consist of a sealess and luminous globe, and peopled with myriads of glorious, honourable, and incorruptible men, of equal rank and station with the angelic host. The means by which He proposed to consummate this magnificent conception were, first by His creative energy ; secondly by His providential arrangements ;

thirdly, by the moral force of truth, argued and attested ; and lastly, by judgment, and recreative energy in the destruction of the wicked and formation of the New Earth.

The principle upon which animal men might attain to the Angelic Order in the Spiritual World of which we speak, He has laid down as a voluntary obedience to His law under the several constitutions He has arranged. Hence, He created man " free to stand and free to fall "—capable of doing, or not doing, as he preferred ; but responsible for the consequences to the extent of the knowledge imparted to him. It is true, God could have ordered things otherwise, and have prevented much present suffering ; but He did not, and the best reason that can be given is, that it was not His pleasure.

2

THE DOGMA OF " IMMORTAL SOULS " SUBVERSIVE OF THE TRUTH

1. *It contravenes the Mosaic account of the Fall.*

MOSES says, that God made Man " a living soul " ; but Orthodoxy says, that God made man an " immortal soul ".

God said, " In the day thou eatest of the Tree of Knowledge, dying thou shalt die " ; but the dogmatist says, " in the day thou eatest thereof thou shalt die figuratively, and thy body shall die literally ; and thus thy immortal soul shall become liable to the pains of hell for ever ".

God said, " Dust thou art, and unto dust thou shalt return " ; the dogmatical theologians say, " Dust is thy body and of the Divine Essence thy soul, and unto dust shall thy mortal body return, and thy soul to me, or else to hell ".

"And the Lord God said, Behold, the man has become like one of us, to know good and evil ; and now, lest he put forth his hand and take also of the Tree of Life, and eat, and live forever ; therefore, the Lord God sent him forth from the Garden of Eden ". The Dogmatists alter this to suit their systems in teaching that the pronoun " he " has reference to his body. With this emendation it should read, " lest he put forth his hand and eat, and his body live for ever ".

But it is easier said than proved, that a " living soul " and " an immortal soul " are identical. They are not the same ; but as diverse as blood and spirit.

It is obvious, that the subject of the penalty is the violator of the law. The eater of the fruit was to die, and the sentence was consummated in the 930th year of his age ; but the record says nothing of liability to the pains of hell for ever.

The expulsion of an immortal from Eden that he might not live for ever is nonsense. The truth is, Man is a living soul ; that is, a living creature. He was created with a susceptibility of death or life eternal, predicated upon his own choice ; which was a quality that distinguished and exalted him above all other animals. In Eden he held a position relatively to the Tree of Knowledge and the Tree of Life. Death and life eternal were before him ; the one the wages of sin ; the other, the reward of obedience, as has been revealed. If he had been created subject to death, death would certainly not have been assigned as a punishment for eating the forbidden fruit ; and had he been formed immortal from the dust, or immortality been breathed into his nostrils, eternal life would not have been connected with any thing exterior to him. The truth is, that his destiny was predicated upon his actions. He disobeyed, and, in transgressing, he came under the sentence of the Law, which said " to dust thou shalt return ". This was a process of many centuries : a process which might have been interrupted. To avert this calamity, the Lord God expelled him from the Garden ; for had he eaten of the Tree of Life he would have lived forever, an immortal sinner, and subject to all the ills of flesh eternally : therefore, because he had come to know evil, the Lord God drove out the man, that he might not " live forever ".

2. *The dogma of the immortality of the soul reduces the Mosaic account to an absurdity.*

When God breathed into man's nostrils the breath of lives, say they, He imparted to him a particle of His own Essence, immaterial, and of course, of a nature kindred to Himself, and this they style the immortal soul. If this be true, what was it that sinned against God ? A particle of God sinned against Himself ! What became liable to the pains of hell forever ? The immortal soul ! Then a particle of God became liable to the pains of hell forever ! Does the immortal soul in rebelling against the law of God show that it is of a kindred nature to the Deity ? What is subjected to glowing torments in hell forever ? The immortal soul, say divines ! Then God consigns a part of Himself to eternal misery for disobeying His own appointments ! If this be wisdom, it is certainly that wisdom which the scripture describes as " earthly, sensual, and devilish ".

3. *The dogma of the immortality of the soul necessitates a change of the words of the Spirit from their proper to a figurative signification.*

It is well known, that death, destruction, corruption, perdition, etc., are all predicated of man in the scripture ; and are often spoken of in connection with the events of a period subsequent to the present life. The literal and proper signification of these words is extinction of the being. But if a part of man, which is of a kindred nature to the Deity, and therefore indestructible and undying, is to be the subject of death, destruction, corruption, and perdition, it is manifest that the meaning of these words must be changed from their proper signification to some other, so as to suit the theory ; for an undying soul cannot die, therefore when it is said, " The soul that sinneth, it shall die ", this must be understood to mean " shall live in torment ". Again, an indestructible soul cannot be destroyed ; hence, when it is written of wicked souls, " Whose end is destruction ", it must be understood to mean " whose end is to be always destroying, but never destroyed ". Again, an incorruptible soul can never be corrupt ; when therefore, it says, " He that soweth to the flesh shall of the flesh reap corruption ", it follows, seeing that all souls are incorruptible, that they shall never corrupt ; no, not even be tainted with corruption, for then the soul would prove to be mortal.

If then, death means life in misery, and destruction, eternal life in torment, by the same legerdemain, life means life in happiness, and immortality, life. For, if life and incorruptibility be predicated of an everlasting life, it is clear that life must have some accessory idea to make the scripture harmonize with the opinions of men. Hence according to the theory of the dogmatists, the *eis anastasin zōēs* which occurs in John 5 : 29, must not be rendered " to resurrection of life " but " resurrection to enjoy life " ; because according to their theory, the soul is living before resurrection, so that resurrection with them is, not in order that a man may live, but that being alive his soul may be united with the dust ; so that being clothed it may enjoy life.

But if man have no constitutional, or magnetic, qualities, but such as are common to him with all animals, which the scripture plainly teaches, then death, destruction, corruption, etc. ; life, incorruptibility, etc., when spoken in reference to his destiny, all have their literal and proper signification. We do not mean to say that these words are never used figuratively ; they are frequently so used. When a living man is said to be " dead in trespasses and sins ", or when it is said, " Let the dead bury the dead ", it needs no uncommon sagacity to perceive that there is a metaphorical as well as a literal sense to the word " dead ", etc. ; but whether literally or figuratively used, their relative connexion must determine.

4. *The dogma of an immortal soul is subversive of the resurrection and the judgment.*

On the supposition of an immortal soul in man, it becomes necessary to provide for a receptacle for it at death. Being, as is supposed, celestial and ethereal, it is judged incompatible with the fitness of things that it should have sepulture in common with the corruptible body. Hence, it became necessary to translate it to some more congenial system than this material world. Elysium or Paradise in Hades by the Jews and Greeks ; and Heaven or the *Aiōn Plērōma* by the Orientals and Latins, were accordingly selected for the happy abode of such souls as were released from corporeal bondage in favour with the priests. From the bed of death to the everlasting region of light, where dwells Jehovah, " Whom no man hath seen or can see ", thither, it is alleged, it wends its rapid flight. Glowing are the descriptions of the beatitude of this Ideal Form which adorn the fancy sketches of " eloquent divines ". It is judged at death. The fact of its translation to heaven proves its acquittal of trespasses and sins. Death is to it " the path of life " : " fulness of joy " is its portion ; and " pleasures for evermore " its present and inestimable reward !

But, though in essence of a nature kindred to the Deity, there are some immortal, immaterial, ethereal souls, which have become contaminated,—contracted ineffaceable defilement in this world ! These are vicious ; irremediably infected with evil—corrupted incorruptible souls ! Such cannot inherit incorruption ; another receptacle must therefore be provided for them, suited to the invincible malignity they have acquired. By some, this receptacle of wicked immortal souls is styled Tartarus, Hell, etc., which are also supposed to be in Hades, where the Devil holds his court, encircled by demons, " ghosts, and goblins damned ". Some suppose it to be surrounded by a brazen wall, and its entrance continually hidden from view by a cloud of darkness, which is said to be three times more gloomy than the obscurest night. Virgil says—and he is good authority, though a pagan, on this side of the question—that it is surrounded by three impenetrable walls, and the impetuous and burning streams of the river Phlegethon. The entrance is by a large and lofty tower, whose gates are supported by columns of adamant, which no power, human or divine, can open. This is described as heaving within the molten surges of glowing lava, whose flaming and sulphurous fires roar with

THE FAITH IN THE LAST DAYS

horrific blast ! To this place of torment, we are told, vicious immortal souls are consigned for ever and ever. I will not undertake to detail the horrors of this " endless hell ". The lovers of the terrific can be satiated with such details upon all common and special occasions elsewhere. We have said thus much concerning the place of vicious disembodied souls, that you may judge if torment can surpass this. Eternal life in burning sulphur, superadded to anguish and remorse, is the hell of the dogmatists, into which these souls, or spirits, are plunged at dissolution.

Now on the supposition that all this is true, I should like to know, what purpose would be answered by the resurrection of the mortal body to life ? One says, the happiness and misery of souls is not perfected until united to the body ; hence the necessity of the resurrection. This is the only hypothesis they can take refuge in ; and manifestly it is of a flimsy texture. We object to this, that there is no such doctrine taught in scripture as the partial, or incomplete, happiness or misery of virtuous and vicious immortal souls in heaven and hell, immediately consequent upon dissolution. If such a dogma be taught let us have direct testimony from the prophetic and apostolic writings. If souls go to God and to the Devil at death, there is then no use in resurrection ; for resurrection is life— it is the " path of life " ; how then, can an immortal soul be said to arise to life, when it shall have been living in heaven for thousands of years ; or a vicious soul to arise to punishment, when it has been agonizing in flames for ages ?

This dogma of immediate flight to heaven or hell at dissolution necessarily flows from the supposition of an immortal soul in man. It is a part of Oriental science " falsely so called ", and was mixed up with Christianity by men " in whom the God of this world had blinded the minds of them which believed not " (the truth in its purity) ; " understanding neither what they say, nor whereof they affirm ". Their " profane vain babblings " have eaten as doth a canker ; of whom were Hymenæus and Philetus, who concerning the truth of the One Hope " erred, saying that the resurrection is past already ; and overthrow the faith of some ".

Hymenæus and Philetus appear to have been conspicuous opponents of the Apostle's doctrine. He alludes to them in 1 Tim. 6 : 20, 21, and names them in his second epistle. They appear to have been professors of Oriental science, which Paul justly avers is " falsely so called ". The dogma of a translation to heaven or hell at death is one item of that profane science, by which they overthrew the faith of some in the resurrection. Their reasonings concerning the tradition of souls, he terms " profane vain babblings, and oppositions of science falsely so called ". This " profane " or Gentile hypothesis rendered nugatory the doctrine of the resurrection ; for, if souls go to heaven when the breath departs from the nostrils, what use is there in resurrection ? Manifestly none ! They saw this clearly, and therefore they concluded, that all the resurrection there would be had " passed already ". If Hymenæus and Philetus were correct in their views of immortal souls, and their direct translation to heaven at death, they were right in affirming that " there is no resurrection of the dead " ; but if " the truth " averred the resurrection of the dead, their hypotheses were " profane vain babblings " indeed, and " oppositions " to the truth, " of science falsely so called " : for the annunciation of a resurrection of the dead to life plainly teaches a previous interruption of man's existence for a time and a subsequent renewal thereof.

Illustrative of this view of the case of these errorists, I adduce the following fact. Justin Martyr, who was contemporary with the Apostle John, testifies that in the primitive Church they hold those not to be Christians, who maintained that souls are received into heaven immediately after death. Irenæus ranks these professors as among the heretical ; and the testimony of the church is uniform on this point down into popish times.

From this we learn, that what is orthodox now concerning souls going to heaven was regarded by the contemporaries of the Apostle as sufficiently pestilential to consign the men that held it to eternal reprobation ; for if they were not to be considered as Christians, it was tantamount to excluding them from the pale of salvation.

It appears that there were persons of this class among the Corinthian Christians. " How say some among you ", Paul inquires of them, " that there is no resurrection of the dead ? " By what " profane vain babblings and oppositions of science falsely so called " do you arrive at so fatal a conclusion ? Have Hymenæus and Philetus been tampering with your faith ? Instilling into your minds their profane legends about immortal souls, and their translation to heaven at dissolution, and thus " overthrowing " your faith in the truth, which I declared to you, concerning the resurrection of the dead ?

Do you not remember how ye were baptized for the dead ? Have you renounced the hope ? Were ye baptized for transla-tion of souls to heaven ; or in hope of the resurrection of the dead ? Now pause, as if he had continued, and reflect upon the fatal consequences of adopting these vain suppositions by which the truth of the resurrection is subverted. You did believe what I declared to you concerning the resurrection of Jesus, who was the " first fruits " or earnest of that great harvest of the dead which is yet to come. But if there be no future harvest, then there are no fruits : for the first fruits argues a harvest in the field waiting to be reaped. Now if souls are immortal, and go to heaven at death, there remains in the soil only perished seed, which will never yield an increase ; there is no waiting harvest —no resurrection of the dead. And if there be no harvest of the dead, there can be no first fruits, and therefore, Jesus did not rise, but must either have perished, or gone to the ever-lasting region of light, according to the science and vain philosophy of the Gentiles.

3
THE HEATHEN DOGMA OF AN IMMORTAL SOUL IN MAN SUBVERSIVE OF THE RESURRECTION OF JESUS

He that professes a principle the logical effect of which is to overthrow a gospel truth, involves himself in the same condemnation as the man who in plain words denies it.

IF we establish the truth of this thesis, we are not responsible for the fearful and startling conclusions to which it leads as it regards the " faith " of the professing world. This faith and the " One Faith " we have long regarded as diverse ; and we are more and more confirmed in our conviction. If the proposition cannot be sustained, happy will it be for those in these days, who teach the Hymenæan heresy as a substitute for the glorious " hope of Israel " ; for which Paul stood before the Rulers of the Synagogue in Rome a prisoner in bonds.

To maintain a principle which makes the resurrection of the dead unnecessary, is tantamount, not only to denying a future resurrection, but to denying the resurrection of Jesus, and therefore also of the saints who appeared to many in Jerusalem. This will appear from the following considerations.

Hymenæus and Philetus affirmed that " the resurrection was past already " (2 Tim. 2 : 18). This was equivalent to saying that " there is no resurrection of the dead " (1 Cor. 15 : 12). From this it would appear that Hymenæus and Philetus admitted that there had been a resurrection in some sense. There were in those days certain professors, of whom, perhaps, Hymenæus and his brethren were some, who taught that Jesus Christ had not come in the flesh (2 John 7) ; yet they received the Apostles' doctrine that he did die, was buried, and rose again according to the Scriptures (1 Cor. 15 : 1-4). These persons are styled " deceivers ", and their disciples " bewitched " ; whose minds were " corrupted from the simplicity that is in Christ " (2 Cor. 11 : 3). They preached another Jesus, whom Paul had not preached ; and another spirit and gospel, which the Corinthians had not originally accepted. The Apostle taught simple truths ; they corrupted their " simplicity ". He affirmed that " Jesus came in the flesh " ; that God, when he was crucified, " condemned sin in the flesh " ; that he was buried bodily ; that his flesh was raised from death to life ; and that he ascended as he rose. Hymenæus and Philetus denied all this ; and affirmed that it was mere appearance, and not reality, and that there was no flesh about him.

Why did these men affirm that Jesus Christ had not come in the flesh ? We answer, that they might be the better able to blend the *gnōsis* of the Orientals and the philosophy of the Greeks and Romans with the doctrine of the Gospel, and so popularize it as to make it more palatable to " the wise and prudent " of the age. The simple truth that Jesus was crucified and buried in the flesh, was a stumbling block in the way of the " vain " notion that " instantly when men die, their souls are received up into heaven ". If they admitted that Jesus was buried, it was tantamount to saying that he did not go to heaven, when he said, " Father, into thy hands I commend my spirit " ; but, denying that he was buried bodily, they could then teach that his " immortal soul " was received up when he made this exclamation. It is therefore evident that the thesis, or proposition, which affirms that Jesus was crucified, buried and rose again in the flesh, and the antithesis, or " opposition ", that Jesus Christ did not come in the flesh, are as opposed as pure truth and unmixed error ; and that the antithesis was affirmed in order to make way for the heathen dogma of the immortality of the soul ; which Hymenæus and his faction sought to mix up with repentance and remission of sins by the name of Jesus.

Those, then, who embraced these fictions received another Jesus, and another gospel than that taught by Paul. They preached Jesus crucified in appearance, and translated instantly to heaven, when his immortal soul left his body. This Jesus, they taught, did not rise in the flesh again ; for being in heaven, resurrection was unnecessary : there would, therefore, be no resurrection of the dead ; for as Jesus had gone to heaven without a resurrection of body, all others through all time might do the same. In the name of such a Jesus as this they preached " another gospel ", even repentance and baptism for remission of sins ; so that their disciples were baptized for translation of soul to heaven at death, and not in hope of a resurrection from the dead as were those who believed on Jesus through the word of the Apostles !

The " immortality of the soul ", then, was the principle by which Hymenæus and Philetus subverted the gospel of life and incorruptibility by Jesus at the resurrection ; so that they affirmed " the resurrection was past already " because there was " no future resurrection of the dead ", seeing that, upon their hypothesis, there was none needed.

The vain babblings and pseudo-scientific antitheses, or " oppositions ", of these men invaded the minds of some of the church in Corinth. They were the dogmas of the Nicolaitanes, whose deeds and doctrine are reprobated in Rev. 2 : 6, 15 ; and essentially opposed to " the knowledge of God ", of which some of the Corinthians were destitute. In his letter to them, Paul shows them the consequences of the principle they held ; and tells them that they are only saved by the gospel he preached to them on condition of their retaining in their minds what he preached to them—" by which ye are saved, *if* ye keep in memory what I preached unto you ". They were permitting what he taught to slip from their remembrance. He had preached that Jesus rose substantially from the dead, the first-fruits of a general resurrection of the righteous dead ; but by rejecting this they were in effect denying that God had raised Jesus ; and the non-resurrection of Jesus in the flesh would leave the Gospel without power, nullify their faith, convict the Apostles of falsehood, leave them in their sins under sentence of death, and leave the believers who had died in hope of a resurrection for ever in the grave. All these consequences flow from the dogma of the innate immortality of man.

But it may be objected that Jesus is risen from the dead, and therefore it matters not whether we believe the dead will rise literally or figuratively, or not at all ; it will not alter the facts in the case.

True, it will not alter the facts abstractly considered ; but relatively to the salvation of the individual, it is of immense importance : for, for him to hold a principle which abrogates the resurrection is virtually to deny the resurrection of Jesus : and by this heathen tradition he renders his own faith void by neutralizing the potential truth, that God did raise up Messiah from the dead. As far as the professor is concerned, to deny that Jesus rose, or to hold a principle which renders his resurrection unnecessary, absurd, superfluous, is the same to him as if he had not risen from the dead at all.

Many of the Corinthians who said that the resurrection was past already, doubtless believed that Jesus rose in the flesh ; yet their denying the resurrection of the dead who fell asleep since Jesus rose was considered by Paul as equivalent to denying that Jesus had risen. Their salvation was conditional. " Ye are saved by the gospel ", said he, " if ye keep in memory what I preached to you ". As if he had said, " If you repudiate from your faith the doctrine of the resurrection of the dead saints, by holding any tradition of men which subverts it, there is no salvation for you by the gospel ; for in forgetting this item of belief, you convert the gospel I delivered to you into ' another gospel ' which cannot save ".

To deny that Jesus rose in the flesh, is to deny that there will be any resurrection of the dead ; and to deny that the dead will rise, is to affirm that Jesus has not risen. The propositions arc inseparable, to wit, Jesus rose ; therefore, the dead in him will rise : Jesus did not rise ; therefore, the dead in him will not rise. The dead in Christ will not rise ; therefore Jesus did not rise. The soul is immortal ; therefore, there is no resurrection of the dead ; therefore, Jesus did not rise ; therefore, Jesus went to heaven without resurrection ; therefore, " death ", not resurrection, " is the beginning of immortality ", as Robespierre affirms. And this is essentially the doctrine of the Hymenæans to this day.

4

THE TREE OF LIFE

The first hint of eternal life in relation to man is contained in this passage :—"And now lest he put forth his hand, and take also of the Tree of the Lives—and eat, and live for ever ; therefore the Lord God sent him forth from the Garden of Eden to till the ground ", according to His sentence. From this we learn that the fruit of this tree had the quality of endlessly perpetuating the living existence of the eater. To have eaten of this would have changed Adam from a living into an ever-living soul ; it would have cured him physically, a. l constituted him an incorruptible sinner, the ever abiding subject of the present state of good and evil. This would have been a fearful consummation ; an immortal sinner in a corruptible estate, so that the earth would have become the abode of immortal giants in crime, without any hope of restoration. But this was not according to the Divine Plan. Immortal saints in a state of unmixed good is the finality of creation, providence, and redemption. The sinner was first to be sanctified, then tried, and afterwards to be immortalized, if approved : therefore, lest Adam should invert this order, and become immortal of body before he should be purified from sin and accounted worthy of acceptance, the Lord God expelled him from the dangerous vicinity of the Tree of Lives. He drove him forth that he should not then become incorruptible and deathless.

The expulsion from Eden forcibly separated Adam and Eve from the means of present immortality ; and whether they should attain to incorruptibility and life depended solely upon the will and philanthropy of God. But the Lord did not content Himself with their simple expulsion. Wayward as they had proved themselves, they would doubtless have conspired to regain Paradise, that they might pluck from the Tree of Lives its immortalizing fruit, and so deliver themselves from the sentence of death to which they were consigned. They were expelled indeed ; but to what will not the inconsiderate recklessness of man impel him ! Apprehending some new act of presumption, the Lord God placed a destroying flame to keep, or defend the tree against their intrusion. Here, as in the Most Holy under the Law of Moses, He placed the emblems of His majesty, styled Cherubim, whose consuming

67

fires infolded " the faces—*peni*—of the Lord ". The Tree was hid by these symbols of the divine presence, and the incorruptibility it was originally provided to impart and shadow forth, became to them a thing of hope and of present desire.

Seeing that they could not eat of the Tree of Lives in the midst of Eden, how could they attain to that incorruptible life which it adumbrated ? In what " way " should they walk ; or in what " path " should they tread that would lead them to it ? The answer is, in the words of Moses, in *The way of the Tree of Life* (Gen. 3 : 24). In chapter 6 : 12, this way is styled ". God's Way ", from which all the Antediluvians, save Noah and his family, had apostatized by corrupting it ; as it is written, "All flesh had corrupted his way upon the earth ". But there was no Bible, nor any priests in those days, from whom the exiles from Eden could learn " the Way leading unto life " ; there were none to say unto them, " This is the Way, walk ye in it ". They knew the Tree of Life was situated in the midst of the Garden, and they knew the path which led to it ; but the destroying flame which swept around it on every side, dared them to approach within its precincts. The Tree of Life was in " the East ". They could look towards it wistfully ; but the decree had gone forth, and they could never eat of that tree, nor even touch it and live. With the way to the Tree in Eden, then, they were acquainted, but of the way of God to the Tree of Life adumbrated by that Tree in the East of the Garden, they had no knowledge. They knew not where the new Tree of Life was planted, how could they therefore know the way ? It remained, then, for the Lord God to enlighten them, for He alone could reveal it. They were consequently " taught of God ". He instructed them what to do in order that they might approach His Cherubim, and bow down before His " faces ", without fear of the devouring flame, all the days of their lives. These instructions revealed to them the Way of Acceptance with Him, which then, as also through all subsequent ages, consisted in doing His commandments that they might have right to eat the Tree of Life, which is in the midst of the Paradise of God (Rev. 2 : 7 ; 22 : 3).

" The Way of the Lord God " is synonymous with what is termed " Religion " ; which may be defined as the way of acceptance with God. Adam and his wife supposed they could appear before God acceptably by devising a way of their own by which to conceal their nakedness from His sight. But He refused to sanction their invention, and stripped them of the foliage they had wrapped around them. The way of the Lord teaches that no man can cover his own sin ; it must be covered for him, and none can appoint the investment but the Lord. Hence, it is written, " The Lord God appointed coats of skin and clothed them ".

The appointment plainly indicates the sacrifice of the animals with whose skins they were clothed. Blood was shed in their investiture ; and their sin was covered by the skins of the sin-offerings in conformity with the principle that " without the shedding of blood there is no remission ". But without faith it is impossible to please God. The mere sacrifice of animals, or offering of the fruits of the ground, will not gain man acceptance with God ; for " it is not possible that the blood of bulls or of goats should take away sins ". Hence the association of something to be believed with the sacrifice of " the firstling of the flock and the fat thereof ", or, in other words, of " the Lamb slain from the foundation of the world ". As the subject matter of this faith, then, the Way of God directed the minds of Adam and Eve to the Seed, or descendant, of the woman, whose heel should be bruised on account of the sin of the world, and who should grow up as a tender plant out of a dry ground, and become the Tree of Life in the Paradise of God, in whom should be deposited the incorruptible life of the race of Man. Eve's son was to be the true Tree of Life, of which if a man shall eat he shall live for ever ! A son, who, as the saviour of his people from their sins, must die for sin ; for without the shedding of his blood he could not be a purification-sacrifice, and such an one was necessary, for the blood of animals was inefficient.

But if the sacrifice without the faith was insufficient, so the faith that the Woman's Seed should be a propitiation, unaccompanied by the appointed sacrifices, would leave the worshipper unaccepted ; or if there were both faith in the promise and an oblation, yet, if the offering were not of divine appointment, the subject was regarded as an evil doer ; for, " to obey is better than sacrifice, and to hearken than the fat of rams ". This is obvious from the testimony that " by faith Abel offered unto God a more excellent sacrifice than Cain, by which he obtained testimony that he was righteous, God testifying of his gifts " ; for, " the Lord had respect unto Abel and unto his offering ". From this we learn that Cain was faithless, and therefore unrighteous. He had no faith in typical sacrifice ; he did not believe that without the shedding of blood there was no remission ; or that a purification-sacrifice typified by the " firstling of the flock " would suffer for sin, and become a Tree of Life of the Lord's planting. Hence he " brought (only) of the fruit of the ground an offering to the Lord " ; while his brother, in addition to this, presented of the lambs of his flock. But God had no respect unto Cain's offering ; for Cain evinced a wilful disposition—a waywardness which corrupted the Way of the Lord.

When he perceived that his unbloody and faithless oblation was not accepted, " enmity " was enkindled within him ; his aspect became lowering and dark with destructive feelings ; and he ceased to behold the Faces of the Cherubim with an upright countenance. While in the presence of these the Lord demanded of him why he was angry, and why he looked so downcast ? Abel had done nothing to offend him ; Abel had " done well ", because he had kept the way appointed, and therefore his sacrifice was consumed. Had he done likewise, his offering would have been accepted too ; as it is written, " If thou doest well, shalt thou not be accepted ? and if thou doest not well, sin lieth at the door " ; by all which we are instructed that the obedience of faith was the condition upon which the family of Adam might obtain a right to that Eternal Life which should be procured for them by the Woman's Seed.

The Lord's Way of righteousness and life, styled " the Way of the Tree of Life ", consisted in faith and obedience. This faith, the Apostle tells us, was " the substance of things hoped for, the evidence of things unseen ". By the belief of these things, Abel, Enoch, and Noah pleased God, and " became heirs of the righteousness " on account of which life and incorruptibility are bestowed upon man. They hoped for the Woman's Seed, who they believed, on the testimony of God, should bruise the serpent's head. Their faith was a living faith, and therefore they kept the Way of the Lord, in offering " the firstlings of their flocks and the fat thereof ", " the fruit of the ground ", and in " walking with God " by being " just and perfect in their generations ". Such was the religion of the righteous among the Antediluvians. They were faithful and obedient ; and, as the earnest of what awaited them in the fullness of time, " Enoch was translated, that he should not see death ; and was not found, because God had translated him ; for before his translation he had this testimony, that he pleased God ". Thus they were taught that the corruptible body should put on incorruption, and "this mortal shall put on immortality ", and so " death shall be swallowed up in victory ".

Almost coeval with the institution of religion, as we have seen, it was corrupted by Cain. He rejected from his system the principle of remission by sacrifice, hence he repudiated the promise, and constituted himself an evil doer. Unbelief and disobedience became the characteristics of Cain and his associates, who dwelt eastward of " the presence of the Lord ". These were termed " men ", while those who " walked with God " were styled " the sons of God ". In the sentence pronounced upon Eve and her posterity, the former are indicated as the Seed of the Serpent ; and the latter, the Seed of the Woman, of whom one was to arise that should destroy him. Between these two classes of Antediluvians there was " enmity " such as was evinced in the fratricidal Cain. But the corruption first introduced by this arch-apostate undermined the principles and overthrew the allegiance of " the Sons of God " ; for seeing that " the daughters of men " were fair, they inter-married with them ; and the earth was replenished with a progeny fit only for capture and destruction. Their wickedness was great, and every imagination of the thoughts of their hearts only evil continually. The Antediluvian Apostasy was complete ; " for all flesh had corrupted the Way of the Lord upon the earth ", which was " filled with violence through them ". The Lord by His Spirit in Noah laboured patiently to reclaim them from their " disobedience " ; but they disregarded His expostulations, " eating and drinking, marrying and giving in marriage, until the day that Noah entered into the Ark, when the flood came and took them all away ". But " Noah found favour in the eyes of the Lord " ; " being warned by God of things not seen as yet, and moved with fear, he prepared an ark to the saving of his house ; by the which he condemned the (faithless) world, and became heir of the righteousness which is by faith ".

Eternal Life has been the Hope of those who have walked with God in all past ages and generations, since the fall. In walking with God they have trod the same path, and journeyed along the same road, which is the only " way that leadeth unto eternal life ". The entrance upon this Way is strait, and its passage narrow, and, though it leads to glory, honour, incorruptibility and life, there are few that find it. Belief in the testimony of God, and obedience to His commandments, are the grand characteristics of " His Way " in its successive manifestations in all time. Dispensations have varied ; but these leading principles have always remained the same. " These are written that ye may believe ", and " Blessed are they that do his commandments, that they may have right to the Tree of Life which is in the midst of the Paradise of God ". " I ", says Jesus, " am the Way, the Truth, and the Life "— " I am the resurrection "—" I am the door, and no man entereth but by me."

5

THE KINGDOM OF GOD

(i) *THE NEW COVENANT*

THE BIBLE is *the Book of the Kingdom of God*, and teaches us that it has already once existed for 1024 years under Moses, Joshua, the Judges, and Kings. With the exception of the two years of Ishbosheth's reign, it was a united kingdom for 92 years of this millennium under Saul, David, Solomon, and the first four years of Rehoboam. From the fourth of Rehoboam it was governed by two dynasties. Ten of its tribes were ruled by kings whom they set up over themselves without regard to the authority of Jehovah to whom the kingdom belonged (Hosea 8 : 4). Thus they raised the standard of rebellion, and rejected the sovereignty of the House of David, which God had chosen to be the royal house of his kingdom as long as the sun and moon should endure throughout all generations.

This usurped royalty of Ephraim, or of the Ten Tribes, continued 256 years ; but Judah yet ruled with God, and was faithful with the Most Holy (Hosea 9 : 12), whose dynasty of the family of David they still continued to acknowledge. In the sixth year of Hezekiah, king of Judah, the Ten Tribes were " removed out of God's sight " (2 Kings 17 : 18), that is, they were driven out of His land or kingdom, and the Tribe of Judah only remained.

In a few years, however, Judah became unmanageable. " The chief of the priests and the people transgressed very much after the abomination of the heathen ; and polluted the temple of the Lord which he had hallowed in Jerusalem. And the Lord God of their fathers sent to them by his messengers, continually and carefully sending ; because he had compassion on his people, and on his dwelling place : and they mocked the messengers of God, and despised the words and misused his prophets until the wrath of Jehovah arose against his people, till there was no remedy. Therefore he brought upon them the king of the Chaldees " (2 Chron. 36 : 14-17). This event happened 134 years after the removal of Ephraim out of his sight, or 390 years from the rebellion against the house of David ; so that during 474 years of this millennium of the kingdom of God, David and his lineal descendants reigned over the House of Judah.

The kingdom of God thus brought to a temporary conclusion has never existed since under the sovereignty of a king or kings of the house of David. Its existence ceased even as a Commonwealth during the captivity in Babylon which lasted seventy years. At the end of this period the kingdom reappeared in Judea ; but it was no longer governed by Jewish monarchs exalted to the throne either by God or the people. Jehovah permitted his kingdom to be subject to the lordship of the Gentiles, until the end of 430 years from the burning of the temple by Nebuchadnezzar. For 122 years after the interposition of the Roman senate, God's kingdom was ruled by Jewish princes of the tribe of Levi, that is, until the Gentile of Idumea, named Herod, became king in Jerusalem, in the 37th year of whose reign Jesus, the Son of God and of David and the rightful heir of the throne of Jehovah's kingdom, was born King of the Jews.

From the commencement of Herod's reign till the destruction of Jerusalem and the temple, a period of 111 years, the kingdom of God was possessed by the Gentiles ; in other words, Israel did not possess the kingdom. From the knowledge of this fact, the reader will be well able to appreciate the force of the question put by the apostles to Jesus after his resurrection, and as a result of their conversation for forty days upon the subject of the kingdom, saying, " Lord, wilt thou at this time restore again the kingdom to Israel ? " (Acts 1 : 6). They knew that he was " The Restorer " ; and believing that " all power was given unto him in heaven and upon earth ", they thought the time had certainly come for the Restoration of all things to Israel spoken of by all the prophets from the days of Moses (Deut. 30 : 1-10). This supposition prompted the question.

But they were too fast. Messiah the prince having come, the kingdom could not be " restored again to Israel " so long as the Mosaic Covenant continued in force. This must be " changed ", the kingdom must be suppressed and desolated, and Jerusalem, the city of the Great King of Israel, be trodden under foot of the Gentiles until their times be fulfilled. They had forgotten these things, and that the kingdom of God was not immediately to appear under the sovereignty of the Son of Man ; but that he was first to take a journey into a far country, where he was to be detained until " the times of the restitution ", called also " the Regeneration ", should arrive (Luke 19 : 11-12 ; Acts 3 : 21 ; Matt. 19 : 28). In the year

74 after the birth of Jesus the kingdom was broken up, and the Mosaic covenant trampled under foot—*not finally abolished, but temporarily suppressed, that it may be " changed" in certain essential and highly important particulars.*

God has had no organized kingdom upon earth since its overthrow by the Roman power. The kingdom in the sense of its territory is where it always was ; and its children, or subjects, " His people Israel ", are to be found in every land, still in hope that the time will come when the kingdom will be restored again to them ; and " God will subdue the people under them, and the nations under their feet " ; for they do not forget the testimony that " the kingdom shall come to the daughter of Jerusalem ", and that " the nation and kingdom that will not serve Zion shall perish ; yea, those nations shall be utterly wasted " (Psa. 47 : 3 ; Micah 4 : 7-8 ; Isa. 60 : 12). The Heir of the kingdom is at the right hand of the Divine Majesty ; and his joint-heirs, the most of them, mouldering and sleeping in the dust, with a few surviving stragglers still existing in the Protestant section of the globe, enduring reproach and tribulation in the hope of its speedy and triumphant restitution.

These are the dissolved and scattered fragments of the kingdom of God. Their reunion is a matter of promise, and consequently of hope. The Gentiles must be expelled the territory ; the twelve tribes must be replanted upon the land ; the sleeping heirs of the government must be awaked, and the living believers in this kingdom changed : and to effect all this, God's Heir, the Restorer of the Kingdom, must come and subdue all things to himself. When these things shall come to pass, God will have " accomplished to scatter the power of the holy people " (Dan. 12 : 7), that is, their power shall be no more scattered, but shall be restored to them : and He will come whose right the kingdom is, and God will give it him (Ezek. 21 : 27).

Having thus presented the reader with a few ideas concerning the kingdom that he may have something tangible and definite before his mind when we refer to it, we shall proceed now to make a few remarks to the inquiry, What is a covenant ?

The kingdom as it was, and the kingdom as it is to be, although the same kingdom, is exhibited in the scriptures under Two Covenants, or constitutions. But before adverting more particularly to these it may be necessary to say a word or two in answer to the inquiry, " What is a Covenant ? " It is a word of very frequent occurrence in scripture, and the representative in our language of the Hebrew *berith*. In English, covenant signifies " a mutual agreement of two or more persons to do or forbear some act or thing ". This, however, is not the sense of the word *berith* when used in relation to the things of the kingdom. Men's compliance or acceptance does not constitute the *berith* of the kingdom a covenant. It is a covenant whether they consent or not, and is enforced as the imperious enactment of an absolute king. It points out God's chosen, selected, and determined plan or purpose, entirely independent of anyone's consent, either asked or given, and is equivalent to a system of government fixed by the Prince, and imposed on the people without the slightest consultation between them. Accordingly, what is called the covenant in one place, is denominated the law in another. As, " He hath remembered his *covenant* for ever, the word which he *commanded* to a thousand generations ; which *covenant* he made with Abraham, and confirmed the same unto Jacob for a *law*, and to Israel for an everlasting *covenant* ". " These are the words of the *covenant* which the Lord *commanded* Moses to make with the children of Israel. Thus saith the Lord, Cursed be the man that *obeyeth* not the words of this *covenant* which I *commanded* your fathers." It is evident from this that covenant and law are used as synonymous and convertible terms.

The statements of the New Testament conduct us to the same conclusion. It may be proper to remark here that a *berith*, or covenant, is expressed in Greek as *diathēkē*. This is the word used in the Septuagint as the translation of *berith*.

The *beriths*, *diathēkēs*, or covenants of the kingdom of God are absolute decrees, which make, or constitute things what they were, and what they shall be. Hence " the Builder and Maker (or constitutor) of all things is God ", " for whose pleasure they are and were created ". But though these covenants are absolute, and the necessity to observe them imperative on all who are placed under them, they are replete with blessings to Israel and the nations, being founded upon " exceeding great and precious promises ". Hence they are styled " the covenants of promise " (Eph. 2 : 12). One of them is styled " the Covenant from Mount Sinai " ; and the other, the Covenant from Jerusalem which is above and free (Gal. 4 : 24-27). The Sinai Covenant is synonymous with the Jerusalem Covenant which now is, that is, as it existed in Paul's day ; while the other covenant is the Jerusalem Covenant which is to be ; and because Jerusalem, which is now

" desolate ", will then be " free ", and " above " Jerusalem in her greatest glory under the Sinai Covenant, she is styled *ano*, that is, above, higher, or more exalted ; and is " the mother of all " who believe the things of the kingdom of God, which will come, or be restored to her, when as " the city of the Great King " she shall have awaked from her present non-vinous inebriation, and have put on " her beautiful garments " (Isa. 51 : 21 ; 52 : 1).

Strictly speaking, the Sinai Covenant, although based on promises, is not one of " the covenants of promise " Paul refers to in Ephesians. These are the Covenant of promise to Abraham, and the Covenant of promise to David ; both of which are elemental principles of the Covenant of the Free Jerusalem, which is to " go forth from Zion " in the latter days (Isa. 2 : 3). The Sinai covenant is styled " the first ", the one to be hereafter proclaimed to Israel, " the second ", although the latter is more ancient than the Sinai law in promise by 430 years, yet as a national *berith* constituting the kingdom of God in its civil and ecclesiastical appurtenances under Messiah the prince and the saints, it is second in the order of proclamation to the Twelve Tribes. The promises of the first covenant, which was added to the ancient covenant (Gal. 3 : 19), were the blessings of Mount Gerizim consequent upon their hearkening to the voice of Jehovah their God (Deut. 28 : 1-14). In these there was no promise of eternal glory and life ; of an everlasting individual and national inheritance of the land ; of universal dominion under Abraham's Seed ; of everlasting righteousness from one atonement ; and of no possible evil coming upon them as a nation. On the contrary, the promises were accompanied with terrible threatenings, which have resulted in all the curses of Jehovah pronounced upon them for not observing to do all his commandments and statutes.

But the Second Covenant of the kingdom of Israel is established, or ordained for a law, upon better promises ; and is therefore styled " a better covenant " (Heb. 8 : 6). It abolishes the remembrance of national offences every year. Under the Sinai covenant these accumulated notwithstanding the yearly atonement, until the magnitude of its guilt crushed the nation, and caused its dispersion into all the kingdoms of the earth, as at this day. The better covenant, however, promises to Israel a great and everlasting amnesty for all past national transgression (Jer. 31 : 31-34), not by virtue of the sacrifice of bulls and goats, which cannot take away sins, offered up by a sinful priest of the order of Aaron ; but by a purification that shall be vouchsafed to the repentant tribes, issuing forth from " a fountain opened to the House of David and to the inhabitants of Jerusalem for sin and uncleanness " ; by the blood of which Jesus has entered into the presence of Jehovah himself, a High Priest of the tribe of Judah, conse-crated after the power of an endless life, who will then have appeared the second time, having returned from the Most Holy to proclaim to his nation that God has been merciful to their unrighteousness, and will henceforth remember their sins and iniquities no more (Zech. 13 : 1 ; Heb. 9 : 24 ; 7 : 16 ; 9 : 28 ; Ezek. 36 : 25-28).

This great national reconciliation being consummated, and the Twelve Tribes grafted into their own olive again, they will then enjoy the better promises of the second Covenant. A new heart, and a new spirit they will then possess. They will be God's reconciled people, and He will be their God. He will call for the corn and increase it, and lay no famine upon them ; and they shall receive no more reproach among the nations. Their land that was desolate will then be as the garden of Eden. Jerusalem will be a rejoicing, and Israel a joy. Their lives shall endure as the days of a tree, and they shall wear out the works of their hands (Isa. 65 : 17-25). These are a few incidents of the national blessedness that awaits Israel, when the kingdom of God shall be restored to them, and established in the second millennium of its independence under the New and Better Covenant.

(ii) THE MOSAIC CONSTITUTION OF THE KINGDOM IMPERFECT.

The kingdom of God is the Twelve Tribes of Israel existing in the land promised to Abraham and Christ. When it existed of old time, the Mosaic Covenant was its civil and ecclesiastical code, which appointed and defined all things. But since the appearance of Jesus in Israel, certain things have come to pass in connection with him, which necessitate a change or amendment of the covenant, or constitution, that provision may be made, or scope afforded, for the exercise of his functions as High Priest and king in Israel ; and for the carrying out of the principles which emane from the dedication or purifica-tion of the New Covenant by his blood.

This is the necessity which existed for a change of the law; "for the priesthood being changed, there is made of necessity a change also of the law" (Heb. 7 : 12). The Sinai Constitution of the Kingdom established a changeable priesthood of the tribe of Levi, the chief of which was an hereditary prince of the family of Aaron, called the High Priest. The high-priesthood is an office divinely created; and no man of Israel was allowed to assume it unless he was called of God as Aaron. It was appointed for the offering for men of both gifts to God, and sacrifices for sins; so that the officiating party becomes a mediator between God and men. But the priesthood of Levi and Aaron was imperfect, and therefore could not impart perfection, so as that he who did the service or the worshippers should have no more conscience of sins, and thereby become heirs of eternal life.

This being the nature of the priesthood under which Israel received the Law, or Covenant, the Mosaic institution was weak and unprofitable, and could make nothing perfect (Heb. 7 : 11, 18, 19; 9 : 9; 10 : 1). This imperfection resulted from the nature of the consecration, or blood of the covenant. Aaron and his sons, the altar and nearly all the things of the law were purified by the blood of bulls and goats, etc.; which, however, could not sanctify to the purifying of the heart, or the flesh from the evil within it which makes it mortal. It was necessary to perfection that sin should be condemned in the flesh of the High Priest, which could not be effected by condemning sin in the flesh of the animals sacrificed under the Law. This necessity would have required the death of a High Priest at the celebration of every annual atonement at least, being themselves sinners; but as this was incompatible with the nature of things, animal sacrifices were substituted. So that Aaron and his successors could not under penalty of immediate death enter into the Most Holy without this substitutionary blood. But then this blood was deficient of the necessary sin-remitting qualities.

The blood required was that of the peccant nature— the human; for it was man, and not the creatures, that had sinned. But even human blood would have been unprofitable if it were the blood of one who was himself an actual transgressor, and a victim that, even if an innocent person, had not come to life again. The Messiah in prophecy asks the question, "What profit is there in my blood, if I go down to the pit? Can the dust praise thee? Can it declare thy truth?"

(Psa. 30 : 9). The answer is, None. For if the Christ had died, and not risen again, he would not have been a living sacrifice, and could not have imparted vitality to the things professedly sanctified by it.

The blood of the Mosaic sacrifices was weak and unprofitable because it was not human ; because it was not *innocent* human blood ; and because it was not the blood of one innocent of the great transgression, who came to life again through the power of the Eternal Spirit. For these three important reasons, the blood of the Mosaic covenant could not take away sins, and therefore the High Priest and the nation, individually and collectively, were all left under the curse of the Law, which was death ; for " the wages of sin is death " (Rom. 6 : 23). The law could not give them life who were under it, being weak through the flesh, and deriving no vitality from the blood peculiar to it ; if it could have conferred a title to eternal life, and consequently to the promises made to Abraham and Christ, then righteousness, justification, or remission of sins would have been by the Covenant of Sinai (Gal. 3 : 21 ; Rom. 8 : 3).

But it may be inquired, if the Mosaic institution could not perfect the conscience, nor give a title to eternal life and the inheritance, but left its subjects dead in trespasses and sins, by what means will the prophets and those of Israel who died before Christ came obtain salvation in the Kingdom of God ? The answer is that what the Law could not do, the bringing in of a better hope accomplished (Heb. 7 : 19). The Mosaic sacrifices were provisional, substitutionary, and representative. They pointed to the sacrifice of Christ, which in its retrospective influence was to redeem those from death, who when living had not only been circumcised, but had walked also in the steps of that faith of their father Abraham, which he had being yet uncircumcised. For the promise that he should be the heir of the world was not to Abraham, nor to his Seed, through the law, but through the righteousness of faith (Gal. 3 : 29 ; Rom. 4 : 12, 13). One object of Christ's death is plainly declared to have been, " for the transgressions under the first testament " ; or as elsewhere expressed, " to redeem them who were under the law " (Heb. 9 : 15 ; Gal. 4 : 5). " By his stripes ", says Isaiah, " we are healed. Jehovah hath laid upon him the iniquities of us all. For the transgression of his people was he stricken." The " *we* ", the " *us* ", and the " *people* " in these texts, are the ancient worthies before and under the

Law, as well as those who have believed the gospel, and after his second appearing shall offer "sin offerings, and meat offerings, and burnt offerings, and peace offerings for reconciliation" under the New Covenant consecrated by his most precious blood.

Under the first or Mosaic Covenant, the priests are said to "make reconciliation with the blood of the sacrifices upon the altar, to make atonement for all Israel" (2 Chron. 29 : 24); so under the second, or New Covenant of the kingdom, Ezekiel speaks of "one lamb to make reconciliation for them" (Ezek. 45 : 15). But withdraw from the premises the death and resurrection of Christ, and faith in them and the promises, and the reconciliation under both covenants is imperfect and vain. Animal sacrifices are necessary to the service as types or patterns, and memorials. The Mosaic reconciliation was typical ; the Ezekiel reconciliation, memorial or commemorative. The typical Mosaic could not perfect the conscience of the worshippers, because Christ had not then died and risen again ; nor could they when he had risen, because they were offered by High Priests, whose functions before God were superseded by a High Priest of the tribe of Judah after another order than that of Aaron, then in the presence of Jehovah himself. The Ezekiel reconciliation, however, will perfect the conscience, because Christ had died and lives for evermore ; which death and resurrection connected with the reconciliatory offerings by faith in the worshipper, and offered to God through the Prince of Israel, the High Priest upon his throne after the order of Melchizedec, will constitute sacrifices of a character such as have not been offered on the earth before.

(iii) *THE PRIESTHOOD OF THE NEW COVENANT.*

The sectarian idea is that after John and Jesus proclaimed repentance there would be no temple service performed by Levites that God would accept. But this is contrary to the sure word of prophecy, which testifies that "the Messenger of the Covenant shall sit as a refiner and purifier of silver : and he shall purify the sons of Levi, and purge them as gold and silver, that they may offer unto Jehovah an offering in righteousness. Then shall the offering of Judah and Jerusalem be pleasant unto the Lord, *as in the days of old, and as in former years* " (Mal. 3 : 3, 4). And again the prophet records Jehovah's declaration, that " David shall never want a man to sit upon the throne of the house of Israel : neither shall the priests, the Levites, want a man before me to offer burnt offerings, and to kindle meat offerings, and to do sacrifice continually. . . Thus saith the Lord, If ye can break my covenant of the day, and my covenant of the night, that there should not be day and night in their season ; then (and not before) may also my covenant be broken with David my servant, that he should not have a son to reign upon his throne ; and with the Levites the priests my ministers ". From this it is manifest that the perpetuity of David's throne, and the perpetuity of the Levitical ministrations, are parallel.

Some say that David's throne is now occupied in heaven ; will these same visionaries affirm that the Levites are offering sacrifices there ? For the testimony says, " They shall do sacrifice continually " ! The truth is that this testimony has regard to the time when the kingdom shall be restored again to Israel. At the time the prophecy was delivered there were unbelievers who, like some in our day, declared that the Lord had cast off the house of Israel and the house of Judah. Therefore said Jehovah to the prophet, " Considerest thou not what this people have spoken, saying, The two families which the Lord hath chosen, he hath even cast them off ? Thus they have despised my people, that they should be no more a nation before them. But if my covenant be not with the day and night, and if I have not appointed the ordinances of heaven and earth : then will I cast away the seed of Jacob, and David my servant, so that I will not take any of his seed to be rulers over the seed of Abraham, Isaac, and Jacob : for I will cause their captivity to return, and have mercy on them " (Jer. 33 : 17-26). It is from the time of this return, then, that the perpetuity begins in relation to David's son, and the Levites. Both houses of Israel are still in captivity ; therefore the return is yet future. When that return is accomplished, then henceforth even to " the end " appointed, shall these gracious promises obtain as notable realities in the land of Israel.

It is therefore a principle of the kingdom of God that the Levites shall be priests in that kingdom under the New Covenant, or constitution, as well as under the Old. As it is written, " Thus saith the Lord, They shall be ministers in my temple, having charge of the gates of the house, and ministering to the house; they shall slay the burnt offering and the sacrifice for the people, and they shall stand before them to minister unto them. They shall not come near unto me, to do the office of a priest unto me, nor to come near to any of my holy things in the most holy place. But I will make them keepers of the charge of the house, for all the service thereof, and for all that shall be done therein " (Ezek. 44 : 9-14). The reason given why they shall not do the office of a priest before God, but shall act as menials in the service, and in relation only to the people, is because under the Mosaic Covenant " they ministered to the people before their idols, and caused the house of Israel to fall into iniquity ". This is the ground of their future degradation from their former rank, to that of the lowest class of the priesthood under the New Covenant.

The next class of priests above them is to consist of the Levites, the sons of Zadok (verse 15). These will have no immediate communication with the people in performing the service, but will officiate immediately between the people's priests and " the Prince ", who is then High Priest, and Jehovah's anointed for ever. Zadok signifies just or justified. Zadok, who was contemporary with David and Solomon, is their representative father in the priesthood, as David is their representative father in the royalty, and Abraham their representative father in the faith. Hence in the priesthood, the saints are " the sons of Zadok " ; in the royalty, " the sons of the Prince " (Ezek. 46 : 16) ; and in the faith " the seed or sons of Abraham ".

Eli and his sons were rejected as representative sacerdotal men, because the sons were wicked, and Eli honoured them above Jehovah. Therefore Jehovah said to him, " I will raise me up a faithful priest, who shall do according to that which is in my heart and in my mind ; and I will build him a sure house ; and he shall walk before mine anointed for ever " (1 Sam. 2 : 29, 35). He must therefore become immortal. Now under the Mosaic Covenant this " faithful priest " was Zadok, who walked before David and Solomon. When Absalom and Israel rebelled against the Lord's anointed, Zadok and Abiathar remained faithful with Jehovah and his king. But when David was about to die, Abiathar, who was descended from Eli, conspired to make Adonijah king instead of Solomon ; while Zadok continued faithful to David. Solomon, however, being established on the throne, " thrust out Abiathar from being priest unto the Lord ; that he might fulfil the word of the Lord, which he spake concerning the house of Eli in Shiloh ". He told him he was worthy of death, but he would spare his life for his father's sake, because he suffered with him in Absalom's rebellion ; he therefore exiled him to Anathoth, and promoted Zadok to the high-priesthood in his room (1 Kings 1 : 7, 39 ; 2 : 22, 26, 27, 35).

Now these were representative events. Jehovah will raise up the faithful of the house of Levi, even Zadok and his sons, and they shall walk before His Anointed for ever—even before the " greater than Solomon " when, in " the city of the Great King ", he sits and rules upon his throne as a priest bearing the glory (Zech. 6 : 12, 13), as Prince of Israel for ever. This superior class of Levites " shall come near to me ", saith the Lord, " to minister unto me, and they shall stand before me to offer unto me the fat and the blood : they shall enter into my holy place, and they shall come near to my table, to minister unto me, and they shall keep my charge." From the seventeenth verse to the end of this chapter are the ordinances for the lowest class of Levitical priests.

Here then is a change in the Levitical arrangements, and not an abolition of them. The " service " will be amended, not abolished. In the service under the Mosaic Covenant there were " divers washings " ; but in the service under the New Covenant of the kingdom " washings " are omitted ; for in the Ezekiel Temple there is no laver, or brazen sea provided. But sacrifices remain ; for eight tables are appointed to be set up in the entry of the north gate on which the lowest class of the priests are to slay them for the people. Paul therefore did not mean that the Levitical service was absolutely and finally discontinued—that it should be revived no more ; but that it should be amended to adapt it to the new circumstances created by the sacrifice and high priesthood of Jesus, which was to supersede the priesthood of Aaron.

If we be asked the reason for the conclusion that Paul meant amendment, and not final discontinuance of the Levitical service, we reply, that it is found in the phrase " until the time of reformation " used by him. His words are *mechri kairou diorthōseōs*. The Levitical service continued unchanged for forty years after the proclamation of " reformation " by Jesus ; so that the *kairos* or definite time for discontinuance was not at his preaching, or even the rending of the temple vail. The Mosaic service was not " imposed until the time of *metanoia* ", which is the word signifying the " reformation " preached. *Metanoeite*, " Repent ye ", said Jesus. No ; it was " imposed until the time of diorthōsis", which is not " repentance ", but emendation, amendment ; from *diorthoō*, to correct, or make right. The subject of the *diorthōsis* is the Mosaic Covenant, not the disposition of men.

The Mosaic Constitution must be amended to make way for a new order of priesthood, and a service which shall show forth the perfection of its character. The work of amendment in regard to its foundation was laid in the death and resurrection of Jesus. It then became necessary to gather out of Judah sons for Zadok, and the Prince. " Behold, I and the children whom God has given me are for signs and wonder in Israel " (Isa. 8 : 18 ; Heb. 2 : 13). These children being separated to Jesus from the tribe of Levi and the nation for the purposes to be accomplished through them at " the restitution of all things ", nothing remained for that epoch, but to give the Mosaic constitution a thorough shaking. This is called shaking the heaven, and was the fulfilment of the prophecy by Haggai reproduced by Paul in his epistle to the Hebrews (Hag. 2 : 6 ; Heb. 12 : 26, 27). " Yet once, it is a little while, saith the Lord of hosts, and I will shake the heavens and the earth." The " little while " was 587 years from the delivery of the prediction ; and about ten years from the date of the epistle. It was the last time the nation of Israel and the constitution of their kingdom were to be shaken. Their commonwealth was to be shaken that " the things made " or constituted, by the Mosaic Covenant, which were incompatible with the rights of the Lord Jesus founded upon " the word of the oath " (Heb. 7 : 21, 28) might be " removed " ; and that " those things which " were in harmony with that word, and which " cannot be shaken might remain ". This then was the first stage of the " emendation ", or as the Gentiles would say, of " the amendment of the constitution ".

The next work in the carrying out the purpose of emendation is thus expressed in Haggai—" I will shake the sea and the dry land ; and I will shake all nations, and the desire of all nations shall come ; and I will fill this house with glory, saith the Lord of hosts ". When this was spoken the temple was in ruins, the foundation only being laid. The people then returned from Babylon said, " The time has not come that the Lord's house should be built " (Hag. 1 : 2, 4, 9) ; that is, the 70 years that it was to lie waste from the time of its destruction are not yet accomplished, 66 years only having elapsed. But

Haggai was sent to them to stir them up to the work, and in four years after, even in the sixth year of the reign of Darius, it was finished (Ezra 6 : 15).

When therefore Haggai said, " This house shall be filled with glory ", he did not refer to the temple which Jesus frequented but to the temple to stand upon the same site which is described by Ezekiel, into which " the glory of the God of Israel ", even the Son of Man in the glory of the Father, " shall come from the way of the east ", and cause the neighbouring earth itself to shine (Ezek. 43 : 2). This is the only interpretation the prophecy will admit of ; for when Jesus came, he was neither " the desire of all nations ", nor was he in glory. The glory of the God of Israel left the temple when the Chaldees were about to destroy it ; and it will not return until Jesus shall sit upon the throne and bear the glory in the era of " the regeneration ".

The shaking of the heavens and the earth, as we have said, refers to " the end of all things " (1 Peter 4 : 7), constituted by the Old Covenant ; but the shaking of the sea and dry land, to the kingdoms of the Gentiles, and is thus explained ; " I will overthrow the throne of the kingdoms, and I will destroy the strength of the kingdoms of the heathen . . . In that day, saith the Lord of hosts, will I take thee, O Zerubbabel, my servant, the son of Shealtiel, and will make thee as a signet ; for I have chosen thee, said the Lord of hosts " (Hag. 2 : 22). This period of overthrow is " the time of trouble such as never was since there was a nation to that same time ", when Michael shall stand up, the Great Prince who standeth for the Israelites, who at that time shall be delivered, even all that shall be found written among the living in Jerusalem (Dan. 12 : 1 ; Isa. 4 : 3).

This is the era of the resurrection of " the heirs " of " the kingdom which cannot be moved ". Michael (*Mi* who, *cha* like, *el* God), the great power of God, even Jesus the great Prince of Israel, appears at this crisis " to subdue all things to himself ", and to complete the work of emendation. He smites the image of Nebuchadnezzar upon its feet (Dan. 2 : 34), and grinds its fragments to powder. He brings the king of the north, who is Head over an extensive region, to his end (Dan. 9 : 45 ; Psa. 110 : 6). He causes Gog to fall upon the mountains of Israel ; and expels the Gentiles out of his land (Ezek. 39 : 4), that they may tread his holy city under foot no more. Having made the nations lick the dust like a serpent, and bound their power as with a mighty chain, he proceeds in the building again of the tabernacle of David, and in the setting up its ruins—that is, in the restoring again of the kingdom of God to Israel, or in " the restitution of all things " belonging to the Mosaic law, compatible with his exercise of the functions of High Priest in Israel. When this work is accomplished the *diorthōsis* or emendation will be complete (Psa. 10 : 16 ; Micah 7 : 16, 17 ; Rev. 20 : 1-3).

If the Mosaic Covenant of the kingdom had been found faultless, then should no place have been sought for the second (Heb. 8 : 7). The priesthood of the Mosaic was changeable, passing from father to son. This was deemed by the Lord a very important defect, which must therefore be amended. He determined therefore that the priesthood should be changed —that it should no longer " be left to other people " ; but should be unchangeable in the hands of Messiah and the saints, or Zadok and his sons. But this purpose could not be carried into effect so long as the Mosaic constitution of the kingdom continued in force ; for this restricted the priesthood to the tribe of Levi, and made no provision for a priest of the tribe of Judah.

Now Jehovah purposed that the High Priesthood of the nation should be changed from the tribe of Levi and the family of Aaron, to the tribe of Judah and the family of David. Hence this change of the priesthood being determined, there was decreed of necessity a change also of the law (Heb. 7 : 12). As Christ's priesthood was not authorized by the Mosaic Covenant, something was necessary on which to found it. This necessity was provided for in the Word of the Oath which runs thus—" I have sworn, and will not repent, Thou art a priest for ever after the Order of Melchizedec ". This oath was uttered by Jehovah upwards of 500 years after the Law was given from Sinai, and constitutes the right of David's son to the priesthood of the kingdom ; as the oath sworn to David also entitles his son to its throne for ever. The grand peculiarity, then, of the new Constitution of the kingdom over the old is, *the union of the high priesthood and kingly office in one person, of the tribe of Judah and family of David unchangeably, or for ever.* Under the Mosaic, the priesthood and royalty of the kingdom were separate, and restricted to two distinct families and tribes— the priesthood to Levi and Aaron ; the royalty to Judah and David. But this will be amended, and the Lord Jesus, in whose veins once flowed the blood of Levi, Aaron, Judah and

David (Luke 1 : 5, 36), will unite in himself the kingly and priestly offices, when he sits and rules upon his throne and bears the glory.

Well, Jesus of Nazareth was manifested to Israel as Son of God at his baptism. It was clearly proved that he was the Christ, and therefore entitled to the things defined in the word of the oaths to himself and his father David. But " he was made under the law " (Gal. 4 : 4), to which he yielded a perfect obedience in all things. He never entered the Court of the Priests, nor the Holy Place ; nor attempted to do service at the altar. Being of the tribe of Judah, the Law forbad him to advance beyond the Court of the Israelites, or to minister in holy things. So long as the Mosaic law continued in practical operation, and he inhabited the land, he must have remained among the people. Had Israel continued in their country under the law to this day, and Jesus had remained with them until now, and they had been willing to acknowledge him, and submit to his government, he would not have ascended the throne until the constitution was dedicated and amended : " for ", says Paul, in view of this condition of affairs, " if he were on earth, he should not be a priest, seeing that there are priests that offer gifts according to the law " (Heb. 8 : 4).

The emendation of the covenant must have been preceded by its dedication. This could only be accomplished by the death of the mediator. The death was the dedication of the covenant in his blood ; as he himself said, " This is the New Covenant in my blood which is shed for many for the remission of sins " (Matt. 26 : 28 ; Luke 22 : 20),—and to show the connection between the covenant and the kingdom, he said, " I will not drink of the fruit of the vine until the kingdom of God shall come ". But when he came to life again after this dedication, he could not even then inherit the kingdom. The Mosaic Covenant must have been changed ; an emendation, however, to which the party in power would by no means consent, as the amendment would have put them all out of the government. Pilate and Herod, Caiaphas and the Council must have surrendered their offices into the hands of Jesus, who would have promoted in their place his own disciples and friends. But they would not hear of such a thing ; therefore it remained only for Jesus to absent himself, and to abolish the kingdom until the time appointed in the wisdom of the Father for its restitution to Israel under a better, more permanent, and perfect order of things.

(iv) *JEWS AND GENTILES IN RELATION TO THE NEW COVENANT*

We come now to the consideration of the difficulty seemingly involved in Paul's doctrine when regarded in the light of Ezekiel's testimony. Jesus is now the High Priest of God, and the only one that exists, or will ever exist in relation to man. He has had no rival since the Mosaic Covenant " vanished away ". He is God's high priest for those, both Jews and Gentiles who have been reconciled to God through his name—that is, who believe God's promises concerning the kingdom, and the things concerning Jesus, and have been united to his name by baptism. This is equivalent to saying, who have been reconciled through the belief and obedience of the gospel of the kingdom—through the obedience of faith. Of the things concerning Jesus are the things pertaining to his divine sonship, his spotless and unblemished character, his sacrificial death and resurrection, etc., constituting him God's Lamb, holy and without blemish, having neither spot, nor wrinkle, or any such thing, of his own free will once offered to bear the sins of many. Thus he was at once the sacrifice and the priest ; for " he offered up himself " ; as he said, " I lay down my life for the sheep. Therefore doth my Father love me, because I lay down my life, that I might take it up again. No man taketh it from me, but I lay it down of myself. I have power to lay it down, and I have power to take it up again. This commandment have I received of my Father " (Heb. 7 : 27 ; John 10 : 15, 17, 18). Being thus the Lamb slain, he resumed his life, and entered into the presence of God before whom he stands as the blood-sprinkled Ark of the Covenant (Rev. 11 : 19), in whom is deposited the Law hereafter to go forth from Zion, and the life of his sheep, whose sins he bears away (Col. 3 : 3 ; Heb. 9 : 28) ; and thus they are sanctified by the dedicated covenant through the once offering of his body : so that " by one offering he hath perfected forever them that are sanctified " (Heb. 10 : 10, 14).

Now these sanctified ones are a purified people, whose " hearts " or minds and dispositions, have been " purified by faith " (Acts 15 : 9)—faith in the promises of God, and in " the blood of sprinkling which speaks better things than the blood of Abel ". The blood of Jesus is the blood of sprinkling which gushed forth from his side as " an offering " or purification " for sin ". The poor in spirit and the meek, the honest and good hearts, that by faith appreciate the virtue of this sprinkled blood, and have become the subjects of repentance and remission in his name, are said to be " sprinkled from an evil conscience " and to have " washed the body with pure water " (Heb. 10 : 22). They are " the children of the promise ", or covenant ; because in becoming Christ's they have believed the promises, and have been purified by " the blood of the covenant ". As yet they walk by faith in the things believed, and not by sight. Faith, which is " the substance of things hoped for, and the evidence of things unseen ", is the mirror which reflects the things of the approaching future, and presents them to the believer's mind as though he were beholding, and personally in the presence of, the very things themselves. Hence, it is said to such, " Ye are come unto Mount Zion, and unto the City of the living God, to Jerusalem the heavenly, and to the myriads of angels, to a general convocation, even to an assembly of first-borns enrolled for the heavens (*en ouranois*), and to God the judge of all, and to the spirits of the just made perfect, and to Jesus the mediator of the New Covenant, and to the blood of the sprinkling which speaks better things than that of Abel " (Heb. 12 : 22-24). Ye are come by faith to these things, which at present ye do dimly contemplate ; but which ye shall see no longer as through a glass darkly, but face to face in the presence of the Lord.

Now these, whose hearts are sprinkled and their bodies washed, are the only people on the earth since the entrance of Jesus into the presence of God, for whom he officiates as " High Priest over the House of God " (Heb. 10 : 21 ; 3 : 6). They are " God's temple " " the true tabernacle which the Lord pitched, and not man " (Heb. 8 : 2). For forty years this temple coexisted with that in Jerusalem ; but since the destruction of the latter it is the only temple of God upon the earth, where gifts and offerings, called " spiritual sacrifices ", are offered acceptably to His name (1 Peter 2 : 5, 9). They become acceptable in being presented through Jesus Christ. They who do the worship (and they are all the faithful) enter into this holy place, or heavenly, which as a whole they constitute, with the sprinkled blood of the covenant upon their hearts. Purified once through faith in the blood-sprinkled covenant of promise, hereafter to become the law of the kingdom, there is in their case no more sacrifice for sin ; " for by one offering he hath perfected for ever them that are sanctified ". Yet, though thus sanctified, they continue to offer spiritual sacrifices. All this is worshipping the Father in spirit and in truth ; which is the only service acceptable to Him while His kingdom is in ruins, and prostrate at the feet of the Gentiles.

But this worship in spirit and in truth (expressed in confession of the hope (Heb. 10 : 23), praise, and prayer ; in baptism ; and in eating and drinking of the symbols on the table of the Lord) is the unburdensome privilege of those only who through faith in the Covenant and its blood have become " heirs of the kingdom ". When this is set up in Palestine, the service is changed in form, but not in principle ; and from social becomes national. In the national service, the higher priesthood, which consists of Jesus and the " children God has given him ", all immortal by resurrection or transformation, though they offer " the fat and the blood ", it is for the people and not for themselves. They need no more sacrifice for sin ; but being " priests unto God " (Rev. 5 : 10), there needs must be something for them to offer on account of the worshippers for whom they officiate. The New Covenant, which we now accept as a matter of faith and hope, has not yet been made with the House of Judah and Israel. If it had, they would now be a united nation in Palestine. It will be made with them when they are grafted into their own olive and not before. At the engrafting, there will be a great national celebration, called " a delivering of the Covenant " (Ezek. 20 : 37) : a delivering of the New Covenant from Zion (Micah 4 : 2), with a glorious, but not such a terrible display of power as when the Covenant was delivered from Sinai. The nation, or Twelve Tribes, having been brought at length to acknowledge Jesus as High Priest and King, are received unto favour ; and being under the New Covenant, as in former years they were under the Old, Jehovah becomes merciful to their unrighteousness, and proclaims everlasting oblivion of all their past individual and national offences by virtue of the royal blood of the Covenant, the preciousness of which they then perceive and appreciate. This amnesty, however, benefits that generation only to which the Covenant is delivered and by which it is accepted. It affects not the generations of Israel's rebellious dead ; they are the " cut off from the people ".

Now, the question remains, when thus reconciled to God through the blood of his Son, is the nation to have a religious service or worship ; and if they are, what is to be its principle, and what its form ? No one who understands the Bible would affirm that the Twelve Tribes of Israel were to live in their own land under the New Covenant for 1,000 years without any national religious worship. To affirm this would be to say in effect that God had prepared a Royal Priesthood for His kingdom, but had provided no service for them to perform. This is not admissible for a moment. There will be a service under the New Covenant as there was under the Old. Its principle will be memorial, not typical ; even the extension of the principle upon which is now celebrated the death and resurrection of Jesus. Hence, the " reconciliation " will be *a memorial reconciliation made perfect by the blood of the Covenant which institutes it.* The reconciliation of the Old Covenant was typical and imperfect ; because the dedication blood, being merely that of bulls and goats, could not perfect the conscience in taking away of sins. When the Prince under the New Covenant " prepares for himself and for all the people of the land a bullock for a sin-offering " (Ezek. 45 : 22), it is memorial of his own sacrifice of himself, and memorial of the reconciliation which the people enjoy through the blood of the Covenant with which, through faith in it, their hearts will be sprinkled then, as the true believers are at present.

Such is the principle of the amended " service which pertains to the Israelites " (Rom. 9 : 4). The form thereof is detailed in Ezekiel more at large than we can present it here. It is a service not of spiritual sacrifices, but of bloody sacrifices of spiritual significance. The lower order of the priesthood, mortal Levites, slay them for the people, and pass the fat and blood from the tables at the north gate to the Altar, where they are burned and sprinkled by the higher or immortal priests, " the seed of Zadok ", before the Lord. The past sins of the nation having been amnestied at the delivering of the Covenant, there is henceforth no more remembrance of sins once a year. The old Mosaic annual atonement on the tenth day of the seventh month, at which the tribes were to " afflict their souls ", is not revived under the New Covenant. It will form no part of the service then. It was one of those things made, or appointed, that was removed when the Lord shook the Mosaic heaven by the Roman power. There will be no laver of water between the Temple and the Altar for the seed of Zadok to wash themselves before they enter the temple. These washings and carnal ordinances are also abolished ; for those who approach the altar and enter in are like their Prince, holy and undefiled, being devoid of evil in the flesh.

6

MOSES AND THE PROPHET LIKE UNTO HIM

MOSES was the great-great grandson of Jacob in the line of Levi, Kohath and Amram. He was born in Egypt in the year of the world 2383, which, according to our computation published in *Elpis Israel*, was 727 years after the Flood, and 350 years after the confirmation of the promise of Canaan to Abraham and his Seed for an everlasting possession. He was named *Moses* by Pharaoh's daughter, importing that he was *saved out of the water*. We do not propose here to compile a history of this, the greatest man of his time, and of the sixteen centuries and a half which succeeded the passage of the Red Sea. It cannot be better related than it is in the admirable writings current in his name. Our object is to call attention to him as *a representative man*—a man representing or typifying another man, even " the Man Christ Jesus ".

The history of Moses is representative from his flight into the country of Midian, Arabia Petrea south of Mount Sinai, to his decease when the Lord hid him from his nation. There was a likeness, indeed, between Moses and Jesus in their infancy ; for while the life of Moses was jeopardized by the decree of Pharaoh, Jesus was also endangered by the mandate of Herod against Rachel's children of two years old and under. But Jehovah preserved them ; and thus were they cast upon Him from their birth, and kept in safety, or " made to hope " upon their mothers' breasts (Matt. 2 : 13-18 ; Psa. 22 : 9, 10). There was a resemblance also in the high qualifications and faithful self denial of these two personages in their manhood. " Moses was learned in all the wisdom of the Egyptians, and was mighty in words, and deeds." This was previous to his attaining the age of forty years. To this time, though the adopted grandson of Pharaoh, and heir apparent of the Egyptian throne, and surrounded by the licentious notables of its court, where the God of Abraham was unknown, Moses was a man of faith—a learned, mighty and faithful man, who might have worn the crown of the greatest monarchy of the age, with all its treasures ; but he renounced them all, and became a fugitive, and companion of oppressed bondmen, that he might share in the kingdom to be established under Abraham's Seed in the adjoining country of the Canaanites (Heb. 11 : 24-26).

Jesus, too, was the most learned and the wisest man of that or any other age before or since. He was wise and learned by divine intuition (John 7 : 15-17) ; and in the language of Cleopas, " was a prophet mighty in deed and word before God and all the people " (Luke 24 : 19). His political self-denial was as conspicuous as that of Moses. Thrice he refused dominion and a crown at the hand of any power inferior to God (Luke 4 : 5-8 ; John 6 : 15). "All these tetrarchal kingdoms of the land ", said their possessor, " will I give to thee, if thou wilt do homage for them to me " ; but on such terms he rejected them. He knew that all upon Israel's land was his, and the world in its widest sense beside. A then present possession would have saved him much suffering, and have exalted him at once to honour and glory. But he knew that to receive even his own at the hand of the enemy would be to forswear the supremacy of Jehovah, and to become Satan's king instead of God's. " Thou shalt do homage to the Lord thy God, and him only shalt thou serve." These were the words of Moses to which he had respect as the words of Jehovah. He knew that to receive the kingdom, glory and dominion of the world from any other power than God would be to descend from the high position of the predestined representative of the Divine Majesty upon the earth for ever, to the degradation of a mere equality with Caesar and the world-ruler of the age. Yea, like Moses, " he had respect unto the recompense of the reward " ; and " for the joy that was set before him " he refused to let the people make him king, " choosing rather to suffer affliction with the people of God, than to enjoy the pleasures of sin for a season ". The " kingdom is not from hence " (John 18 : 36). It can only be received with eternal honour and glory from thence ; that is, from God, not from Satan nor the people. Moses and Jesus understood this well ; therefore Moses forsook Egypt, and Jesus forsook Palestine, that they might receive the royalty from God at the appointed time.

Thus far the resemblance between Moses and Jesus is complete. Cradled in peril, saved of God, and hopeful of the same promise, they were men of renown in word and deed, whose faith was " made perfect " by their works after the example of their father Abraham (James 2 : 22), leaving behind them illustrious exemplifications of the truth that the enjoyment of the pleasures of sin for a season is incompatible and fatal to an inheritance of the kingdom of God.

But here the present similitude between them is suspended. Moses and Jesus were indeed the rejected of the nation, as is already implied in the allusion to their departure from their people, the one into Midian, where he met with God in the bush ; and the other to a far country, where he is still in the presence of Him whose glory illumined the rocky Arabia : but as yet, unlike the case of Moses, Jehovah has not sent Jesus from " holy ground ", shining unapproachable light, to be a ruler and a deliverer, to bring the tribes of Israel out of the land of the enemy, even those tribes which said unto him, " Who made thee a ruler and a judge ? Away with such a fellow ; we will not have him to reign over us ! "

But Moses, whom they refused, they afterwards received as their commander, legislator, and king. They placed themselves under him as Jehovah's representative, through whom the nation should obtain political independence and organization, and by whom it should be put into possession of a country, even of that country from which their fathers came before they migrated into Egypt, and which was promised to Abraham and his Seed for an everlasting possession (Gen. 12 : 1-3 ; 13 : 14-17 ; 15 : 7, 8, 18-21 ; 17 : 5-6).

This was an acceptance of Moses which finds no counterpart in the annals of Israel and the history of Jesus. They have refused him as they refused Moses, but a like acceptance of him is yet to come.

From the accession of Moses to the leadership of the Twelve Tribes of Israel, his history is that of the nation also. He is no longer to be contemplated as an individual isolated from his people ; but as a prophet (Deut. 34 : 10), a mediator (Exod. 24 : 2 ; Deut. 5 : 5 ; Gal. 3 : 19), a lawgiver, a man of war (Exod. 14 : 25-27 ; Num. 21 : 34), and a king (Deut. 33 : 5). These were his relations to Israel from his *second appearing* in their midst to the end of his career. He was a mediator-prophet, a lawgiving-prophet, a warrior-prophet, and a royal-prophet. He was not simply a man through whom God spoke to the tribes of Israel as he spoke to them through Ezekiel—a man whose functions were restricted to the utterance of the divine purpose ; but a man who was not only to speak but to execute the will of Jehovah, whose servant he was.

Now the reader will see by consulting the references that Moses was precisely the kind of prophet we have indicated. During his administration of the national affairs, Jehovah spoke by him alone. At the commencement of his career, before he was accepted by the nation, he was sent to the people as a prophet-preacher, announcing that the time had arrived to redeem Israel from the power of them that hated them, and to establish the kingdom of God in the promised land—that glorious kingdom of which they were to be the priestly and holy nation (Exod. 19 : 5, 6). This proclamation of " the Everlasting Gospel " they believed for a while ; and in consequence placed themselves at the disposal of Moses, that they might obtain its promises at his hand. " The gospel ", says Paul, " was preached unto them " ; that is, by Moses : but it did not profit that generation, because their faith failed them. They had faith enough to escape from Egypt, but they had not faith enough to enable them to enter the promised country, and to possess it Mosaically ; much less faith had they to obtain a right to it everlastingly, under the covenant which provides for the priesthood and royalty of Christ.

But, as is well known, the character of Gospel-preacher was merged into that of the prophet-judge of Egypt, and the warrior-prophet of Israel ; for Moses, having preached salvation to the tribes, executed judgment upon their oppressors, and by the hand of Jehovah his strength gave the nation baptism into himself in the cloud and in the sea, as its sovereign under God. Henceforth, Moses was every thing to the Twelve Tribes. When they had once heard Jehovah's voice thundering forth the Decalogue from Sinai's cloud-capped, burning, and trembling mountain, He granted the petition of their terror-stricken hearts that henceforth He would speak to them only through His servant Moses, lest they should die. Jehovah spoke to Moses in their hearing thus that they might *believe him for ever* (Exod. 19 : 9) ; for if they should believe Moses, they would not fail to believe in him of whom he was afterwards to write. As Moses was to Aaron, so he was to all Israel, " in the place of God ". He gave them the bread of heaven to eat, and water out of the flinty rock to drink, and clad them with raiment that waxed not old upon them. What a prophet-king was this ! Truly the father of his people, who sustained them in life and food and raiment, and taught them wisdom from above. What nation ever had such a king as Moses ? and what were David and Solomon to Israel after him ? As the servant of Jehovah, he gave the nation an existence, ushering it into being, amid storm and fury, and the ruin of a mighty host, from the depths of the sea ; he sustained it from the stores of heaven for forty years ; beat down their enemies, and trampled them as the mire of the streets ; gave them a holy, just and good, but inexorable law ; and brought them to the verge of Canaan's land, a well trained and disciplined nation, fit and prepared to take possession of it under the conduct of a successor worthy of himself. He was Jehovah's servant, " faithful in all his house, for a testimony ", or representation, " of those things which were to be spoken after ". He was the greatest character the world has known, with one exception. The world's great ones are not to be named in the same breath. Moses ! What meekness, disinterestedness, faithfulness, self-denial, wisdom, knowledge, power, honour, glory, and exaltation, doth that name represent !

Dost thou not, O thoughtful reader of the living oracles, recognize in the foregoing sketch the Moses of the Pentateuch ? Yea, verily, it is a true portrait of the original in outline, left unfinished in detail, that thou mayest fill in the lights and shadows of the picture at thy convenience. Study Moses, and see if he was not the kind of prophet herein described. Do you think you would have a true conception of his prophetic character, if you knew no more of Moses than as a preacher of the gospel to Israel before he visited the court of Pharaoh ? No indeed. You must know the whole written history of the man to be able to say, " I know the prophet Moses " : for Moses was a prophet to the end of his career. You cannot separate his prophetic office from his mediatorship, or his legislatorial, or regal functions. His code is a great symbolic as well as verbal representation of the truth—a speaking prophecy to the eyes and ears of his nation, and to all others who comprehend it. You must contemplate him in the entirety of his mission ; you must view him as a whole, and then, and not till then, will you be able to say if Ezekiel or any other prophet be " *a prophet like unto him* ".

Moses, the prophet thus fully manifested in Israel, was a representative man. This is evident from the following passage in his writings. Addressing the Twelve Tribes he says, " Jehovah thy God shall raise up unto thee a *Prophet* from the midst of thee of thy brethren, LIKE UNTO ME ; and unto him ye shall hearken ; according to all that thou desirest of Jehovah thy God in Horeb in the day of the assembly, saying, Let me not hear again the voice of Jehovah my God, neither let me see this great fire any more, that I die not. And Jehovah said unto me, they have well spoken what they have spoken. I will raise them up a Prophet of their brethren, *like unto thee*, and will put my words into his mouth ; and he shall speak unto them all that I shall command him. And it shall come to pass that whosoever will not hearken unto my words which he shall speak in my name, I will require it of him " (Deut. 18 : 15-19). This passage attests the truth of what we have said. It plainly and explicitly declares that the prophet Moses was typical of a future prophet who was to appear in Israel. In other words, that this future prophet was to be like Moses.

Now, beloved reader, suppose you and I had been living at the time Jehovah spoke these words by His servant Moses, with whose extraordinary history, which was national, we were quite familiar, what should we have expected would be the mission of the prophet to come ? I say, " the mission " ; for it is the mission that supplies the characteristics of the prophet by which his resemblance to Moses can be determined. Should we not expect the Moses-like prophet to preach the ever-lasting gospel to the Tribes of Israel ; to overthrow their oppressors ; to baptize the nation into himself as their deliverer by its passage through the sea ; to stand between them and Jehovah to speak to them all that He should command him ; to give them a law ; to build a temple in their midst ; to organize the nation ; and to fit and prepare it for entrance into the land of Israel under the covenant of an everlasting possession, which is the nation's hope ? Should we not expect a prophet whose mission should be to accomplish something like this ? Should we not expect him to perform these things in the midst of the Twelve Tribes after the manner of Moses ? Certainly we should.

This Moses-like prophet was expected for sixteen centuries and a half. During all that long period, though many prophets appeared in Israel, not one of them was accepted as the one like unto Moses. None of them claimed to be like him, not even Elijah. Yet why should he not, if a great miracle-working prophet were the sum of the similitude to Moses ? At length Jesus came, " a prophet mighty in deed and word before God and all the people " ; and some of them said, " We have found him of whom Moses in the Law, and the Prophets, did write, Jesus of Nazareth, the son of Joseph " ; while others said, " This is of a truth that prophet that should come into the world " ; and as the result of their conviction meditated the taking of him by force and making him a king (John 6 : 14, 15). This shows what sort of a Moses-like prophet the people expected, to wit, a prophet-king ; hence Nathanael, when he saw the man announced by Philip as the prophet foretold by Moses, recognized him as Son of God, and Israel's king.

Zacharias, the father of John, thus defines the mission of the prophet-king ; " Jehovah hath raised up an horn of salvation for us in the house of his servant David, as he spake by the mouth of his holy prophets, which have been from the beginning of the age ; that we should be saved from our enemies, and from the hand of all that hate us ; to perform the mercy promised to our fathers, and to remember his holy covenant— the oath which he sware to our father Abraham, that he would grant unto us, that being delivered out of the hand of our enemies we might serve him without fear, in holiness and righteousness before him, all the days of our life ". These are the ideas imparted to Zacharias by the Holy Spirit with which he was filled. They define the work to be accomplished by the Moses-like prophet, who is styled " a Horn of Salvation for Israel ".

This is just the sort of prophet Moses was. He was a Horn or power through whom Jehovah saved the tribes from Egypt. Moses was raised up in the house of Levi, but the Horn or power like unto Moses was raised up in the house of David. His mission was as stated. It was Mosaic : first, to deliver Israel from their oppressors ; and secondly, to perform the good thing promised to their father in the holy covenant, and confirmed by an oath to Abraham. The work which Moses performed was but the earnest of that to be executed by the Moses-like prophet. Moses delivered Israel, but the deliverance was not the everlasting salvation of the nation. They fell under the power of their adversaries again, and their condition has become worse than Egyptian. In the days of Jesus ten-twelfths of the nation were outcasts among the nations beyond Parthia ; and the other two, though still occupants of the land, were oppressed by the Roman Power. The Holy Spirit in Zacharias taught them to expect that the child about to be born would complete the work that Moses had begun in saving the Twelve Tribes with an everlasting deliverance, so that they " might serve Jehovah without fear in holiness and righteousness before him all the days of their life ".

The mercy promised to Israel's fathers is the execution of judgment and righteousness in the land of Israel by the Branch of righteousness which was to grow up to David (Jer. 33 : 14, 15). In perfecting this work, the Holy Covenant confirmed by an oath to Abraham would find its manifestation in the kingdom of God restored again to Israel. The tabernacle of David which is fallen down, and whose ruins are trampled under foot, will then have been built as in the days of old (Acts 15 : 16 ; Amos 9 : 11). This work accomplished, and the Restorer will stand in the midst of Israel as the Moses-like prophet in full manifestation. His resemblance to Moses must be based on the historical representation of that distinguished man as the prophet-sovereign of the Twelve Tribes.

No account is taken of Moses in the history during his forty years' absence from Israel further than that he was a keeper of sheep in an obscure country. Figuratively speaking, this is the employment of his antitype. He is superintending the affairs of his " little flock " in this nether wilderness—making reconciliation for his household—until the time shall arrive to leave " holy ground ", where the glory of the God of Israel shines upon him. But in this there is no similitude between him and Moses as a prophet in Israel. The Moses-like prophet must be present in Israel's midst, surrounded by the Twelve Tribes, and discharging the duties which it is the function of a High Priest, or mediator, to perform. Of the mission of Moses' antitype suffice it to say here that Zacharias testifies that it is *to save Israel from their enemies and all that hate them* ; *and to convert what Jehovah promised to Abraham into an accomplished fact.*

The Holy Spirit testifies, I say, that the babe of Bethlehem was the Horn provided in David's house to perform this work, which is as political, national and warlike a mission as that of Moses. When this goodly child attained to manhood, did he save Israel from all, or even any of those that hated them ? Did he not on the contrary strengthen those very enemies, and send them against them to slay them, to burn up their city, and scatter them abroad ? O, but we hear some word-corrupting mystic of world-wide celebrity " piously " observing, their real enemies that hated them were their sins and the devil, not sinners ; and that when the Jews " confessed the Lord ", and " obtained a hope " or " got religion ", or were " baptized for the redemption of sins ", they were " the saved " ; and consequently " saved from their enemies and all that hated them " in the spiritual sense of the words ! We pray for patience when we hear such stupid nonsense. The spiritual sense of the words is the obvious sense, which is in strict accordance with the grammatical or literal. " The Lord added to the church daily ", not the saved, but *tous sōzomenous*, the present participle passive, " the being saved " (Acts 2 : 47)— persons, the subjects of a salvation which begins with the remission of their past sins, and is perfected when, having been raised from the dead, they inherit for ever " the kingdom restored again to Israel " at their national reconciliation with Jehovah, and deliverance from their enemies, and the power of all that hate them. Hence Paul says, " *we are saved by the hope* ", if we be not moved away from it, but keep in memory what he preached (Rom. 8 : 24 ; Col. 1 : 22, 23 ; 1 Cor. 15 : 1, 2).

But granting that salvation is complete at baptism, in some sense, the baptized of Israel were certainly not saved from all that hated them, which is the salvation under Jesus the words of Zacharias call for. The opposite is true ; for those that hated them prevailed against the saved, delivering them over to torture and death, as they have prevailed against them to this day, and will prevail against them till the Ancient of Days come, and the saints possess the kingdom, and dominion, and the greatness of the kingdom for ever under the whole heaven (Dan. 7 : 18, 21, 22, 27), *not above it.* Seeing, then, that Israel is not saved, but continue " a people scattered and peeled, a nation meted out and trodden under foot, whose land invading armies have spoiled " ; that there is no king in Israel executing judgment and righteousness in their land ; and that the holy covenant sworn to Abraham has only been dedicated with the precious blood of his Seed, and beyond this no more performed than in the days of Moses ; the conclusion is inevitable, that the Lord Jesus has not yet accomplished his mission, and that he has not yet appeared as a prophet like unto Moses.

Now because this conclusion is true, and cannot be refuted, the Jews of our time refuse to confess Jesus as their ruler and judge ; " whose goings forth have been from of old, from everlasting " (Micah 5 : 1, 2). Gentile theologists rightly affirm that he is the prophet of whom Moses wrote ; but they do not affirm the truth in maintaining that in his appearing he resembled or was " like unto " him. So long as they occupy this ground the conversion of Jews by them to any respectable extent is impossible. " The testimony of Jesus is the spirit of the prophecy "—the testimony of the prophecy is the spirit which testifies of Jesus (Rev. 19 : 10 ; John 15 : 26 ; 16 : 13, 14 ; 6 : 63 ; 1 John 2 : 27).

This spirit-testimony defines the mission of Christ which the apostolic history plainly demonstrates was performed by Jesus to a very limited extent ; and they who affirm it was fully accomplished aver what they cannot prove ; and convict themselves of profound ignorance of the spirit-word, and exclude themselves also from that worthy company styled " the brethren of John having the testimony of Jesus ". Instead of giving " death-blows to Jewish. infidelity ", they are stumbling-blocks in the way of Jewish acceptance of Jesus as the prophet like unto Moses, whom Jehovah promised to raise up in the midst of Israel. "Admitting ", say the Jews, " that all affirmed of Jesus in the New Testament narratives be true, proving him to be a true man and no impostor, still he is manifestly from that account not the Messiah promised in Moses and the prophets, if, as Gentile philosophers teach, he is to appear no more upon earth, and to do no more for the Twelve Tribes of Israel, as such, than feeding a few thousands at two meals, and healing the diseases of a few sick Jews, as reported of him."

This is an impregnable position, well fortified by the testimony of God. The New Testament history proves Jesus to have been Son of God, a great prophet, mighty in deed, Son of David raised from the dead and translated from the earth ; but, deny that he is to appear in Palestine again and to reign there in the midst of the Twelve Tribes of Israel on David's throne, wearing the crowns of all earth's kingdoms— deny this, and prove that he is to remain for ever where he is, and you deny that Jesus is the Christ, the prophet like unto Moses, concerning whom Jehovah hath testified in His word since the foundation of the world was laid.

On the other hand, that our Jewish friends may not boast themselves against Jesus, however justly they can exult over his pretended friends, we remark that if any prophet should appear among them, and re-establish them in Palestine, and make them a great nation, rebuilding the temple and restoring the law, and reigning over them in Jerusalem, yet he would not be the person of whom Moses in the law and the prophets did write, if he had not previously been the subject of all the New Testament narrates concerning Jesus. He might be Moses, or Elijah ; but the Messiah of whom Moses wrote, impossible. Such a king could not maintain them in everlasting possession of their land ; he could not give them rain from heaven and fertility of soil ; he could not blot out their transgressions as a thick cloud ; neither could he bestow upon any of them eternal life ; in brief, he could not perform the oath sworn to Abraham by God that " they might serve him without fear, in holiness and righteousness before him, all the days of their life "— as a nation to die no more by the hand of hating Gentile tyrants ; and as individuals under their own vines and fig-trees, none daring to make them afraid.

Jesus, the great power of God, alone can accomplish this. It is the great work for which he has been prepared—a preparedness to which he has attained through suffering unto obedience and perfection. Moses suffered affliction before he was exalted to the throne of Israel. He was an abscondant homicide keeping sheep in the desert—a fugitive from his people before he exchanged his crook for the sceptre of Jeshurun's king. This is Jehovah's rule—probation before exaltation. Israel's Messiah cannot be exempt from this law— a principle working out its results to this day in the experience of all who with him are " the heirs of God ".

7

MEDIATORSHIP

" The Law " is a term applied in the Scriptures to that system of things enjoined by Jehovah upon the Twelve Tribes of Israel through Moses. " The Law was given through Moses " (John 1 : 17), and hence it is styled " the Law of Moses " ; not because it originated from him as the French code did from Napoleon, or certain laws of Greece from Draco and Solon ; but because it was transmitted through him as the medium of communication between the Lord of the Universe and the descendants of Abraham in the chosen line of Isaac and Jacob, whom He surnamed Israel, of whom He condescended to become the King. " He gave them a fiery law " (Deut. 33 : 2), which He caused to be delivered to Moses for promulgation. He did not leave His throne in the light to commune with Moses in His own proper person ; for " no man shall see him and live " (Exod. 33 : 20 ; 1 Tim. 6 : 16) ; but He imparted His will to the angels of His presence, " who do his commandments, hearkening unto the voice of his word " ; and these, as faithful ministers of His pleasure (Psa. 103 : 20, 21), handed to Moses His high, and holy, and just decrees, with all the sanctions of Sinai recorded in " the Book ". Thus " the law was ordained by angels in the hands of a Mediator " (Gal. 3 : 19), who was Moses, occupying middle ground between Israel and their King.

Terrified with the thunder-tones in which the Decalogue was delivered, which made even Moses quake with fear, they besought Jehovah to speak to them only through the medium of their brother. In making this request they proposed a Mediatorship, and suggested the appointment of Moses to the office. They had acknowledged themselves Jehovah's nation, and now they wished that the communication between them should be through an intermediate person with whom they could confer without terror. The proposal pleased Jehovah, who said " they had well spoken what they had spoken ", and their request was consequently complied with. From this time the Mediatorship became an ordinance in Israel ; Moses was the first that held the office, in which he officiated as a priest, prophet, legislator and king. After the nation was planted in Canaan, the high priests acted in the character of mediators, being Jehovah's supreme magistrates over the people, for the pontificate was always above the kingly office, though many of the kings treated the high priests with indignity. Moses was the only complete representative of a mediator that has yet appeared in Israel. He was Jehovah's representative in all His relations to the nation. David and Solomon shared the mediatorship with Zadoc the high priest, but it was only as kingly, not priestly and legislative, representatives of Jehovah. They were mediatorial administrators of Moses' law ; and representative men in the offices they sustained—Jehovah's representatives, individually representative in their historical outlines of the Mediator like unto Moses, who shall hereafter appear as king in Jeshurun.

No other nation besides Israel has received a law " ordained in the hand of a mediator ". The constitutions and laws of the nations have been given to them by evil men who have subdued them ; or by men no holier, whom they may have chosen to rule over them. Hence their organizations are evil, and the spirit which actuates them, satanic. The supreme power is one, and the people is another, and there is no mediator— " no daysman betwixt them that might lay his hand upon them both ". Their laws and institutions being human, purely so, they have no intercourse with God ; for if they spoke to Him and He should answer, seeing that they have no mediator, they would be as terror-stricken as Israel of old, and cry out, " Let not God speak with us, lest we die ! " Never did a people before hear the voice of God speaking out of the midst of the fire and live ; nor besides Israel has any nation heard Him speak at all. Jehovah speaks only to Israel, in Israel, and through them ; and if the nations are addressed, it is through the mediation of the tribes ; for what Moses was to them, so are they to the world at large.

Mediation being an Israelitish institution, and there being no other between Jehovah and the population of the earth ; and it being admitted that no man can come to God save through a mediator approved of Him ; it follows that both individuals and nations can obtain access to " the throne of the Majesty in the heavens " only through the mediation which pertains to Israel. Now this mediation is through the Mosaic law. Obviously so ; because according to that law there is no acceptance except through sacrifice offered in Jerusalem by the priesthood of Levi. So long as Jerusalem is trodden under foot of the Gentiles, this is impossible ; Israel, therefore, like the rest of the nations, although they trust in Moses, are as destitute of mediation as though the mediatorship pertained to the Chinese and not to them. If blindness had not happened to them, they would certainly see this ; for it is written in Moses, " Cursed is every one that continueth not in all things written in the book of the law to do them ". But what one thing, not to mention all things, do they observe in the letter or spirit of it that is written therein ? They practice circumcision. But that is not of the law ; yet by the practice they become debtors to do the whole law. By offending in the least they are guilty of the whole ; for Moses curses every Israelite who continueth not in all.

Cursed, then, are they of Moses in whom they trust ; yet were they ever so willing to obey him, they are circumstantially prevented. The Turks possess their holy city and land,* and by the sword are prepared to suppress every attempt to re-establish the Mosaic commonwealth. Alas for Israel ! They are " without a king, without a prince, without a sacrifice, without an image, without an ephod, and without teraphim " (Hosea 3 : 4), and the king, prince, sacrifice, image of the invisible God, they will not receive ! But if Israel's case is forlorn, that of the nations is worse ; for while Israel refuses him who speaks from the right hand of God, the Gentiles, who profess to acknowledge him, pay no regard to what he says. Redemption awaits Israel (Dan. 12 : 1) ; but anger and wrath, and sore distress, to all the world besides. How shall this trouble be eschewed ?

Escape there is none save for those who obey the truth. The door is not yet shut ; " He that believeth and is baptized shall be saved " ; but mark the words which follow—" He that believes not shall be condemned ". What is that thing which, when not believed, brings condemnation to man ? The context answers this question in two words—" THE GOSPEL " (Mark 16 : 15, 16 ; Rom. 1 : 16). So that you may even be baptized, or rather immersed, but if you believe not " the gospel " you cannot be saved. The gospel announces to every man, both Jew and Gentile, who believes it, access to Jehovah and His restored kingdom through His son Jesus, on his accession to the mediatorship in Israel.

The law of Moses was ordained by angels in the hand of the mediator. But that law as originally ordained has been impaired by the manifestation of some of its antitypes ; and

*Written in 1853.

being therefore no longer an exact representation of the knowledge of the truth, and incompatible with the nature of things as modified by the appearance of the prophet like unto Moses, it needs to be amended. This emendation is ordained by Jehovah in the hand of a mediator, as well as the original promulgation of the law. Moses received it from the angels as the ministers of God ; but Jesus, who is greater than Moses, " being a son over his own house ", in which Moses was only a servant (Heb. 3 : 5, 6), receives the amended law direct from Jehovah ; for, says God, " I will put my words in his mouth ; and he shall speak unto them (Israel) all that I shall command him ; and whosoever will not hearken to my words which he shall speak in my name, I will require it of him ". Angels brought the words of God to Sinai, and there delivered them to Moses for him to speak to Israel ; but the Holy Spirit, in the form of a dove, descended from before the throne, and abode on Jesus. He needed no angels to tell him what to speak, for the Father dwelt in him by His spirit, and moved his tongue to utterance. " The Father is in me. I speak not of myself ; the Father dwelling in me doeth the works." Though that Spirit forsook him when he yielded up his life upon the cross (Matt. 27 : 46, 50 ; Luke 23 : 46), it was only till he rose again by its life-imparting energy (Col. 2 : 9 ; John 1 : 16). The fullness of the Godhead now dwelleth bodily in him ; and of that " fullness have we all ", says an apostle, " received, even grace for grace " (John 1 : 16). When he shall depart from " holy ground " to revisit the arena of suffering and reproach, angels will escort him to his kingdom, full of Jehovah's words of truth and mercy to His people ; for " he shall roar out of Zion, and utter his voice from Jerusalem ; and the heavens and the earth shall shake : but he will be the hope of his people, and the strength of the children of Israel. So shall they know that he is the Lord their God dwelling in Zion his holy mountain : Jerusalem shall then be holy, and strangers shall pass through her no more " (Joel 3 : 16, 17).

Thus will he utter his archangel voice from Zion, amid the echoes of Jehovah's trumpet sending forth its blasts as on Sinai in the days of old. That trump will awake the dead (1 Thess. 4 : 16 ; 2 Thess. 1 : 7, 8). And where will be his foes ? Though gathered together to battle against Jerusalem a mighty host, of what account will they be, when the crashing thunder of that dead-awakening shout, rattling through the flaming heavens, shall boom upon their ears ? Madness will seize upon them, and upon their horses blindness and astonishment. The burden of Jerusalem will be heavy upon them, and a cup of trembling to them all (Zech. 12 : 1-7 ; 14). But drink it to the dregs they must ; for their wickedness will be great (Joel 3 : 13). Jehovah's first interview with His nation at Sinai was attended by a terrific demonstration preceded by the overthrow of Israel's enemies. Under the sanction of this display of power and glory He presented Moses to the people as His representative over them. But the time is not very remote when the crisis that is now forming will necessitate a second interview between Jehovah and the Tribes. They have to be delivered from those that hate them ; and to be impressed with a spirit of prompt obedience and submission to the Moses-like prophet, who is to be the mediatorial representative of Jehovah in their midst for a thousand years to come. Nothing short of a Sinaitic demonstration will accomplish this ; for Israel is as stiff-necked a people today as thirty-four centuries ago. The battle of Armageddon and the war which it inducts with all the attendant manifestations of power and great glory, will inaugurate, with all subduing majesty, Jehovah's king in Zion, the hill of His holiness. The mediatorship will then have reappeared in Israel under the new covenant, dedicated upwards of eighteen centuries before by the blood of the Mediator, who speaks the words commanded of the Father in sending forth the amended law from Zion, and the word of Jehovah from Jerusalem (Isa. 2 : 3) ; not to Israel only, but to the residue of men who then seek after the Lord, and to all the nations called by His name (Acts 15 : 17). Great, glorious, and free, will Israel then be in the midst of enlightened, obedient, and happy nations. The Kingdom of God, for which Jesus taught his apostle to pray, will have come to Zion, and his Father's will performed on earth as it is in heaven. As the woman's seed he will have bruised the serpent's head, and have delivered his brethren from evil, because the kingdom is his, the power and the glory for ever, amen.

Thus then will the amended law be ordained by Jehovah in the hand of Jesus, the Mediator of the New Covenant, even the law initiated by Moses for a single nation ; but perfected and adapted to a consociation of all nations, by the prophet like unto him, the future king and lord of all the earth (Zech. 14 : 9). When that which is perfect hath come, the ordering of things terrestrial will have obtained the permanency of a thousand years, as exhibited in the following descending series :

JEHOVAH,

Lord of the boundless universe ; dwelling in unapproachable light ; whom no man hath seen, or can see and live ;

JESUS,

Jehovah's High Priest and King over all the Earth on David's throne in Zion ;

THE SAINTS,

Associates with Jesus in the enlightenment and government of the world ;

LEVITICAL PRIESTHOOD,

Priests to Israel and the Gentiles who come up to worship Jehovah at the Temple in Jerusalem ;

TWELVE TRIBES OF ISRAEL,

The Kingdom of God, or Jehovah's First Born of the many nations constituted His sons in Abraham, their federal paternal chief ;

THE NATIONS,

The inheritance of Jehovah's king to the ends of the earth.

8

REPRESENTATIVE THINGS

THE acquisition of knowledge by mere verbal signs is tedious and generally difficult. All kinds of teachers, from the teachers of babes to the dignified professors of the highest branches of philosophy and science, are so convinced of this, that where the case admits of it they endeavour to exemplify by representations addressed to the senses of their disciples. Thus the teacher of a child is not content with telling his pupil that H O U S E stands for *house*, but he demonstrates it by presenting him with the representation or picture of a house. This impresses the idea on the child's mind indelibly, so that whenever he sees the word *house* this representative word is immediately succeeded in his mind by the idea or image of the thing itself. The professor of mathematics points to his representative diagrams ; the chemist to his experiments ; and so forth, all of them for the common purpose of making more intelligible the precepts they inculcate.

Knowledge of all things gains access to the human mind by all the senses—by seeing, by hearing, by tasting, smelling and feeling. If only one sense be engaged in the acquisition of it, it is not likely to be so quickly and comprehensively acquired as when two or more senses are employed. The prophets of Israel were sometimes made to see, hear, taste, smell, and feel in relation to one and the same subject before they were permitted to make known, or deliver their message to the rulers and people of the nation. This gave them a full assurance of knowledge which could not be made more certain, seeing that there remained no other avenue to their minds, no sixth sense to receive additional impressions.

It is manifest from the divine oracles that God teaches men as they teach one another, not by precept only, but by example, type, or representation also. This is apparent from the many visions seen by the prophets, who in describing what they saw delineate and paint it, as it were, on the minds of those that read their descriptions ; so that in this way the visions are transferred from their minds to them. Vision, however, is not the only representative mode of instruction exhibited in the sacred scriptures. The events of Israel's history, the leading men who figured in their several generations, the temple furniture, national festivals, and other institutions of their law are all representative things, that is, things illustrative or shadowing forth a something God has declared shall be. The proof of this is contained in the following passages : thus it is written in I Cor. 10 : 6 : " These things were our examples (*typoi*, types) to the intent we should not lust after evil things, as they also lusted ". The things here referred to were the overthrowings of the Israelites in the wilderness because of the displeasure of God at the faithlessness and obduracy of their hearts, although He brought them safely through the tempestuous sea, fed them with " angels' food ", and slaked their raging thirst with water from the flinty rock. The food, the drink, and the rock were styled " spiritual meat ", " spiritual drink ", and the " spiritual rock ", the spirituality of which they did not perceive. The word spiritual in this place is *pneumatikon* in the original text, and evidently means figuratively, typically, or representatively ; for, says the apostle, " that Rock was ", or represented, " the Christ " from whom rivers of living waters were to flow. The Rock in Horeb was indeed a beautiful and expressive emblem of the Lord Christ ; for when Moses smote it Jehovah's representative stood upon the top of it, thereby connecting the Lord and the Rock as the sign and the thing signified. From the seventh to the tenth verses of this chapter the apostle cites various instances of the perverseness of Israel in the wilderness notwithstanding the goodness of God to them, and finishes his citations by declaring that " all these things happened unto them for ensamples ", or types ; " and they are written for our admonition upon whom the ends of the world ", or ages of the Law, " are come ". The deduction from which is that the gospel was preached to the generation of Israel that came out of Egypt, as well as to the generation contemporary with the apostles ; but that it did not profit them because, although baptized unto Moses, they did not continue in the faith but turned back in their hearts to Egypt ; so also the belief of the same gospel would be unprofitable to those who are baptized unto Christ, if they continue not in the faith, but commit sin even as they.

But these representative things, or " ensamples ", do not find their full and complete significancy in the spiritualities pertaining to the believers of " the truth as it is in Jesus ". They have a meaning which will appear only at the engrafting of Israel again into their own olive tree. The passage of the

Red Sea and baptism of the Twelve Tribes into Moses is an historical event which has an individual and a national signification. Thus as the national baptism into Moses released Israel after the flesh from their bondage to the Egyptian adversary, so an individual baptism into Christ releases the believers of the same gospel, or Israel after the spirit, from their moral bondage to the adversary, or sin incarnate in the flesh. But the national baptism into Moses also represents the future national baptism of the twelve Tribes into Jesus as the Christ and prophet like unto Moses, whom the Lord their God was to raise up unto them from among their tribes. They have sung the song of Moses, but they have yet to sing the song of Moses and the Lamb on the shores of the Egyptian sea in celebration of their Second Exodus from the house of bondage. The man whose name is the Branch, even Jesus and not Moses, will be the king in Jeshurun who will divide its waters, and lead them in triumph to the eastern shore. Then will the nations rejoice with Israel ; for the Lord will have avenged the blood of His servants, and have rendered vengeance to His adversaries, and have been merciful to His land, and to His people (Deut. 32 : 43).

The testimony which writes these things upon our hearts is found in nearly all the prophets ; a quotation or two must therefore suffice in this place : let the reader consult the eleventh and twelfth chapters of Isaiah. There he will find that a branch is to grow out of Jesse's roots who is to judge the poor with righteousness, and to strike terror into the hearts of his adversaries, at a time when the earth shall be full of the knowledge of the Lord as the waters cover the sea. In that day of glory and intelligence, he is to stand as an ensign for Israel and the nations, around which they will all be gathered in one glorious dominion. The introduction of that day of rest is to be characterized by the assembling of the outcasts of Israel and the gathering together of the dispersed Judah from the four wings of the earth a second time. A return from Egypt is especially referred to in the eleventh and fifteenth verses, in the latter of which it is declared that " the Lord (that is, the Branch) shall utterly destroy the tongue of the Egyptian Sea (that is of the Red Sea) ; and with his mighty wind shall he shake his hand over the river (Nile), and shall smite it in the seven streams (or mouths), and make go over dry shod ". This can only refer to the future, for there has been no second gathering of the Ten Tribes called Israel, or of the Two Tribes styled Judah, since the first gathering of the latter from the Babylonish Captivity. The Branch, whose name is the Lord our Righteousness (Jer. 23 : 5, 6), is the ensign and the gatherer ; for Jehovah formed him from the womb to be His servant, to bring Jacob's tribes again to Him, and to restore the desolations of Israel (Isa. 49 : 5, 6, 8). He is Jehovah's servant, then, to do all these things, which are the exact antitype of what Moses effected, and therefore illustrated or represented by the redemption from Egypt ; as it is written, " there shall be a highway for the remnant of his people, which shall be left from Assyria, like as it was to Israel in the day that they came up out of the land of Egypt ". The result of this second national redemption from civil and ecclesiastical bondage among the Gentiles will be the restoration of political harmony and concord among the Twelve Tribes, their national supremacy over the rest of the world, and their drawing water out of their own country's wells in safety, and therefore termed " the wells of salvation " in their song of joyful thanksgiving for the restoration of their land and kingdom by " the Repairer of the breach, the Restorer of the paths to dwell in " (Isa. 58 : 12).

Once more. The national probation in the wilderness of Egypt for forty years under Moses is also representative of the individual probation of believers subsequently to their baptism into Christ and of the national probation of the Twelve Tribes in the wilderness of the people previous to their being brought into the bond of the covenant, and into the land of Israel. That the Mosaic probation is representative of spiritual or individual probation appears from the apostle's reasoning in the third and fourth chapters of Hebrews. The exhortation in the ninety-fifth Psalm, which he quotes, he applies to the believers in Jesus, and to Israel at large, by connecting the two classes of the commonwealth together in his reasoning. The testimony in Ezekiel shows its applicability to the Twelve Tribes hereafter as well as to " the children of the promise " in the days of Paul. Let the reader consult that prophet in the twentieth chapter from the thirty-third to the thirty-eighth verse inclusive. He will there find that similar things are to be enacted over again as have already transpired in the days of Moses. Israel is to be brought out from the countries wherein they are scattered with a mighty display of divine power ; they are to be brought into a wilderness, where, says the Lord, " I will plead with you face to face. Like as I pleaded with your fathers in the wilderness of the land of Egypt, so will I plead with you ". The carcasses of the rebels are to fall there, so that although brought into the wilderness from their present houses of bondage " they shall not enter, saith the Lord, into the land of Israel " ; in other words, " they shall not enter into his rest " under Christ when he sits upon the throne of David in the land.

The twofold representative character of the " ensamples " supplied by the history, the typical history, of Israel in the flesh arises from the nature or constitution of things pertaining to the kingdom which is to be restored again to Israel, styled the kingdom of God and of Christ. There are two classes belonging to this kingdom the members of which must necessarily be proved before they can be admitted to its organization. Neither class can be dispensed with in this organization, yet both must previously " pass under the rod " that the approved may be manifested. These two classes are " the children of the kingdom " (Matt 8 : 12) after the flesh, or the natural descendants of Abraham in the line of Isaac, and Jacob ; and " the children of the kingdom " (Matt. 13 : 38) after the spirit, or those of Israel and the Gentiles who believe the promises, " the exceeding great and precious promises of God ", and are therefore styled also " the children of the promise who are counted for the seed " (Rom. 9 : 8). Israelites according to the flesh are the natural born subjects of the kingdom, and therefore God's people in a political sense. The generation that came out of Egypt was proved and found to be unfit to occupy the land as the subjects of the kingdom and commonwealth under the first or Mosaic constitution. It was therefore destroyed in the wilderness, and their children of the next generation previously trained by Moses were planted in the land promised to the fathers. The descendants of this generation of the tribes of Jacob, now scattered among the Gentiles, are as unfit to occupy the land of Israel as the subjects under its new, or second, divine constitution or covenant, as their fathers were whose carcasses fell in the wilderness. Nevertheless, unfit as they may be they will not be condemned unproved should the kingdom be established contemporarily with the present generation. They will be made of necessity to pass under the rod that the turbulent and rebellious spirits among them may be purged out ; for if they were permitted to occupy the land under Jesus as the " king of the Jews ", they would prove as ungovernable and disloyal as their fathers who exposed him to ignominy upon the accursed tree.

But the generation of Israelites according to the flesh, which shall be approved as fit to occupy the land when the kingdom and throne of David are re-established, will not furnish inheritors of the thrones of David's house. These are taken out from Israel and the nations upon the principle of faith in the gospel of the kingdom perfected by good works. A son of David, such as Solomon or Hezekiah, cannot occupy the throne of David under the future constitution simply because he is David's son according to the flesh. The flesh profiteth nothing in relation to the honour and glory, might and majesty, dignity and renown, of the kingdom. The throne must be occupied by that son of David who has been made perfect through sufferings, who though a son of God, yet learned obedience by the things which he suffered. Probation must precede the introduction of either class as elements of the kingdom, which though essentially dissimilar, yet pertain to one and the same institution, in the relation to one another of rulers and the ruled.

The King having passed through a probation of great suffering to the joy that yet awaits him, it is not to be supposed that those who are to rule with him shall enter into that joy without probation also. The co-rulers with Christ must be proved as well as he ; for none can reign with him who do not suffer with him in some way or other. A tried and approved nation, and tried and approved rulers, will constitute the Kingdom of the Age to Come. The probation of these, that is, of the nation and of the rulers at different periods is represented by the things that happened to the nation and rulers under the law ; the one constitution of things being typical of the other. Hence the twofold signification of the types.

The law of Moses constituted things which are remarkably representative of the realities of the age to come. These realities are styled the substance or body, of which the institutions of Moses are " the shadow " ; and because of this intimate relation between them he was strictly enjoined by Jehovah to see that he made all things precisely according to the pattern he had showed him in the mount. Hence they are styled " the pattern of things in the heavens ", which things in the heavens will be manifested when the kingdom and throne of David are established by Jesus under the new constitution. The patterns are the representative things of the law, which

115

constitute " the form of the knowledge and of 'the truth "
(Rom. 2 : 20 ; Heb. 9 : 23).

Among the representative things pertaining to Israel under
the law are certain men who are styled in the English version
" men wondered at ", or as it reads in the margin, " men of
sign ", that is, typical, or representative men—men representing
some other person than themselves. Joshua the son of Josedech
and his companions are expressly set forth as typical men. So
are Isaiah and his children. He said to Ahaz, " Behold I and
the children whom the Lord hath given me are for signs and
for wonders in Israel from the Lord of hosts, who dwelleth
in mount Zion ". Paul quotes this in Hebrews and applies it
to Jesus and his brethren, the children of God. Hence the
prophet and his children, Shear-jashub and Maher-shalal-
hash-baz, were signs or types of Jesus and the saints who are
appointed to perform wonders in Israel when the Lord returns
to build up Zion.

9

THE DAY OF ATONEMENT

" Behold, now is the Time of Acceptance ; now is the Day of Salvation ".

THE day of atonement, its numerous sacrifices, and the various rites enjoined, all deserve our most careful attention ; not only from the supreme importance attached to them under the Mosaic Law, but from their frequent mention in the New Testament, and from their typical bearing on the events of our own time, or those which will shortly come to pass.

By the Jews, it is called emphatically THE DAY. It is the day of condemning, avenging, and coverings of Sin, *yom hak-kiphpurim*—a Day of Coverings : on it the sins of the whole Jewish nation are covered over ; on it the High Priest per-formed all the functions of ordinary priests ; and on this day only he entered the Holy of Holies, or the most holy chamber or division, of the temple beyond the Veil. This day was considered as a Sabbath, or rest, a festival, and the strictest of fasts ; and it concentrated in itself the solemnities proper to each of these, and it had a longer period of preparation preceding it than any other holy day required.

The High Priest performed all those services appointed for the Tabernacle—the daily, the sabbatical, and the festival services, as well as those peculiar to this day, and he finished by reading to the people.

Tisri was the first month of the Civil Year, and the seventh of the Ecclesiastical Year, and the 10th of Tisri was the Day of Coverings, termed in the English Version, " the Day of Atonement ". From the first to the seventh are called *days of conversion* ; because in them they turned to Yahweh in prepara-tion for the 10th. The 8th and 9th were styled *terrible days*. On these they clothed themselves with sackcloth, and began to afflict their souls. At sunset on the 9th Tisri the fast began. No food was allowed, except in cases of extreme necessity, and even then the quantity was limited to what a date shell could hold. Seven days before the fast, the High Priest took up his abode in the temple, purifying himself, and practising those various sacrifices, and other offices on the 10th. On the 9th he fed sparingly, concluding before sunset ; during the night he was attended by the younger priests, who read to him, and prevented his sleeping, lest his dreams should be unholy. Others watched for the approach of day, and at the first streak of dawn, they roused the High Priest to the arduous duties of the day. There were fifteen victims which he must slay, divide, wash, and offer in sacrifice, as far as possible with his own hands. *He must wash his whole body five times* ; wash his hands and feet ten times ; and change his garments six times during the day ; and the fast must be as strictly observed by him as by the rest of the people. He went into the Holy of Holies four times during the day ;

1. With the incense ;
2. With the blood of the bullock ,
3. With the blood of the goat ;
4. At the conclusion of the sacrifices to bring out the Incense.

When the Day of Coverings dawned, the High Priest *put off* his ordinary garments, immersed his whole body, and five times washed his hands and feet ; he then *put on the holy garments*, and addressed himself to the service of the day.

He first slew the daily sacrifice, a lamb, burnt its members, offered the morning incense, trimmed the lamps, and went through the ordinary morning service. He then offered the bullock, and seven lambs, appointed for extraordinary significant days, and again washed his hands and feet. He then put off the golden garments, bathed himself, and put on the *linen garments* appropriate to the day (Lev. 16 : 4) ; and now began the service peculiar to it.

He first went to his own bullock (ver. 6), which was between the temple and the altar, and putting both hands upon his head, confessed his sins. Leaving the bullock in the hands of a keeper, he went to cast lots for the two goats in the north-east quarter of the Court below the altar. The lots were inscribed, the one " For Yahweh " ; the other, " For Scapegoat ". After drawing them, he tied a scarlet fillet on the horns of the Scapegoat, when it was taken to the east gate of the temple, which looked towards the Mount of Olives, whence it was to be sent into the wilderness in due time, the victim-goat remaining where it was.

He returned to his bullock, and confessing again over him his own sins, and those of the sons of Aaron and of the holy people, he slew the bullock, and gave the blood to a priest, who stirred it up to prevent coagulation.

He now took the censer, filled it with burning coals from the Brazen Altar ; then took a *handful* of incense from a vessel which was brought to him, and threw it into another dish. He took the censer of coals in his right hand, the dish of incense in his left, and entering the *first* time into the Holy of Holies through the Veil placed the burning censer in front of the Ark of the Covenant, poured the incense into his hand, scattered it on the coals, waited till the place was filled with smoke, and then came out backwards, his face being towards the Ark.

On reaching the Court of the Priests, he took the blood of the bullock, which had been kept stirred, and sprinkled it upon the Mercy Seat, eastward ; and before it seven times. Coming out again from the Most Holy, he left the remaining blood in the *Holy Place*. He now went out, and slew the victim-goat, and going with his blood into the Holy of Holies a *third* time, sprinkled it also before the Mercy Seat. Coming out, he set it down in *the Holy Place*, and sprinkled the blood of the bullock *before the Veil*, then the blood of the goat also. He then *mingled both bloods* in one vessel, and sprinkled the Golden Altar, and vessels of the sanctuary ; and going out, poured the remaining blood under *the Brazen Altar*.

These things transacted, he next sent away the Scapegoat, having laid his hands on his head, and confessed the sins of the people. While the Scapegoat was being conveyed away, the High Priest went on with the service of the day. He divided the bullock and goat he had slain, and whose blood he had taken within the Veil : he burnt their fat and inwards upon the Brazen Altar, but sent their carcasses to be burnt *without the camp* or city. By this time the Scapegoat had reached the wilderness, which event, they say, was known by the whitening of the scarlet fillet on the door-post.

The High Priest then read certain sections of the Law, recited eight prayers, washed his hands and his feet, *put off the linen garment*, bathed, *put on his golden garments*, and washed his hands and feet. He then offered a ram for himself, another for the people, and seven lambs as extra oblations for this day. At length he offered the daily evening sacrifice, washed his hands and feet, *put off the golden garments*, bathed, put on the linen garments, washed his hands and his feet, and going *a fourth time* into the Holy of Holies, brought out the censer and the dish, which he had left there at the beginning of the service of the day. Washing his hands and feet, he put off the linen garments, bathed, put on the golden garments, washed his hands and feet, offered the evening incense, and trimmed the lamps. Then finally washing his hands and feet, he put off the golden garments, resumed his ordinary dress, and went home, followed by the people, and congratulated by his friends.

In solving the enigma of this Mosaic Day of Coverings, it should be remembered, that Christ's person, Christ's office, Christ's sacrifice, and one time of offering it, the Eternal Spirit in Flesh, or *Christ alone* could fill—to show forth any *one* of these, several types combined ; and as each type requires its own time, there must be for each one of Christ's offices several times in the types. The Christ, in his single person, embodies the paschal lamb and its blood of sprinkling ; the victims of the Day of Coverings and their blood of sprinkling ; the bodies burnt without the camp ; and the High Priest who entered the Holy of Holies. All the types concenter in the Eternal Spirit Incarnate—the Christ ; and therefore in applying them *to him*, we are under the necessity of giving our whole attention to the meaning of the emblem, not to its circumstances. We must stop, in our application of the types to Christ, at that point where they foreshow his person or offices, and not apply to the Great Antitype the various times, places and circumstances which are only meant to give necessary locality to the several types. But when the finished work of the Christ comes to be applied to the faithful, or to successive generations ; or when we endeavour to trace out the course of his future manifestations, the time and order observed in the type become important features in our inquiry, and an attention to this distinction removes some difficulty in the case.

The Day of Coverings was a day of sacrifice in a preeminent degree—a day of death, of burning, and of blood— "A day of blood, and fire, and cloud of smoke ". It was a day also of confession of sin, tribulation, and pardon ; so that it became " a time of acceptance, and a day of salvation ". This was the character of the Mosaic Pattern ; of a single day in every year of the Times of the Ages ; and it foreshadowed a day of like character—a " Now ", which, Paul says, is the time of acceptance and the day of salvation (2 Cor. 6 : 2).

This Antitypical Day of Coverings has already continued for many centuries. Its preparation began with the entrance of the Eternal Spirit into its personal Temple (John 2 : 21) when he descended on Jesus in the form of a dove ; the slaying of the bullock and the goat, the burning of their carcasses without the camp ; and the carrying of the burning censer into the Holy of Holies, have been fulfilled in the death and resurrection, and ascension of Jesus, who, like the Scapegoat, is absent from the camp of Israel. The *handful* of incense, the prayers of the little flock, still smokes before the Ark. The censer remains there ; yea, and must remain there till the day is terminated, and its service complete. While it is smoking before the Ark, blood flows and the fire burns. Sin has been condemned in the flesh ; and the household or sanctuary of the Eternal Spirit reconciled ; but all its members have not yet been brought in. When these are complete, " the Hour of Judgment ", the last hour of the day of atonement, will have come. The law will then be proclaimed from Zion by the High Priest in his golden garments. The Jubilee trumpet will sound, and Israel shall return. In this terrible crisis, Babylon falls, the harvest is reaped, the vintage gathered, the wine-press trodden, and the times of the Gentiles fulfilled. Their kingdoms become the kingdoms of Yahweh ; Israel is pardoned ; the nations blessed in Abraham and his Seed ; the Day of Atonement consummated ; and the Feast of Tabernacles, the feast of the 15th of Tisri, inaugurated to the joy of all the earth.

SACRIFICE IN THE AGE TO COME

THE answer to the question, *Will burnt offerings and sacrifices be offered in the Age to come ?* must be sought for in the testimony of God. He only can tell ; and He has graciously condescended to do so. He instructs us in His Word that the sacrificial offering of beasts shall be a part of religious worship or service in the World or Age to Come. Of this there can be no doubt with those who believe the prophets ; but, whether we can reconcile the restoration of sacrifice with the sayings of Paul (Heb. 10 : 6 ; Eph. 2 : 15 ; Col. 2 : 14) without being led to a denial of either, or to the affirmation that a contradiction exists, is another thing, and a question to be settled, not by the opinions of the learned, but by reason enlightened by the handwriting of God.

The first witness to be summoned in the case is Malachi. He testifies that a time shall come when, " from the rising of the sun even to the going down of the same, my name, saith Jehovah of armies, shall be great among the nations, and in every place incense shall be offered to my name, and a pure offering ; for my name shall be great among the nations, saith the I-shall-be of armies ". This is evidently in the future, because it has never obtained in the past. Now when the time for the offering of this incense and pure offering in every place shall have arrived, a purified priesthood will have been prepared to offer it among the nations : for the same witness testifies, saying, " The Messenger of the Covenant . . . shall sit as a refiner and purifier of silver : and he shall purify the sons of Levi, and purge them as gold and silver, that they may offer to Jehovah an offering in righteousness. Then shall the offering of Judah and Jerusalem be pleasant unto Jehovah, as in the days of old, and as in former days " (Mal. 3 : 1-4).

The next witness we shall call up is Isaiah. He testifies that at the time when " the Lord God gathereth the outcasts of Israel ", " the sons of the stranger that join themselves to the Lord to serve him, and to love the name of the Lord, to be his servants, every one that keepeth the Sabbath from polluting it, and taketh hold of my covenant, even them will I bring to my holy mountain, and make them joyful in my house of prayer : their burnt offerings and their sacrifices shall be accepted on my altar ; for mine house shall be called an house of prayer for all peoples " (Isa. 56 : 6-7). When these words were written, the temple of Solomon was still standing as the house of prayer for Israel. But the prophet speaks here of a future temple which should be a house of prayer, not for Israel only, but for all peoples. That house has not yet been erected, but will certainly be, for Zechariah testifies that the man whose name is The Branch " shall build the temple of Jehovah "— a temple very minutely described by Ezekiel. Upon the altar of this temple, then, the burnt-offerings and sacrifices of the sons of the stranger will be accepted : offerings which shall be selected from the flocks of Kedar, and the rams of Nebaioth. For, says Isaiah, the Gentiles shall come to the light of Jerusalem, and kings to the brightness of her rising, when she shall arise and shine, and the glory of the Lord is risen upon her ; and " they shall bring gold and incense ; and they shall show forth the praises of the Lord. All the flocks of Kedar shall be gathered together unto her, the rams of Nebaioth shall minister unto her : they shall come up with acceptance on mine altar, and I will glorify the house of my glory " (Isa. 60 : 6-7).

Again, Isaiah tells us that in a time, which has hitherto never obtained, when the Egyptians shall serve with the Assyrians, and Israel shall be the third with Egypt and Assyria, a blessing in the midst of Palestine—then " they shall cry unto the Lord because of oppressors, and he shall send them a Saviour, and a Great One, and he shall deliver them. And Jehovah shall be known to the Egyptians, and the Egyptians shall know Jehovah in that day, and shall do sacrifice and oblation ; yea, they shall vow a vow unto Jehovah, and perform it " (Isa. 19 : 19-25).

When they do sacrifice and oblation thus, it will be at the yearly festival of Tabernacles ; for " every one that is left of the nations which came against Jerusalem shall even go up from year to year to worship the King, the I-shall-be of armies, and to keep the feast of Tabernacles " (Zech 14 : 16). Now the feast of Tabernacles cannot be kept without sacrifice, as will appear by consulting the law by which the festival was decreed, which reads thus : " The fifteenth day of this seventh month shall be the feast of Tabernacles, seven days unto Jehovah. On the first day shall be a holy convocation ; ye shall do no servile work therein. Seven days ye shall offer an offering made by fire unto Jehovah, on the eighth day shall be a holy convocation ; ye shall offer an offering made by fire unto Jehovah ; it is a solemn assembly, and ye shall do no servile work therein ". For the Gentiles to keep this feast, they must observe it as the Israelites did before them, according to the law ; and not as they " keep the Sabbath " now, observing the first or eighth instead of the seventh day, after a fashion of their own, and omitting those requirements which are inconvenient.

The Feast of Passover is also to be observed in the Age to Come ; which, however, cannot be kept without sacrifice. Jesus said to his disciples, " I will not any more eat of the Passover, until it be fulfilled in the kingdom of God ". This was equivalent to saying, "When the Passover is fulfilled in the kingdom of God I will eat of it ". Hence we find its restoration testified by Ezekiel in these words : " On the fourteenth day of the first month ye shall have the Passover, a feast of seven days ; unleavened bread shall be eaten. And upon that day shall the Prince prepare (by the priests who offer his burnt-offerings and his peace-offerings, Ezekiel 46 : 2) for himself and all the people of the land, a bullock for a sin-offering. And seven days of the feast he shall prepare a burnt offering to Jehovah, seven bullocks and seven rams without blemish, daily the seven days ; and a kid of the goats daily, for a sin-offering. And he shall prepare a meat offering of an ephah for a bullock, and an ephah for a ram, and a hin of oil for an ephah ". And in the next verse the feast of tabernacles is thus referred to : " In the seventh month, on the fifteenth day of the month, shall he do the like in the feast of the seven days, according to the sin-offering, according to the burnt-offering, and according to the meat-offering, and according to the oil " (Ezek. 45 : 21-25).

The reader will observe, however, that the Passover is a feast for Israel's observance, not for that of the nations. The Prince, or High Priest, is to prepare it, " for himself, and for all the people of the land ", that is, of Palestine ; because the passover is the memorial of the deliverance of the Twelve Tribes and their rulers from the power of all that hate them. In this deliverance, when it is fulfilled in the Kingdom of God, the nations are punished after the manner of the Egyptians ; become a sacrifice at the hand of the destroyer, while he passes over Israel whom he comes to save. The Passover is the Fourth of July for Israel—the anniversary of the independence of their nation ; which can only be celebrated by those Gentiles in the Age to Come who acquire citizenship in their land.

In respect of the Feast of Tabernacles, or Feast of Ingathering, the nations may well rejoice with Israel in the celebration thereof; for it will memorialize their ingathering into the Abrahamic fold when they shall all be blessed in Abraham and his Seed. But the possibility of national ingratitude for so great a benefit is implied in the following words of the prophet : "And it shall be, that whoso will not come up, of the families of the earth, unto Jerusalem to worship the King, the I-shall-be of armies, even upon them shall be no rain ". But this would be no punishment to Egypt, because rain does not fall there : her fertility is maintained by the inundations of the Nile. It is therefore decreed that, " If the family of Egypt go not up and come not, that have no rain, there shall be the plague wherewith Jehovah shall smite the nations that come not up to keep the feast of tabernacles. This shall be the punishment of Egypt, and the punishment of all nations that come not up to keep the feast of tabernacles " (Zech. 14 : 16-19).

This same witness concludes his testimony relative to the constitution of things in the Age to Come by declaring that sacrifice shall be offered in a temple in Jerusalem. His words are : " The pots in the house of Jehovah shall be like the bowls before the altar. Yea, every pot in Jerusalem and in Judah shall be holiness to the Lord of armies : and all they that sacrifice shall come and take of them, and boil therein ; and in that day there shall be no more the Canaanite in the house of the I-shall-be of armies ". This can only relate to the future ; because the sacrificing is to be practised at a time when the Canaanite no more intrudes where it is unlawful for him to go. " The Canaanite " is a phrase put for the enemy of Israel— the enemy shall no more be in the house of Jehovah. But the enemy is now lord of Jerusalem, and has established a temple of his superstition upon the site chosen of Jehovah for the house of His name. The Ottoman is for the present the Canaanite of the Holy City—the desolating abomination of the glorious land. But better times are fast approaching, when the last of the Canaanites shall be ignominiously expelled. Hear what Zephaniah says upon this subject : " Sing, O daughter of Zion ; shout, O Israel ; be glad and rejoice with all the heart, O daughter of Jerusalem. Jehovah takes away thy judgments, he casts out thine enemy ; the King of Israel, Jehovah, is in the midst of thee : thou shalt not see evil any more " (3 : 14-15). Then shall the stone refused of the builders have become the head of the corner ; and those of the city who behold him shall say, " Blessed be He that comes in the name of Jehovah ! The mighty one is Jehovah who showeth us light : bind the sacrifice with cords to the horns of the altar . . . O give thanks unto Jehovah; for he is good ; because his mercy is for the age ! " (Psa. 118 : 26-29).

When the daily sacrifice was taken away by the Fifth Horn of the Grecian Goat in the days of Titus, it was only an interruption, not a final abolition, of sacrifice. It was a suppression of it for " many days ", at the expiration of which it will be restored with other things suppressed. This is apparent from the testimony of Hosea, who saith, " The children of Israel shall abide many days without a king, and without a prince (or High Priest), and without a sacrifice ; afterward (after the " many days " have expired) shall the children of Israel return (to Palestine) and seek Jehovah their God, and David their king : and shall fear Jehovah and his goodness in the latter days " (Hos. 3 : 4-5). These " latter days ", then, succeed the " many days " which have not yet expired. When they arrive, Israel will again have a king, a prince, and a sacrifice ; and that king will be David II, who will be a prince, likewise, after the order of Melchizedec, for one thousand years. And to this agrees the testimony of Jeremiah, who, speaking of the perpetuity of David's throne from the commencement of the reign of the man whose name is The Branch, saith, " In those days shall Judah be saved (which cannot be affirmed of Judah yet) and Jerusalem shall dwell safely ; and this is the name which shall be proclaimed to her—Jehovah our Righteousness ". And here is the reason given for Judah's salvation and Jerusalem's safety : " For ", continues he, " David shall never want a man to sit upon the throne of the house (or kingdom) of Israel : neither shall the priests the Levites want a man before me to offer burnt-offerings, and to kindle meat-offerings, and to do sacrifice continually." Here is an offering of sacrifices by Levites contemporarily with the reign of a son of David upon the throne of Israel. It is evident, therefore, that the " never " in the text commences with a henceforth, which is yet in the future. The epoch of that henceforth is the salvation of Judah, and the placing of Jerusalem in such a position that she may be safely inhabited, which cannot be till her enemy is cast out. From that time David shall never be without a successor in the throne of Israel ; and that successor shall be Messiah, during whose priestly reign Levites shall do sacrifice continually.

Reader ! Canst thou break Jehovah's covenant of the day and of the night, that there should not be day and night in their season ? If thou canst, " then also may my covenant, saith Jehovah, be broken that I have made with David my servant, that he should not have a son to reign upon his throne : and with the Levites, the priests, my ministers ". This is equivalent to saying that no combination of powers on earth or in heaven can prevent the Messiah, who is David's son, reigning on Mount Zion where David reigned ; or the Levites superseding the Mohammedans, Greeks, Latins, and Protestants in Jerusalem, and doing sacrifice there continually.

From the evidence, then, of these witnesses it is clear that sacrifice and offering will be elements of divine service in the Millennial Age. They will be " pure " and " pleasant " offerings to Jehovah ; because they will be perfect offerings, and offered in righteousness by a purified priesthood. They will be perfect, because they will be perfected by the sacrifice of Him whose expiatory death they represent. They will be pure offerings and pleasant, because the offerers will present them with enlightened faith and purified hearts. The Levites, refined as gold and silver, will slay the sacrifices of the peoples ; while the Sons of Zadoc, once dead, but then alive for evermore, and " kings and priests for God ", with the Prince of Israel in their midst, will approach and stand before Jehovah to offer unto Him the fat and the blood : they shall enter into His sanctuary, and come near to His table, to minister unto Him ; and shall keep His charge (Ezek. 44 : 15).

Such, however, was not the case in the Mosaic Age. The offerings were neither perfect, pure, nor pleasant to Jehovah. They were imperfect, not having been perfected by the expiation they typified ; but keeping up a remembrance of unpardoned offences every year. This will not be the case with the perfect offerings of the Age to Come. These will not be remembrancers of transgressions unforgiven ; but memorials of pardon through the sacrifice of Messiah the Prince. There is no day of annual atonement in the future age. Israel's offences are blotted out once for all as a thick cloud when the New Covenant is made with them on their re-settlement in the Holy Land when that age begins ; a forgiveness of national offences which lasts for ever, as it is written, " I will be merciful to their unrighteousness, and their sins and iniquities I will remember no more ".

But, the Mosaic offerings were not always unpleasant to Jehovah. It was the abominations of the offerers that made them disgusting in His sight. The High Priests and their sacerdotal households, who ought to have been " Holiness to Jehovah ", were very often men of reprobate character setting an example to Israel which they were not slow to follow, thus verifying the sayings, " Like priests, like people ", and " The leaders of my people cause them to err ".

This view of the matter accords with the handwriting of Jehovah by Malachi. " Judah ", saith he, " hath dealt treacherously, and an abomination is committed in Israel and in Jerusalem ; for Judah hath profaned the holiness of Jehovah which he loved, and hath married the daughter of a strange god. Jehovah will cut off the man that doeth this, the master and the scholar, out of the dwelling-places of Jacob, and him that offereth an offering to Jehovah of armies. And this have ye done again, covering the altar of the Lord with tears, with weeping, and with crying out, insomuch that he regardeth not the offering any more, or receiveth it with good will at your hands. Ye have wearied Jehovah with your words : yet ye say, Wherein have we wearied him ? When ye say, Every one that doeth evil is good in the sight of Jehovah, and he delighteth in them ". The saying, " insomuch that he regardeth not the offering any more, or receiveth it with good will at your hand ", implies that there was a time when He did regard the offering, and did receive it with good will, or pleasure, at their hand. Indeed the Spirit saith so in so many words when testifying of the purification of the sons of Levi ; as it is written, " Then shall the offering of Judah and Jerusalem be pleasant to Jehovah (or regarded, and received with good will) as in days of old, and as in former years ".

In reading Jehovah's reasons for taking no pleasure in the sacrifice and offering ; and burnt offerings, and offering for sin which were offered in Judah by the law, we are forcibly reminded of the sectarian practices and dogmas of our day. When ecclesiastics want to " bring down the Holy Ghost ", they assemble the people to what they call " the altar of the Lord ", which, like Judah's priests of old, they " cover with tears, with weeping, and with crying out ". This was the practice of Baal's worshippers, from whom the Jews learnt it ; and it is the idolatrous custom in these times of those who profess to go to the Lord to " get religion " ! But the reader will perceive from the words of Jehovah Himself that He despises such religion-getting, and turns His back upon it ; so that the fruit of these ecclesiastical demonstrations are not of God, but of the carnal mind unenlightened by His truth.

The priests also who practised this Baalism held a dogma essentially the same as Universalism. They taught that " Every one that doeth evil is good in the sight of Jehovah, and he delighteth in them ". This was in effect affirming that men would be saved however evil they might be ; for it is only in the saints that Jehovah delights. Such doctrine and practices, then, as these caused Jehovah to take no pleasure in the sacrifice and offering He had ordained in the Mosaic law ; and therefore Messiah came to do, or establish, the Second Covenant—to bring it into force through the offering of the body the I-shall-be had prepared for Himself. It was not possible, besides, for the blood of bulls and of goats offered by the law, to take away sins. They needed perfecting in their antitype— the restored body of Jehovah. " Therefore coming into the world, he saith, Sacrifice and offering thou requirest not : but *ears hast thou restored to me* ; in burnt offerings and sacrifices for sin thou hast no pleasure. Then said I, behold, I come (as it is written of me in the volume of the little book) to do that which is thy will, O God. Saying above, Sacrifice and offering and burnt offerings and offering for sin thou desirest not, neither hast pleasure, which are offered according to the law : then said he, Behold, I come to do that which is thy will, O God. He taketh away the first, that he may establish the second. By which will we are sanctified through the offering of the body by the anointed Jesus once only " (Heb. 10 : 5-10).

Messiah having thus been obedient unto death, and brought the Abrahamic Covenant into force, will, when he comes again in power and glory, carry out the purposes of the New or Second Covenant, and in so doing cause to be offered to Jehovah by the sons of Levi in Judah's midst, pure offerings that will be pleasant to Him as in the days of former years ; his own one offering having perfected for a continuance the things which the Mosaic Law could not ; for nothing was perfected by it.

As to Eph. 2 : 15, the subject of the discourse is the aboli- tion of the cause of enmity between Jews and Gentiles, which was " the law of the commandments in ordinances " which prevented peace between them. This ground of enmity he abolished when by the one offering of his body on the cross he took it out of the way, and established the " better covenant " which promised good things to Jews and Gentiles upon the same conditions. If Christ had not died and risen again, the Mosaic law would have continued in force to this day ; and there would have been no union of Jews and Gentiles in " one body ", and consequently the Gentiles would have continued helplessly, " without Christ, being aliens from the Commonwealth of Israel, and strangers from the Covenants of Promise, having no hope, and without God in the world ". To enable us to get at Christ, by becoming citizens of the Commonwealth of Israel, it was necessary to remove the Mosaic law out of our way, and to introduce another that would be more favourable. By becoming proselytes of Judaism, Gentiles might come to be with Moses, and citizens of Israel's commonwealth under his law ; but as this could not make alive, they would remain under sentence of death ; and enjoy nothing beyond the temporal advantages of a residence in the Holy Land in common with the natives. It could give them no right to be citizens in the Age to Come, and to reign for ever with Messiah over Israel and the nations for a thousand years. This right is derived from that Covenant which Jesus established or confirmed in dying and rising again. If we take hold of it by believing the things promised in it ; and *also* take hold of him, by faith in him, as the confirming sacrifice, or Mediator, thereof : and become obedient to the " law of Faith ", which commands such believers to be baptized into the name of the Father, of the Son, and of the Holy Spirit, we become the children of the covenant ; and through Jesus acquire citizenship in the Israelitish Commonwealth of the Age to Come. To such obedient believers, " who have received the knowledge of the truth, there remaineth no more sacrifice for sins " ; but a looking for the Second Appearing of Jesus unto salvation.

The text in Col. 2 : 14 relates to the same topic as that in Ephesians ; namely, the taking away the cause of division between Jews and Gentiles, the Mosaic law, or handwriting, which made it " an unlawful thing for a man that is a Jew to keep company, or come unto one of another nation ". While this handwriting was in force, there could be no union between Jews and Gentiles in " one body ", as members of which they were to love as brethren. The law divided them, and set them at variance ; as the gospel now separates those that obey it from all religious fellowship with disobedient unbelievers.

The Abrahamic Covenant, which was ratified by God for Christ—*eis Christon*—430 years before the law of Moses was given, knows nothing of that law. The law was an addition, not to it as a codicil, but as a distinct covenant, additionally presented and enjoined upon the natural descendants of Abraham, Isaac, and Jacob, until The Seed, or Christ, should come, to whom the promise of the everlasting possession of the Holy Land was made in the Covenant ratified for him. " It was added because of transgressions " among the Israelites, who while in Egypt served the gods of the Egyptians ; and were fast merging into forgetfulness of the good things covenanted to their nation under Christ.

The Abrahamic Covenant contains no cause of enmity between Jews and Gentiles ; for it promises among other things that " In Abraham's Seed (Christ) shall all nations of the earth be blessed ". All nations, include Jews and Gentiles. Not so the law, however. It was a " fiery law ". In itself " holy, just, and good " ; but notwithstanding its intrinsic excellence, " it was weak through the flesh " in which, Paul says, " no good thing dwelleth ". On account, therefore, of this weakness, the holy, just, and good Mosaic law, was " found to be death " to every Israelite ; for it said, " cursed be every one that continueth not in all things written in the book of the law to do them " ; which was too great a demand upon poor weak humanity to accord. Even Jesus, who was without sin, no fault being found in him, was cursed by it, saying, " Cursed be everyone that hangeth upon a tree " ; thus he became a curse for us. This law, then, was found to be death to him ; can it therefore after this be found to be life to any other mortal ? By no means ! Hence it condemns to death every Israelite, and every one else that seeks justification by it. And if God's people Israel with their King were sentenced to death by it, of what avail can it be to us Gentiles ? Certainly of none ; and therefore it is written, "Are we Jews better than they the Gentiles ? No, in no wise : for both Jews and Gentiles are all under sin " ; so that " all the world becomes guilty before God ".

Here, then, we behold mankind in an awful dilemma— naturally, under the sentence pronounced upon Adam, which is death ; and Mosaically, cursed to death by a law humanity is too weak to keep. If the state of the case had continued thus " the gates of Hades " would have prevailed for ever over Jew and Gentile, patriarch and prophet, from the first transgression to the natural extinction of the race, Enoch, Moses and Elijah alone excepted as exceptions to the rule.

The wisdom of God in a mystery, however, devised a happier result than this. The world " being dead in sins ", that is, dead Adamically and Mosaically because of transgression, He sent Jesus into the world to take the Mosaic handwriting out of the way by nailing it to his cross. And this he did by fulfilling all the righteousness shadowed forth in that law which cursed him on the tree ; a part of which representative righteousness was the atonement for sin by blood. Being nailed to the cross as the result of his voluntary surrender of his life, he may be said to have nailed himself to the cross by the hand of sinners ; for, saith he, " No man taketh my life from me, but I lay it down of myself. I have power to lay it down, and I have power to take it again. This commandment have I received of my Father " ; and therefore it was not suicide, but, " obedience unto death ". In being without sin and in perfecting the sacrificial righteousness of the law, he nailed it to the cross, when he nailed himself there. Now, being the Mediator of the Abrahamic covenant, he had therefore of necessity to die that it might come into force. Having therefore perfected the righteousness of the law in himself, the shadow was no longer necessary as the substance had come. In dying, consequently, he proclaimed " It is finished ! " and being perfected, in a few years after " it vanished away ". Thus, he blotted out the handwriting of ordinances that was against us, which was contrary to us, and took it out of the way, nailing it to his cross ; having in this way divested the authorities and the powers of Israel (for they derived their ecclesiastical and civil authority from the law), triumphing over them in rising from the dead, he exposed them with boldness of speech by the apostles.

The Mosaic Covenant being taken out of the way by the sacrificial death of Jesus, the Abrahamic was brought into force by the same means ; for the blood of Jesus which perfected the Mosaic Sin-offerings, also rendered purifying or consecrated the Abrahamic covenant, called " The New " though made before the law, because it came into force on nailing the Mosaic to the cross. The Abrahamic covenant, I say, was rendered purifying by the blood of Jesus ; so that " whosoever believeth " the things of the covenant, his faith and resulting disposition shall be counted to him for repentance and remission of sins in his name.

The Abrahamic Covenant, however, does not exclude the use of sacrifice. It was typically ratified or confirmed by the sacrifice of animals consumed by fire from heaven before the Mosaic law was given ; so, when the things it covenants are fully accomplished in the Age to Come, sacrifice will be restored, not as typical of the future, but as a memorial of the past. Blood shedding in the Age to Come will commemorate the shedding of the blood of Jesus in the end of the Mosaic Age. It will occupy the position in " the Service " that the breaking of the loaf does now to mortal believers of the truth in hope of the glory of God. " This do in remembrance of me." The broken bread and poured-out wine are remembrancers, or memorials, of the body broken and blood of Jesus shed for the remission of the sins of those who should become his brethren. When he appears a second time this form of remembrance will cease ; for it was to be observed, to use his words, " Until I come ".

Shall we say that when this unbloody memorial of his sacrificial death shall cease by the statute which limits it, there will be no memorial ordained to keep it in remembrance throughout the Age to Come ? If we affirm this we must reject all that testimony adduced in the former part of this article, which declares the restoration of sacrifice. Its restoration is certain. And when restored, upon what principle will it exist ? Will it represent the sacrifice of a future Christ ? That is impossible. Then it will not be typical. Will it be as the procuring cause of the remission of the sins of the people living in that age ? That would be to ignore the death of Jesus, which is inadmissable. Will it be to render purifying a new covenant ? None such exists to be confirmed and dedicated. Will it be for the cleansing of the resurrected saints ? For them, there is " no more sacrifice for sins ", having been by the one offering of Jesus sanctified and perfected for ever. It is upon none of these principles. There remains, then, but one other principle upon which sacrificial bloodshedding can be restituted in the Age to Come ; and that is, the one already set forth, even as a memorial of the consecration of the Abrahamic Covenant by the blood of Jesus, styled " the blood of the covenant " ; by the which the future rulers of the world are now sanctified ; and the future nations of that world, Gentile and Jewish, will be made holy through the dedicatory offering of Jesus Christ once. Thus will " God have justified the nations through faith " as he promised to Abraham, saying, " In thee shall all nations be blessed ". So that then " they which be of faith ", be they individuals or nations, " will be blessed with faithful Abraham ".

11

JESUS THE HEIR TO DAVID'S THRONE

" *Call his name Jesus. He shall be great, and shall be called the Son of the Highest ; and the Lord God shall give unto him the throne of his father David ; and he shall reign over the house of Jacob for ever ; and of his kingdom there shall be no end* " (Luke 1 : 30-32).

IT was revealed unto Nebuchadnezzar, king of Babylon, through the prophet Daniel, that in the " latter days " the God of heaven would set up a kingdom that should not be destroyed ; which kingdom should not be left to other people, as the kingdoms of Babylon, Medo-Persia, Greece and Rome have each successively been ; or as the ten kingdoms into which the Roman empire is at present divided should be ; but a kingdom which " shall break in pieces and consume all these kingdoms (of men) and itself shall stand for ever " (Dan. 2 : 44). Some years subsequent to this, in the first year of the reign of Belshazzar, the king of Babylon, Daniel himself had a vision of the rise and fall of the great monarchies above alluded to. After viewing them until their dominion was taken away, in his account he says, " I saw in the night visions, and behold, one like the Son of Man came with the clouds of heaven, and came to the Ancient of days, and they brought him near before him. And there was given him dominion, glory and a kingdom, that all people, nations, and languages should serve him ; his dominion is an everlasting dominion, which shall not pass away, and his kingdom that which shall not be destroyed " (7 : 13, 14). Mark ! this person like the Son of Man had given unto him, dominion, glory, and a kingdom ! There will be no difficulty in proving that the individual whom Daniel saw receiving these high honours was no less a personage than our Lord and Saviour Jesus Christ.

The reader will at once perceive an intimate connection between this prophecy of Daniel and a parable which Jesus spake to " some who thought that the kingdom of God should immediately appear ". He said, "A certain nobleman went into a far country, to receive for himself a kingdom, and to return " (Luke 19 : 12). The " certain nobleman " designates Jesus, who was " born to be a king " ; the " far country " the heavens into which he ascended, and in which he will remain " until the times of the restitution of all things " ; the " kingdom " that which Daniel saw given to him, and which the Lord God has promised to give him ; and " to return " his coming again, " in his glory, and all the holy angels with him, when he shall sit upon the throne of his glory ", " and judge the living and the dead at his appearing and his kingdom ". No one will deny that Jesus alludes to himself in this parable, and that he teaches in it—that he was to possess royal dignity on his return. This is no isolated doctrine of the Bible, but is fully corroborated by the testimony of prophets and apostles.

John the Baptist, the herald of the Messiah, announced the approach of Heaven's King, and declared that he was then in the midst of the people, and in order that he might be manifest to Israel, he had come immersing in water (John 1 : 26-34). Jesus and his apostles taught the nation of the Jews that the kingdom of the heavens had come nigh unto them, and that they were therefore to repent, or amend their lives. Jesus frequently illustrated the nature of the kingdom by striking parables and apt illustrations, and declared who should and who should not enter into it. " Blessed are the poor in spirit ", said he, " and those who are persecuted for righteousness' sake, for theirs is the kingdom of heaven ". " Except your righteousness exceed the righteousness of the scribes and Pharisees, ye shall in no case enter into the kingdom of heaven " (Matt. 5 : 3, 10, 20). " Whosoever shall not receive the kingdom of God as a little child, he shall not enter therein." " How hard it is for them that trust in riches to enter into the kingdom of God ! It is easier for a camel to go through the eye of a needle, than for a rich man to enter into the kingdom of God " (Mark 10 : 15, 24, 25). " Except a man be born of water and the Spirit, he cannot enter into the kingdom of God " (John 3 : 5). Such were the teachings of Jesus in reference to this kingdom.

He likewise intimated on various occasions that the Son of man should administer the affairs of the kingdom of God— reward his servants, and punish his enemies. He also claimed this kingdom as his own. Hence he promised the apostles that they should eat and drink at his table in his kingdom (Luke 22 : 30). And when at Pilate's bar, accused by the Jews of making himself a king, he did not deny the accusation, but said, " My kingdom is not of this world : if my kingdom were of this world, then would my servants fight that I should not be delivered to the Jews : but now is my kingdom not from hence. Pilate therefore said unto him. Art thou a king then ? Jesus answered, Thou sayest it, I am a king. To this end was I born, and for this cause came I into the world, that I should bear witness unto the truth " (John 18 : 36, 37). There are some who infer that because Jesus declared his kingdom not to be of this world, that therefore it must be out of the world. This is not correct. Literally he said : " My kingdom is not of this *kosmos* "—a word which means order, arrangement, or constitution of things. His kingdom will not be of the order of things which prevailed in Judea at that time, but will be arranged according to a heavenly constitution of things. Hence it is styled " the kingdom of the heavens ". Jesus also said that he was born to be king ; and in consequence of witnessing this " good confession before Pontius Pilate ", suffered death. And for " the suffering of death he was crowned with glory and honour ", and has obtained " a name which is above every name ", even " King of kings, and Lord of lords ".

The future dignity and glory of the son of Mary is noted by the angel Gabriel in his message to the virgin : " He shall be great, and shall be called the Son of the Highest ". Did not the Father acknowledge him before witnesses that he was His Son ? Did not the mighty works which he performed and to which he frequently appealed in proof of his Messiahship, also prove that he was the Son of God ? And the apostle Paul says that " he was declared to be the Son of God with power, according to the Spirit of holiness, by the resurrection from the dead " (Rom. 1 : 4). The writer to the Hebrews says that " God hath in these last days spoken unto us by his Son, whom he hath appointed heir of all things ". And alluding to his greatness he says, " When he bringeth his first-begotten into the world he saith, And let all the angels of God worship him. Unto the Son, he saith, Thy throne, O God, is for ever and ever : a sceptre of righteousness is the sceptre of thy kingdom : thou hast loved righteousness and hated iniquity ; therefore God, even thy God, hath anointed thee with the oil of gladness above thy fellows " (Heb. 1 : 2, 6-9).

We will now inquire more particularly concerning the throne and kingdom which Jesus will ultimately possess. We have already seen that the diadem of universal dominion shall be placed upon his head ; that regal honours shall be given to him ; but as yet we have not ascertained his right and title to all this glory. This is hinted at in our text in the following words : " The Lord God shall give unto him the throne of his father David ; and he shall reign over the house of Jacob for ever ".

This language is sufficiently clear to show that the kingdom which Jesus will possess is the kingdom of David—that the throne which he will occupy will be the throne of David—that the subjects of his kingdom will be everlasting—and that he is the legitimate heir and son of David.

In order to understand this important matter fully, we must refer to the covenant which Jehovah made with David, for He made " an everlasting covenant with him, ordered in all things and sure ". This covenant is recorded in 2 Sam. 7 : 12-16 ; also in Psa. 89, from which we make a few extracts : " I have made a covenant with my chosen, I have sworn unto David my servant, Thy seed will I establish for ever, and build up thy throne to all generations . . . My covenant will I not break, nor alter the thing that has gone out of my lips. Once I swore by my holiness that I will not lie unto David. His seed shall endure for ever, and his throne as the sun before me. It shall be established for ever as the moon, and as a faithful witness in heaven " (Psa. 89 : 3, 4, 34-37). Again, " The Lord hath sworn in truth unto David ; he will not turn from it ; Of the fruit of thy body will I set upon thy throne " (Psa. 132 : 11). The Lord, by the prophet Jeremiah, reiterates this covenant. He says, " Thus saith the Lord, If ye can break my covenant of the day, and my covenant of the night, and that there should not be day and night in their season ; then may also my covenant be broken with David my servant, that he should not have a son to reign upon his throne " (Jer. 33 : 20, 21).

The covenant requires, then, that the heir to the throne of David be of a character approved by Jehovah. Hence we find this specified in the last words of David in the following manner :— " The God of Israel said, the Rock of Israel spake to me, He that ruleth over men must be just, ruling in the fear of God . . . Although my house be not so with God ; yet he hath made with me an everlasting covenant, ordered in all things and sure ; for this is all my salvation, and all my desire, although he make it not to grow " (2 Sam. 23 : 3, 5). David looked forward to the time when such a righteous king should occupy his throne ; " who shall judge the poor of the people, save the children of the needy, and break in pieces the oppressor " ; a king " in whose days the righteous shall flourish " ; a king who shall have universal dominion, and before whom all kings shall bow, and become tributary ; and a king " who shall live ", or be immortal, whose name shall endure for ever, and in whom all men shall be blessed (see Psa. 72).

And yet history shows that the sons of David did not all of them walk in the steps of their father, nor regard the God of Israel. Even Solomon, the immediate successor of David, and who is claimed by some as the one referred to by the covenant, grievously sinned against the Lord. And the house of David became so corrupt that Jehovah frequently warned the kings of Judah of the result of their wickedness. By Jeremiah he said to them : " O house of David, thus saith the Lord : Execute judgment in the morning, and deliver him that is spoilt out of the hand of the oppressor, lest my fury go out like fire, and burn that none can quench it, because of the evil of your doings " (21 : 12). And because they repented not, but rather increased in wickedness, the Lord determined to deprive them of the royalty, and overthrow the kingdom. Hence Ezekiel said to Zedekiah, the last of Judah's kings, " Thou profane wicked prince of Israel, whose day is come when iniquity shall have an end, Thus saith the Lord God ; Remove the diadem, and take off the crown : this (man) shall not be the same ; exalt him that is low, and abase him that is high. I will overturn, overturn, overturn it : and it shall be no more, until he come whose right it is ; and I will give it him " (21 : 25-27). This dreadful catastrophe was prophetically seen by the Psalmist. Hear his lamentation : " But thou hast cast off and abhorred, thou hast been wroth with thine anointed. Thou hast made void the covenant of thy servant : thou hast profaned his crown by casting it to the ground. Thou hast made his glory to cease, and cast his throne to the ground " (Psa. 89 : 38, 39, 44). And the prophet Hosea says, " The children of Israel shall abide many days without a king, and without a prince, and without a sacrifice, and without an image, and without an ephod, and teraphim. Afterward shall the children of Israel return, and seek the Lord their God, and David their king ; and shall fear the Lord and his goodness in the latter days " (3 : 4, 5).

And now let us pause to inquire whether that method of interpretation can be correct which disregards the covenant which Jehovah made with David—a covenant confirmed by an oath, and the concurrent testimony of the prophetic word ? We think not. Nor will it do to say the various items of that covenant are fulfilled, unless a descendant of David is now on his throne, reigning in his kingdom, over the tribes of Jacob, who is righteous, powerful, glorious, and immortal. This cannot be ; for the kingdom and throne are yet in the dust, and Israel in captivity. And no one of Adam's race has yet appeared who fills the character of David's Son and David's Lord, except Jesus of Nazareth. But let us examine the testimony a little further.

Our text says, that " Lord God shall give unto him the throne of his father David ", from which we infer that he is the promised son and heir according to the covenant. Jesus was " the son of David according to the flesh ". His genealogy, both on his father's and mother's side, proves it. He is frequently styled the son of David in the Gospels. Zacharias, the father of John the Baptist, inspired by the Holy Spirit, designates Jesus as the Messiah long desired by the Jewish nation. He says, " Blessed be the Lord God of Israel, for he hath visited and redeemed his people, and hath raised up a horn of salvation for us in the house of his servant David ; as he spake by the mouth of his holy prophets, which have been since the world began " (Luke 1 : 68-99). This horn of salvation is called " the horn of David " in Psa. 132 : 17 ; and " the horn of the house of Israel " in Ezek. 29 : 21. A horn is an emblem of strength or power ; behold, then, how appropriate when applied to Jesus. The angel of the Lord said to Joseph, " Thou shall call his name Jesus ; for he shall save his people from their sins " (Matt. 1 : 21). Hence Paul says, " So all Israel shall be saved ; as it is written, There shall come out of Zion the Deliverer, and shall turn away ungodliness from Jacob ; for this is my covenant unto them, when I shall take away their sins " (Rom. 11 : 26, 27).

Again, Jesus declares himself to be both " the Root and Offspring of David " (Rev. 22 : 16), which throws us back on the prophecy of Isaiah 11 : "And there shall come forth a rod out of the stem of Jesse, and a branch shall grow out of his roots . . . And in that day there shall be a root of Jesse, which shall stand for an ensign of the people ; to it shall the Gentiles seek ; and his rest shall be glorious ". This prophecy is quoted by the apostle Paul and applied to Jesus Christ (Rom. 15 : 12), thus proving the fact that the Messiah was of the seed of David, according to his gospel (2 Tim. 2 : 8).

Again, Jesus says that he has " the key of David " (Rev. 3 : 7), and Jehovah says of him by Isaiah, " The key of the house of David will I lay upon his shoulder " (22 : 22). The word *key* signifies authority or government ; this is evident from what we read in Isa. 9 : 6, 7 : " Unto us a child is born, unto us a son is given ; and the government shall be upon his shoulder ; and his name shall be called Wonderful, Counsellor, The mighty God, The everlasting Father, The Prince of Peace. Of the increase of his government and peace there shall be no end, upon the throne of David, and upon his kingdom, to order it, and to establish it with judgment and justice, from henceforth even for ever ". Compare this passage with the one at the head of this article, and it will be very evident that Jesus is the one who bears the key of David, and who will exercise the authority which it imparts. And Jesus declared before his ascension that " all power is given unto him in heaven and in earth " ; and Paul says, " God hath highly exalted him, and given him a name which is above every name : that at the name of Jesus every knee should bow, of things in heaven, and things in earth, and things under the earth ; and that every tongue should confess that Jesus Christ is Lord, to the glory of God the Father " (Phil. 2 : 9-11). Again he says, " God hath set him at his own right hand in the heavenly places, far above all principality, and power, and might, and dominion, and every name that is named, not only in this world, but also in that which is to come ; and hath put all things under his feet " (Eph. 1 : 21, 22).

The apostle Peter also teaches the glory and exaltation of Jesus : " Him hath God exalted with his right hand to be a Prince and a Saviour, for to give repentance to Israel, and forgiveness of sins " (Acts 5 : 31). " Let all the house of Israel know assuredly that God hath made that same Jesus, whom ye have crucified, both Lord and Christ " (Acts 2 : 36). And this exaltation to his Father's right hand is only for a set time : " Until I make thy foes thy footstool ". This glorious consummation will take place in the times of the restitution of all things, when God shall send Jesus Christ to bless Israel and the nations.

Without pursuing the investigation of this subject any further, we conclude by saying that the testimony of prophets and apostles agree in declaring Jesus to be the heir to David's throne, and that, having received the royalty of his Father, God, he will " return, and will build again the tabernacle of David that is fallen down, and close up the breaches thereof ; and will raise up his ruins, and build it as in the days of old "

(Amos 9 : 11 ; Acts 15 : 16) ; that he will " restore the kingdom again to Israel " (Acts 1 : 6) ; " make him that was cast far off a strong nation " (Micah 4 : 7) ; establish " Jerusalem as the throne of the Lord " (Jer. 3 : 17) ; and as " the Ruler in Israel ", and " Prince of the kings of the earth ", " shall stand and rule in the strength of the Lord, in the majesty of the name of the Lord his God, and he shall be great unto the ends of the earth " (Micah 5 : 4).

12

MOMENTOUS TRUTHS*

(i) *THE HOPE OF THE WORLD AND "THE HOPE OF ISRAEL"*

THE caption of this article has been selected as expressive of a startling truth, in which all men, profane and pious, are equally interested. There are in the world two great objects of desire, which all profess to hope for and to which all who profess them aver that God has called them ; hence, they may be still further characterized as the Two Hopes of the Two Callings These two hopes are different in all their details ; they are opposite and antagonistic, and so contrary, therefore, the one from the other, that if one be demonstrated to be God's truth, the other is thereby proved to be no hope at all, because in fact a mere vain imagination. For this reason Paul, in writing to the brethren who were sorrowing for some Christian relatives, who had fallen victims to the power of the enemy, exhorts them not to mourn as did " the others ", the Pagan Gentiles, " who had no hope " ; for they should embrace them again, when Jesus should raise them from the dead (1 Thess. 4 : 13).

We say that the phrase " the others ", in Greek, *hoi loipoi*, with the definite article *the*, imports the Heathen Gentiles. This will be still more evident from Eph. 2 : 12, where Paul defines the state of Gentiles out of Christ. " Remember ", says he to the Adopted Israelites of the Ephesian Body, " that ye, in time past, were Gentiles in the flesh, and styled the Uncircumcision by the circumcised Jews " : " at that time ye were *chōris Christou*, separate from Christ, being aliens from the Commonwealth of Israel, and strangers from the Coven-ants of Promise, having no hope, and atheists—*atheoi*, i.e. without God—in the world." Not to multiply quotations, it is clear from this that the Gentiles not in Christ and in God are " the others who have no hope ". Let it then not be forgotten by any, pious or impious, that the scriptures write that man hopeless who is an alien from the Jewish State or Polity. " The Hope of Israel " is not such a Gentile's hope even though he

---

*As a result of preparing this and the next two articles, Dr. Thomas recognized that when he was immersed by Walter Scott he was ignorant of the One Hope : see Introduction, pages 11-45. *Momentous Truths* was an appropriate title.

may speculatively believe it ; what shall we say of those pietists who repudiate its details, general and particular, as " husks " and " useless speculations " ? Their hope it is not ; they also are self-convicted as hopeless of the truth.

This then is certain, namely, that *it matters not what a man hopes for, if that hope be false or spurious ; if it be not the Hope promised in the Covenants of the Promise, he is repudiated as hopeless in the scriptures of truth ;* and further, that even if in theory he believe it, if he continue in his Gentilism, i.e. if he become not an Adopted Citizen of the Jewish Polity (*politeia*), he is without Christ, without hope, and without God. Let the prophets and diviners of the living age, the leaders of the people, professors, editors and preachers give ear to these things ; for we speak to them especially as to those who cause this people to put their trust in things which form no part of the truth of God.

But indeed, though the heathen were hopeless of the true hope, and atheists as respected their acknowledgement of the one only living and true God, they had a hope and a godliness of their own imagining. These are termed by the apostle in 2 Cor. 10 : 5 *logismoi* (reasonings), which exalt themselves against the knowledge which comes from God ; and speaking of them to the Christian Disciples at Rome, he says in chapter 1 : 21, that they were " vain in their imaginations (*dialogismoi*, reasonings or dialogues, such as Plato's *Dialogue on Laws*) and their foolish heart was darkened. Professing themselves to be *sophoi*, wise men, they became fools ". They hoped for things relating to souls which were vain dialogisms or speculations. Believing in the inherent immortality of corruptible flesh, because they imagined it to be pervaded by an immaterial soul, they hoped at death to be delivered from present evils by the reabsorption of their immortalities into the Divine Essence. To them the idea of a resurrection of the mortal body was a monstrous absurdity ; hence they laughed Paul to scorn when he announced it on Mars' Hill at Athens. They deceived their foolish heart by the vain imaginings of the translation of their souls on the wings of demons to the Elysian fields in the region of everlasting light. The terms being changed, angels being substituted for demons, and heaven for the Elysium, the hope of the present generation of Gentiles is identical with the heathen dialogisms of the apostolic era.

We repeat it. Let the reader examine into this matter, and he will find, that the hope of the Catholic, Protestant, Mohammedan, and Pagan communities of the 19th century, is the same, substantially the same, though philologically metamorphosed, as the hope of the heathens of Greece and Rome. Episcopalians, Presbyterians, Methodists, Universalists, Baptists, etc., all teach it as the " one hope of their calling " ; the translation of their immortalities at death from earth to heaven on angels' wings is believed by the people and preached by the clergy, and advocated by partisan editors as the revealed truth of God ! They pray for it in prayers, eulogize it in their rhapsodies, and sing it in their hymns, as the consummation most devoutly to be wished !

We shall not pause here to argue against these absurdities ; when we show what the true hope is, they will be as conspicuous as the sun at noon-day. We shall now content ourselves with affirming simply that the scriptures do not teach these things. They belong to the New Platonism of the Egyptian Theology. To sing these things is to pour into the ear of the Deity what is not of the truth, and therefore as saith the apostle, lies ; for what is not of the truth is a lie.

Nevertheless, these are all items of the hope, both of the pious and undevout of this generation. Suppose we grant that it is the true hope ; it must then be the hope of Israel, and if so, it will be found in the Covenants of the Promise made to the Fathers, and confirmed by the oath of God. Will any one be kind enough to show us where any such hope has been promised to Israel ? And if this were promised, how comes it that Paul saith the Gentiles had no hope, seeing that they had indulged in these items of expectation almost from time immemorial ?

Here then is one of the hopes—the hope of the pious, the hope of the impious, and the hope of the hypocrite as well ! A hope which the scriptures aver is no hope, and that all who trust in it are doomed to utter and irretrievable disappointment.

We have already hinted what we now affirm, namely, that the character of a man's faith, whether it be living or dead, may be determined by the hope he assuredly entertains.

The One Faith embraces the things which relate to repentance and remission of sins in the name of Jesus, as well as to those which pertain to the hope ; whereas the hope relates to things in the undeveloped future ; hence the apostle says " hope that is seen is not hope : for what a man seeth, why doth he yet hope for ? But if we hope for that we see not, then do we with patience wait for it " (Rom. 8 : 24).

A man may believe all things relating to repentance, and the remission of sins, but if his faith do not embrace the true hope, he does not possess that faith which pleases God. This appears from Paul's teaching in Hebrews. " But ", says he, " we are not of a drawing back unto destruction, but of a faith unto an acquisition of life. Now faith is an assured expectation (*hypostasis*) of things hoped for ; a conviction of things unseen." Having thus defined the Faith unto Life, which is nothing less than a belief of " things which are eternal ", he tells the Hebrews, that " without it, it is impossible to please God " (chap. 10 : 39 ; 11 : 1, 6). This was saying in effect, that unless their faith comprehended the things contained in the Covenants of Promise, they could not be saved ; for, says he elsewhere, WE WERE SAVED BY THE HOPE (Rom. 8 : 24) ; that is : " Christian disciples in Rome, when ye were saved from your past sins through the name of Jesus, it was not only by faith in his death, in the sin cleansing efficacy of his blood, and in his resurrection abstractly considered ; but by an assured expectation and conviction of the things unseen and eternal, which are comprised in the hope of the Gospel ". " For ", as if he had continued, " even the redemption of your mortal bodies from corruption is purely conditional on your adhesion to the hope."

We wish here to be distinctly understood. We affirm that *no man hath the remission of past sins, a title to the Kingdom of God, nor will he obtain possession of it, unless his faith include a belief of the true hope, and unless he keep this hope in mind stedfast to the end.* Now let the prophets and diviners of this age give ear to the proof we now present for their conviction.

In Hebrews 3, the apostle is discoursing concerning the One Hope, or " Rest which remains for the people of God " : " Holy brethren ", says he, " partakers of the heavenly calling, consider Christ Jesus ; whose house we are IF indeed we hold fast the confidence and the hope firm unto the end. For we have become associates of Christ, IF indeed we keep in mind the principle of the assured expectation (*hypostasis*) stedfast to the end " (verses 1, 6, 14). You see here what is predicated on an " if ". If you possess not the assured expectation, you are neither of the house, nor associates of Jesus.

Again, in 1 Cor. 15, Paul discourses of the hope into which the Christian disciples in Corinth had been immersed. In this chapter he speaks of the Resurrection of the Dead, the Second Advent of Jesus, the delivering up of the Kingdom, the duration of his reign, the complete subjection of his enemies, baptism for the resurrection of the dead, the nature and appearance of the saints when glorified, the impossibility of mortal men inheriting the Kingdom, the instantaneous transformation of the saints in the flesh into incorruptible and immortal persons, the abolition of death, the subjection of the Son to the Father, etc. He treats of all these things as of so many items of the glorious hope, which made the things he delivered to them glad tidings or Gospel. These astonishing revelations to the heathen mind, were all predicated on the fact of the resurrection of Christ according to the Prophets. If he had risen, as Paul testified, all these things would come to pass ; but if he had not, then none of them would happen. It was certain that Jesus had risen from the dead ; their belief, or disbelief, would not alter the fact ; though it would materially affect themselves individually : for if they denied the true hope in relation to the resurrection ; if they affirmed that there was no future resurrection, or, what was equivalent to it, that " the resurrection was past already ", as some of them did—then they were in effect denying the resurrection of Jesus, and by implication, everything consequent upon it.

But upon what ground did they conclude that there was " no resurrection of the dead ", or that " it was past already ", by which conclusion their faith was overthrown, and shipwrecked ? The foundation of their error was the adoption of the " profane vain babblings, and oppositions of a false *gnosis*, or science ", which was then being taught pretty extensively in the churches by such men as Hymenæus and Philetus. These sophists inculcated the reveries of Plato, and other heathen philosophers, about souls, immortality, heaven, hell, etc. They taught that all men were inherently immortal, because of the immaterialities which pervaded their bodies ; and that at death, the immortal part of man went direct to heaven or hell. Hence resurrection and the judgment day, the Second Advent of Jesus, the waiting for the Kingdom of God, etc., were all superfluous incumbrances, which might very well be dispensed with as so many " useless speculations ", which tended only to prejudice the literary and philosophic community against the doctrine of remission of sins in the name of Jesus, and the acknowledgement of the one God, " without making men any better, or increasing the Christian virtues ! " Professing to be wiser than the Apostle, they became fools ; nevertheless, many embraced their notions as less unpopular than the teaching of Paul.

Now to these pious professors of another hope, and therefore of " another gospel ", the apostle says, if you hold these profane or heathen notions, which are subversive of the true hope, you profess a vain faith ; ye may indeed believe that Jesus died for our sins according to the prophets ; that he was buried, and arose again as predicted ; but if you abandon the hope of Israel, for which I hazard my life daily, and embrace the heathen philosophy concerning the " immortality of the soul ", " ye are yet in your sins ", and consequently " without Christ, aliens from the Jewish Polity, strangers from the Covenants of the Promise, having no hope, and atheists in the world ". You thus become heirs of perdition, and the horizon of your destiny is limited by the things seen and temporal. Alas for you ; for, " if in this life only you have hope, ye are of all men most miserable ! "

Now let this make an indelible impression upon our minds, namely, that these Christian disciples at Corinth had attended Paul's reasonings in the Synagogue every Sabbath Day, by which they had been persuaded of the truth, both Jews and Greeks (Acts 18 : 4). Having heard, many of the heathen Corinthians also believed and were baptized (verse 8). In writing to these persons, he tells them that " they are washed, sanctified (or made saints) and justified in the name of the Lord Jesus, and by the Spirit of God " (1 Cor. 6 : 11). But upon what principle ? Upon the very same as were the Christian disciples in Rome : they were saved by the hope.

Their salvation, then, from their past sins, and their continuance in a saved state, were conditional. Hear what Paul saith to them : " But I now make known to you, brethren, the glad tidings which I myself announced to you ; by which also ye are saved, if ye hold fast a certain word (*tini logō*) I myself brought to you, unless indeed ye have believed it to no purpose " (1 Cor. 15 : 1, 2). What was this certain word, or *tis logos* ? The things he recalls to their recollection in this chapter ; and which he predicates on the death, burial, and resurrection of the Messiah, as *en prōtois*, among the first things, he delivered to them. If they did not hold fast to this word, or hope, which made his annunciation glad tidings, he declares that they would go to perdition, although they had been washed, sanctified and justified as aforesaid.

Again : in Colossians the Apostle also makes the hope of Israel the topic of discourse. No one, we presume, will venture to affirm that the hope of the gospel is not identical with the hope of Israel, for which Paul was bound in chains and carried prisoner to Rome. We say then that he discourses in this epistle of the hope of Israel, because he treats of the hope of the Gospel. This hope is contained in the " word of the truth of the gospel " which he preached. He says he was made a minister of the hope, that he might fully preach the word of God concerning it. He styles it, " the Mystery which hath been hid from previous ages and generations, but now (in his time and by his agency) is made manifest to his saints : to whom God would make known what is the riches of the glory of the Mystery among the Gentiles, which is Christ in you the Hope of Glory " (chap. 1 : 5, 25, 27). As the minister of this glorious hope, wherever he went he proclaimed it to the people ; and so indefatigable were he and the rest of the Apostles that within thirty years from the Ascension it had been made known " to every creature under heaven ". The Colossians had received it. It taught them that their " life was hid with Christ in God " ; and that " when Christ their life shall appear, then shall they also appear with him in glory " (3 : 3, 4). It taught them this, which excluded all speculation about going to glory at death, and having immortal life within them. Still they were no more than others proof against the *Gnosis* of the Hymenæus and Philetus class of preachers, whose word ate like a canker, as is evinced in this day. Like a phagedenic ulcer upon the body, it has eaten out and thoroughly eradicated from the human mind almost all vestiges of the Hope of Israel. Where is the prophet, where the divine, where the scribe, that does not inculcate the " profane babblings " of Hymenæus and Philetus ? " Beware ", says the Apostle to the Christian disciples at Colosse, " lest any man spoil you through philosophy and vain deceit, after the tradition of men, after the rudiments of the world, and not after Christ " (2 : 8). He knew how that men from among themselves would arise, teaching " perverse things to draw away disciples after them ". Hence, he exhorts them to " let no man judge them in meat, or in drink, or in respect of a holy day, or the new moon, or of the Sabbath ; nor beguile them of their reward in a voluntary humility and worshipping of angels, intruding into those things which he has not seen, vainly puffed up in his fleshly mind " (2 : 16, 18).

These teachers were " false apostles, deceitful workers transforming themselves into apostles of Christ " (2 Cor. 11 : 13). Paul styles them " fools " (verse 19) ; who preached " another Jesus, another Spirit, and another gospel " (verse 4), by which, " as the serpent beguiled Eve through his subtility " they corrupted the minds of the brethren from the simplicity that is in Christ (verse 3). Now, says he to them at Colosse, of such men " beware ". Be on your guard, lest ye slip your cable ; for the safety of your vessel depends on holding fast to the anchor. Remember, that formerly ye were alienated and enemies in your minds by wicked works, but now are reconciled, that ye may be presented holy, and unblameable, and unreprovable in his sight (chap. 1 : 21, 22).

Ah ! exclaim the Diviners, here is a case in which the reconciliation is absolute, and not at all conditional upon holding fast to the hope of Israel ! Not so fast. The presentation of these Christian disciples before the King, as " holy, unblameable, and unreprovable " persons, is predicated on the following conditions, namely : " IF ye continue in the faith, grounded and settled, and be not moved away from the hope of the gospel, which ye have heard, and which was preached to every creature under the Heaven ; whereof I, Paul, am made a minister " (Col. 1 : 23).

Here, then, are two indispensable conditions of salvation,
1st.—*A continuance in The Faith without vacillation ;*
2nd.—*Immobility from the Hope of the Gospel.*

The first condition implies that The Faith has been embraced ; for a man cannot continue a believer unless he primarily believe. The second presupposes that his primary belief comprehended the knowledge of the Hope of Israel ; for it is enjoined upon him that he " hold fast to it stedfast to the end ", that is, " be not moved away from it ".

You perceive then, if a man would be saved, he must have the right kind of a hope. If he hopes for things which God has not promised, he hopes for things which will never exist, and therefore his hope is a mere delusion. Now the scriptures style God, " the God of hope " ; is He God of a true hope, or of a false hope ? If of a false one, then He is God of no hope ; but, if of the true one, then be assured that as men are saved by the hope, God will save them only by that which is true. This is just, however calamitous to the man ; for, if one hope that his " immortal soul " will go to the right hand of the majesty in the skies at the instant of death, he would be exceedingly disappointed at finding himself on earth at the coming of Jesus ; and that he had never been where he hoped he should have been at all. If a man hope for a nonentity he has no hope ; and therefore being *de facto* hopeless, he is an heir not of salvation, but of destruction.

Thus, then, we have shown,

1st.—That the heathen Gentiles had a hope of immortality, predicated on the speculation of man being constituted of two principles, the one material and the other immaterial, and therefore immortal ;

2nd.—That, though they had a hope yet as it was a false one, the scripture regards them as having none ;

3rd.—That the hope of the ancient heathen is substantially the hope of the Romanist, Mohammedan, Pagan and Protestand communities even to this day ; and therefore no hope, but purely a delusion ;

4th.—That the character of a man's faith is determined by the things which he hopes for ;

5th.—That the hope of the Gospel relates to things in the undeveloped future ;

6th.—That a faith destitute of the true hope is displeasing to God ;

7th.—That men are saved by the Hope of the Gospel ;

8th.—That salvation by the true hope is conditional on not being moved away from it ;

9th.—That the " profane vain babblings and oppositions of science falsely so called ", taught by the ancient heretics, Hymenæus, Alexander and Philetus, " whose word " hath " eaten like a canker ", constitute the theology inculcated from the pulpits and presses of the present age ;

10th.—That this speculative and corroding theology has not only eaten out " the One Hope of the Calling ", so that the world has lost all knowledge of it ; but it has popularized the religion of Jesus, stultified the public mind, seared its conscience, and lulled it into a profound sleep ; and shut the Kingdom of God against the people ;

11th.—That the spurious hope inculcated by the ghostly leaders of the world is subversive of the Gospel, and therefore, inimical to the well-being of mankind ;

12th.—That the hope which saves through Jesus was unknown until it was announced by the Apostles ;

13th.—That the command to preach this hope " to every creature " was executed within thirty years after the Ascension, by the Apostles ; hence, no rational expectation of converting the world by stationary or missionary clergy, founded upon the text in Matt. 28 : 19, 20, can be entertained : it is not salvation, but damnation, which awaits the sapless, fruitless and faithless Gentiles of these latter times ; and

14th.—That teachers of a false hope are deceiving and being deceived.

(ii) *THE ONE HOPE*

It remains for us to show,

1st.—*That there is but One True Hope ;*

2nd.—*That it was this hope contained in " the Word of the Truth ", which made that word Glad Tidings, or Gospel, to the world ;*

3rd.—*What this Hope is.*

First then, the Apostle in writing to the Christian disciples in Ephesus, discourses at some length concerning that undeveloped reality which makes " the Word of the Truth " he announced the Glorious Gospel of the Blessed God. In the fourth chapter, he tells them that he is a prisoner ; and, in Acts 28 : 20, we are told on what account he was deprived of his liberty ; " for the Hope of Israel ", says he, " I am bound with this chain " : therefore because he was bound for that which Jehovah had promised to the Fathers of Israel, he styles himself " the prisoner of the Lord ". " I therefore ", says he, " the prisoner of the Lord, beseech you that you walk worthy of the vocation with which ye are called " ; that is, walk worthy of the Hope of the Gospel. Then, further on he exhorts them to " endeavour to maintain the unity of the Spirit in the bond of peace " (4 : 3), which can only be done by " contend- ing earnestly for the Faith originally delivered to the Saints ", as we are commanded to do. In the verse immediately following he enumerates the grand integral parts which in combination make up the unity of the Spirit's teaching, styled in verse 13, " the unity of the faith, and of the knowledge of the Son of God ". This unity is constituted of seven particular units, namely, " One Body ", or aggregate communion of Christian disciples ; " One Spirit ", " One Hope of the Calling ; one Lord, one Faith, one Baptism, and one God ". Thus the unity is defined by the Apostle ; and thus we prove that " the unity of the faith and knowledge of the Son of God "—or, in other words, " The truth as it is in Jesus "—recognizes only one Hope. Another argument in proof of this is derivable from the use of the definite article *the*. It is not a hope, but the Hope of the Gospel.

Thus, " God, willing more abundantly to shew unto the heirs of the promise the immutability of his purpose, confirmed the promise by an oath : that we might have strong consolation, who have fled for refuge to lay hold upon the hope set before us ; which hope we have as an anchor of the life, both sure and steadfast, and which hope enters (or penetrates) into that (dispensation of things) within the vail (which conceals them from our sight) " (Heb. 6 : 17-19).

The importance, as well as unity, of this hope may be inferred from the position it occupies in " the armour of God ". " Take ", says the Apostle, " the helmet of salvation " ; and that we may know what the helmet is, he says, " let us who are of the day be sober, having for a helmet the hope of salvation " (1 Thess. 5 : 8)—not the hope of being saved from hell, but having an assured expectation of the things God has promised to the Fathers of Israel.

Much more proof of this point might be adduced, but it is not necessary. We shall proceed now to show,

2.—*That it was the hope contained in " the Word of God " which made that word Glad Tidings, or Gospel, to the world.*

This is illustrated and proved by the following consideration. When the Word was preached by the Apostles, and their collaborators, they revealed secrets to the people which made them rejoice with inexpressible joy. Does the reader think that this effect would have been produced by persuading them that they should obtain forgiveness of sins in answer to prayer, or by a disquisition on the immortality of the soul, which they had professed to believe for many previous ages ? Let the reader examine himself, and say if such preaching, nay, if even baptism for remission of sins—ever kindled within him joy inexpressible. But in the minds of the ancients, such a joy was produced by what they heard. Does not this prove that the pious of this age have not heard, and therefore have not believed, the same things as gospel, as those announced by the Apostles ? If they had, their feeling and morality would be identical.

How was it with the Christian disciples of Pentecost ? " They ate their meat with gladness and singleness of heart " (Acts 2 : 46). How was it with " the multitude of them that believed " in Jerusalem ? " They were of one heart, and of one soul : neither said any of them that aught of the things which he possessed was his own " (Acts 4 : 32) ; there was no covetousness among them ; this was a Christian union which no " Protestant Union " will ever attain to—a union which the world will never witness again till Messiah comes ; for Protestantism contains not within it the self-destroying, self-crucifying, principles of the Word.

How was it with the Samaritans ? " There was great joy in that city " (Acts 8 : 8). How was it with the officer of the Ethiopian Queen ? " He went on his way rejoicing " (verse 39). How was it with Paul himself ? " I take pleasure in infirmities, in reproaches, in necessities, in persecutions, in distresses for Christ's sake " (2 Cor. 7 : 10) ; " I count all things loss for the excellency of the knowledge of Christ Jesus ; for whom I have suffered the loss of all things, and do count them dross, that I may win Christ " (Phil. 3 : 8). Here was " knowledge " for which he was willing and did sacrifice every thing to realize. How was it with the Antiochians ? " They were filled with joy " (Acts 13 : 52). How was it with the Philippian Jailor and family ? " He rejoiced, believing in God with all his house " (Acts 16 : 34). How was it with the Ephesians ? " Many of them which practised curious arts brought their books together, and burned them before all ; and they counted the price of them, and found it 50,000 pieces of silver. So mightily grew the Word of God and prevailed " (Acts 19 : 19). Do such sacrifices result now from the belief of preaching ? How was it with the Galatians ? They received Paul " as an angel of God, as Christ Jesus himself ". They spake of the blessedness, and if it had been possible, would have plucked out their eyes and given them to him (Gal. 4 : 15). And how, lastly, was it with the Christian disciples throughout Asia Minor and the adjacent countries where they believed the preaching of the Word ? " They rejoiced with joy unspeakable and full of glory " (1 Pet. 1 : 8).

Now, it is not in human nature to rejoice with such ecstasy in believing the abstract doctrine of forgiveness of sins through prayer, or baptism ; or of going somewhere beyond the skies, to " that undiscovered bourne whence no traveller has returned ", when they are called upon to be dissevered from property and friends, by the shaft of " the King of Terrors " as they style him. The most vivid conception of the Elysian Heaven has never excited in professors " a joy unspeakable " ; on the contrary, their extreme anxiety to continue in the present state of existence evinces its impotency and their own incredulity of its desirableness.

The fruit of this doctrine, universally believed in our own day, proves that it is devoid of a refining influence upon society ; it fails to humanize or moralize ; and leaves the believer of it still subject to bondage through fear of death.

But the fruit of the word preached by Paul was altogether different. It caused them who believed it to " deny themselves of all ungodliness and worldly lust, and to live soberly, righteously, and godly in the present age ". It taught them to " look for that blessed hope, even the glorious appearing of the great God, even of our Saviour Jesus Christ " (Titus 2 : 13). By believing it, this potent word formed Christ in the hearts of men—The Hope of Glory ; and that they might win him, they hazarded with joy, life, liberty, everything, for in him is the fullness of God.

He informs Titus, that " the Grace of God ", or his Word, " that bringeth salvation had appeared to all men ", that is, to Jews and Gentiles ; " teaching them", etc. ; and among the things it teaches is the " Blessed Hope ", according to his own saying. This was the " blessedness " of which the Galatians spake with such intense interest ; it was the great feature of the Word of the Truth as it is in Jesus, which made its announcement such exciting and joyful news. Much more might be said under this head ; but this is enough for the present ; we pass on therefore, to the next thing to be shown.

3.—*What this blessed Hope is, that makes the word Glad Tidings or Gospel.*

Paul, in the third chapter of Galatians and the eighth verse says, " the scripture, foreseeing that God would justify the nations through faith, preached before the gospel to Abraham ". This is an important declaration. On Paul's authority then, we are informed that the Gospel was preached about 1954 years before the day of Pentecost. Was the Gospel thus preached, remission of sins by the Holy Spirit in answer to prayer ? Or, was it repentance and remission of sins in the name of Jesus Christ ? Or, was it the truth, that Jesus is the Christ the Son of the living God ? Reader, mark well what we say ; it was none of these ; but, in the words of the Apostle himself, it was this, namely, " IN THEE (ABRAHAM) SHALL ALL NATIONS BE BLESSED ". This was an announcement of " blessedness "—a blessedness on nations, on all nations placed constitutionally as nations " *in* " Abraham, the details of which, when the Galatians heard Paul unfold them, caused them so much joy that if it had been possible they would have plucked out their eyes, and given them to him. This is that gospel to which he refers when he says, " I was separated to the Gospel of God, which he had promised afore by his prophets in the Holy Scriptures " (Rom 1 : 2).

Concerning this blessedness which he styles " The blessing of Abraham " (Gal. 3 : 14)—quoting from the prophet Isaiah, he says, " eye hath not seen, nor ear heard, neither have entered into the heart of man the things which God hath prepared for them that love him " (1 Cor. 2 : 9). Hence this emphatic declaration excludes from God's gospel all the foolishness of men, current as wisdom before the Apostolic preaching, and which the clergy now preach for truth : the hereditary immortality of the soul, and translation to heaven at death are no part of this blessedness ; for these had for ages previous entered into the hearts of the heathen philosophers of Greece and Rome.

Now, the things of this unseen and unheard of blessedness make up " the hidden wisdom of God ". It was announced in general terms to Abraham ; but its details were hidden and remained secret for ages. Hence, it is styled, " the Wisdom of God in a Mystery ", which none of the princes of Paul's age knew (1 Cor. 2 : 7, 8). He also says in another place, " the Mystery has been kept secret since the time of the ages "— that is, from the time the Gospel was preached to Abraham (Rom. 16 : 25). Again, he says " the Mystery of Christ in other ages was not made known to the sons of men " ; and again, " the Mystery hath been hid in God from the beginning of the ages " (Eph. 3 : 5, 9). Also repeated thus, " The Word of God—the Mystery—hath been hid from the beginning of the ages and generations " (Col. 1 : 26). These quotations are sufficient to prove that all the speculation in the world concerning the destiny predetermined of God for mankind, were the mere blunders of heathen men.

" In thee, Abraham, shall all the nations be blessed." Was not this an announcement of something future—" shall be blessed " ? Was it not, then, presented to Abraham as a matter of hope ? If then, also, this were the gospel preached to the Father of the Faithful, was it not the hope of the Gospel ? Certainly it was. Well, does not Paul tell you, that the details of this hope were kept secret ? Because they were so, therefore

he styles them " the Mystery of the Gospel " in Eph. 6 : 19.
Let it then be noted that the one Hope of the calling is the
Gospel—*the very ancient Gospel itself*—preached to Abraham
and secreted as to certain details from human knowledge for
ages. Let us ascertain now when its mystery was made known.

Paul says he was " an Apostle separated for the Gospel of
God " (Rom. 1 : 1). He explains this by saying, " Be not
moved away from the hope of the gospel, whereof I, Paul,
am made minister ; fully to preach the Word of God, even
the mystery which hath been hid ; but now is made manifest
to his saints : to whom God would make known what is the
riches of the glory of this mystery among the Gentiles ; which
is Christ in you (dwelling in your hearts by the belief of these
things) the Hope of Glory " (Col. 1 : 23-27). This is the definition of Paul's apostleship to the Gentiles—to make known
to them God's intention concerning them.

Again ; " The mystery is NOW (1,800 years ago) made
manifest, and by the scriptures of the prophets, according to
the commandment of the everlasting God, is made known
to all nations for the obedience of faith " (Rom. 16 : 26).
From this we learn also that all the nations of the old Roman
civilization once knew what this long-hidden, but then-
revealed mystery was ; but since that order of things faded
away before the Dark Ages, it has been entirely blotted out
from their remembrance, and now demands to be resuscitated
from the book of God for the obedience of faith among those
who are watching for the Lord's return.

Concerning the unseen and unheard-of Blessed Things,
Paul saith, " but God hath revealed them unto us by his
Spirit " (1 Cor. 2 : 10) ; and they are placed on record in the
New Testament.

" By revelation Jesus Christ hath made known unto me,
Paul, the Mystery ; which in other ages was not made known
as it is now revealed unto his holy apostles and prophets by
the Spirit : unto me is this grace given, that I should preach
among the Gentiles the unsearchable riches of Christ ; and
to make all see what is the fellowship of the mystery, which
from the beginning of the ages hath been hid in God who
created all things (*dia*) on account of Jesus Christ : to the
intent that now unto the principalities and powers in the
heavenly places (kings, governors, councils, etc.) might be
made known through the church the manifold wisdom of
God, according to the eternal purpose which he purposed in

Christ Jesus our Lord " (Eph. 3 : 1-11). Thus the eternal purpose of God was made known to the ancient nations by Paul's preaching of " the Word of Truth, the Gospel of their salvation " ; we would now like to know what was this eternal purpose, which, when announced by the apostles, produced such joyousness in the hearts of the people ?

Hear what the scripture saith : " God has made known the mystery, or secret, of his will which he hath purposed in himself ". Well, what is it He hath willed, or predetermined ? Let us read it wide awake ; it is this that He hath resolved upon, namely, " That in the dispensation of the completion of the times appointed, he might gather together in one (imperial monarchy) all things under Christ, both the things which are in the heavens (kingly governments, etc.) and which are on the earth (people, nations and languages) under him, in whom we have obtained an inheritance " (Eph. 1 : 10).

But perhaps the correctness of the parentheses interjected may be disputed. We will, therefore, quote a declaration of God's eternal purpose (not the Mystery, but the Will) from one of the prophets of Israel. Here it is :—" In the days of these kings (represented by the ten toes of Nebuchadnezzar's image, and now existing) shall the God of heaven set up a kingdom which shall never be destroyed ; and the kingdom shall not be left to other people, but it shall break in pieces and consume all these kingdoms, and it shall stand for ever " (Dan. 2 : 44). "And I saw in the night visions, and behold there was given to the Son of Man (Jesus Christ) empire, glory, and a kingdom, that all people, nations and languages should serve him ; his empire is an everlasting dominion, which shall not pass away, and his kingdom one which shall not be destroyed " (Dan. 7 : 14). From this, then, it appears, that God's intention is to establish an Imperial Monarchy upon the ruins of all kingdoms and republics extant ; and to put the sceptre of absolute and universal dominion into the hand of the Son of Man. This will be an indestructible kingdom ; and those who are appointed to its honours, dignities, offices, in the beginning of it, will retain them as long as it lasts ; and as it is everlasting, it is very obvious that flesh and blood, or mortal men, cannot inherit it.

Paul saith to Timothy, " Preach the Word " ; that is, preach the Hope of the Gospel, or Kingdom of God. Invite the people to take office under God's King ; tell them what God hath said in the prophets, how that " the saints shall take away the dominion of their oppressors to consume and destroy it to the end. And the kingdom and dominion, and the greatness of the kingdom under the whole heaven, shall be given to the people of the Saints of the Most High, whose kingdom is an everlasting kingdom, and all rulers shall serve and obey him " (Dan. 7 : 27). Tell them, " When the Lord shall build up Zion, he shall appear in his glory (Psa. 102 : 16) ; and that then, " The high praises of God shall be in their mouth, and a two-edged sword in their hand ; to execute vengeance upon the heathen, and punishments upon the people ; to bind their kings with chains and their nobles with fetters of iron ; to execute upon them the judgment written ; this honour have all his saints " (Psa. 149 : 6). Tell them, "All things are theirs —-the world, life, death, things present and to come, all are theirs ; and they are Christ's, and Christ is God's " (1 Cor. 3 : 21). Tell them these things, O Timothy ; reprove, rebuke, exhort, and let no man despise thee.

Now " the People of the Saints " are those who believe the Hope of Israel, and obey the King of Israel. They are styled, " kings and priests unto God " in the New Testament, because they are chosen on the principle of an obedient faith to act as kings and priests in the Messiah's Kingdom of the Coming Age. " Do ye not know ", saith Paul, " that the saints shall judge the world ? " (1 Cor. 6 : 2)—shall reign as kings and officiate as priests in the new imperial monarchy to be founded—in the everlasting kingdom of Jesus Christ ?

But this kingdom is yet future ; and generation after generation of God's royal priesthood hath succumbed to the power of the enemy : what then must needs occur before the saints can possess the kingdom ? They must rise from among the dead ; or if any such be living when the kingdom is set up, they must be changed from flesh and blood, which is corruptible, and therefore mortal, into flesh and spirit, a combination which is incorruptible and deathless ; for, as we have said, the offices of the kingdom and empire do not change hands : the gifts and calling of God being without repentance ; hence, the glory, honour, and dignities of the Empire require that they who obtain appointments to them be immortal. Thus, then, " glory, honour, incorruptibility, life ", and blessedness in all its manifestations, are announced as the attributes of the kingdom of God ; hence, to preach the kingdom of God is to proclaim all these things through it as an incorruptible institution. The Resurrection of the Just is not the hope of the Gospel ; it is only an item thereof ; yet it is vastly important ; for it is the path of life—the strait gate of life ; and holds a similar relation to the Future Age that our birth of the flesh does to the present ; the resurrection gives us introduction to the kingdom of God.

(iii) *THE CHARACTER OF THE KINGDOM*

We have ascertained what the purpose of God towards our world is for 1,000 years to come. We find both the prophets and apostles testifying the same thing. Let us, then, discourse in brief about this glorious Kingdom.

First, then, a kingdom whose offices are never vacated requires the administration of immortals. Hence, the King must be immortal. Now, as he is to be a Son of Man, from whom is he to descend ? Hear the scripture : " How goodly are thy tents, O Jacob ; and thy tabernacles, O Israel ! Their king shall be higher than Agag ; and his kingdom shall be exalted. I shall see him, but not now ; I shall behold him, but not nigh : there shall come a Star out of Jacob, and a sceptre shall rise out of Israel, and shall smite through the princes of Moab, and destroy all the children of Sheth. Out of Jacob shall come he that shall have dominion " (Num. 24 : 5-7, 17, 19). This King, then, is to arise out of the Jewish nation ; but whose Son is he ?

" When thy days be fulfilled, and thou shalt sleep with thy fathers, O David, I will set up thy seed after thee, and I will establish his kingdom. He shall build a temple for my name, and I will stablish the throne of his kingdom forever. I will be his Father and he shall be my Son " (2 Sam. 7 : 12-14). Thus speaks Jehovah to the second King of Israel. We learn from this that the throne of the Kingdom of Israel is an everlasting throne ; that the King destined to fill it must be both Son of David and Son of God.

Behold, then, the Covenants of the Promise made to Abraham and to David. They belong to Israel and to the adopted citizens of their State. " To Israel pertain the adoption, and the glory, and the covenants, and the giving of the law, and the service, and the promises " (Rom. 9 : 4). Great and glorious is the destiny of Israel ; but infinitely more so that of those who shall inherit the **Kingdom** and Empire of Israel's King.

The hope of this Kingdom in all its relations was the hope of Israel. In one of the national songs they say, " The Lord Most High is terrible ; he is a great King over all the earth. He shall subdue the people under us, and the nations under our feet " (Psa. 47 : 2, 3). They refer also to the same thing in another, saying, "All the ends of the world shall remember and turn unto the Lord ; and all the kindreds of the nations shall worship before thee. For the kingdom is the Lord's ; and he the governor among the nations " (Psa. 22 : 27, 28). " In his days shall the righteous flourish, and there shall be abundance of peace so long as the moon endureth. He shall have dominion also from the sea and from the River (Euphrates) to the end of the Land. They that dwell in the wilderness (the Arabians) shall bow before him ; and his enemies shall lick the dust. The kings of Tarshish (the present rulers of the Anglo-Indian Empire) and the kings of the Isles (of all Gentile countries) shall bring presents : the kings of Sheba and Seba shall offer gifts. Yea, all kings shall fall down before him. All nations shall serve him " (Psa. 72 : 7-11). Shall serve him ; David's Son and Israel's King. This, we repeat, was, and still is, the Hope of Israel ; and the revelations of God concerning it are the " good tidings of great joy ", or gospel, " which shall be to all people " (Luke 2 : 10).

But who, among all the tribes and armies of Jacob, is the son of David, Son of God, and King of Israel ? We answer upon the testimony of the apostles that Jesus of Nazareth is he. Hence, then, the Glad Tidings of the glorious Kingdom must be preached in his name, for he is the hereditary and rightful sovereign thereof.

The hope of Israel, then, is the hope of the Gospel which was preached by the apostles in the Word of the Truth. In this, this Kingdom of God is announced ; a Kingdom to be established in the Holy Land under the sovereignty of Jesus Christ, when the times appointed for the continuance of existing human governments shall have run out. This Kingdom, as we have seen, is to absorb all other dominions ; and to exist as a New Dispensation for a thousand years.

But an empire of this magnitude will require officers to administer its affairs ; one King, however powerful and absolute, could not in the nature of things, judge, or rule, the world of nations alone. What was necessary to be done in this emergency? Send a proclamation among the Jews and Gentiles, and invite them without respect of persons to accept glory, honour, and dignity as well as office, in the new government. This is precisely what God did by Jesus Christ and his Apostles. Jesus says, " I must preach the kingdom of God to the cities, for therefore am I sent " (Luke 4 : 43). "And it came to pass that he went throughout every city and village, preaching and showing the glad tidings of the kingdom of God " (Luke 8 : 1). And he sent his twelve disciples to preach the Kingdom of God, and they went through the towns preaching the Gospel (Luke 9 : 2, 6). Hence, to preach the Gospel is to preach the good news concerning the Kingdom of God. When Jesus, therefore, said to his apostles, " Go ye into all the world, and preach the Gospel to every creature ", it was equivalent to saying, " Go, and preach the Good News concerning the Kingdom which the God of Heaven intends to set up among the nations, as saith the prophet Daniel ; he that believes what you preach and is baptized shall be saved " ; that is, he shall inherit the kingdom, if he be not moved away from the hope of it. They obeyed the mandate. It was preached on the Day of Pentecost ; also in the Temple Porch ; and Philip preached it in Samaria ; for, " when the Samaritans believed Philip, preaching the things concerning the kingdom of God, and the name of the Lord Jesus, they were baptized, men and women " (Acts 8 : 12). Paul preached it in Thessalonica, in Athens, in Ephesus, in Rome, and everywhere he went ; in private houses, in jails, in market places, in fora, in palaces, and wherever else the people would listen to him. " I know ", says he, to the Ephesian Christians, " that ye all, among whom I have gone preaching the kingdom of God, shall see my face no more " (Acts 20 : 25) ; while there, " He went into the synagogue, and spake boldly for the space of three months, disputing and persuading concerning the kingdom of God " (Acts 19 : 8 and 28 : 31).

Thus we have condensed from the Word of Truth an answer to the question, " What is the hope of the Gospel by which we are saved, if we believe it ? " This subject is now fairly broached, but infinitely far from being exhausted. We have placed before the reader the Two Hopes : the Hope of the World lying under the Wicked One, and the Hope of Israel, irradiated by the light of the glorious gospel of the Blessed One. This is that to which Paul refers, saying, " I stand and am judged for the hope of the promise made of God unto our fathers (Abraham, Isaac and Jacob) : unto which promise our twelve tribes, instantly serving God night and day, hope to come. For which hope's sake, King Agrippa, I am accused of the Jews. Why should it be thought a thing incredible with you, that God should raise the dead ? " (Acts 26 : 6-8). " For the hope of Israel am I bound with this chain " (Acts 28 : 20). Was Paul judged and chained for the hope of his soul's soaring, at the instant of death, through the skies on an angel's wing to the right hand of the Majesty in the Heavens ? If so, when and where did God promise this to the Fathers ? He never promised any such thing ; and let him who affirms the contrary prove it.

In conclusion we have shown,

1.—That there is but " One true Hope which is a seventh item of the unity of the Faith and of the Knowledge of the Son of God " and that as the Spirit revealed them, they constitute " the unity of the Spirit " ;

2.—That this one Hope is styled " the hope of the calling ", " the vocation ", and " the heavenly calling ", because the Apostolic proclamation was authorized by heaven and calls to a future Kingdom which the God of heaven will set up ;

3.—That it is this Hope which made the apostles' preaching glad tidings of great joy to all people ;

4.—That the pious and ungodly of these times are equally in the dark respecting it ;

5.—That the hope of Christendom is powerless for the regeneration of the world ;

6.—That the ancient Gospel cannot be preached without the proclamation of the Blessed Hope ;

7.—We affirm that the man who does not believe in the literal advent of Jesus in power and great glory to set up the kingdom cannot preach the ancient Gospel that Paul announced ;

8.—That the nations of the Roman civilization understood this Hope, but did not nationally accept the call ; that they entirely lost the knowledge of it through the apostasy of the Church, and the overshadowing of the Dark Ages ;

9.—That the indestructible kingdom is the basis of the one Hope, the attributes of which constitute the " recompense of the reward " ;

10.—That all existing empires, kingdoms and republics in their political and ecclesiastical arrangements will be soon abolished, their rulers ejected from place and power, and the government of the world transferred to Messiah and his associates ;

11.—That to obtain office in the new imperial kingdom men must believe the glad tidings concerning it ; believe the things relating to Jesus Christ ; and thus believing, become the subjects of repentance and remission of sins in his name, by being immersed into the name of the Father, Son, and Holy Spirit ; thenceforth, he must walk worthy of his high destiny in the light of Holy Writ ;

12.—That for such persons to obtain possession of the kingdom, if dead, they must rise from the dead ; and if living they must be changed into immortal men, by the power of God ;

13.—That Jesus Christ is the Son of God, and that there is remission of sins in his name by immersion to him who believes this truth, is not the ancient Gospel ; it is not Paul's gospel ; a man may believe these things, but fail of remission, because his faith includes not the Blessed Hope ;

14.—We should continually pray, " Thy kingdom come, and thy will be done on earth as it is in heaven ", until this prayer be accomplished.

13

AARON AND CHRIST

JEHOVAH (that is, I shall be, *Ehyeh*, Exod. 3 : 15) said to Moses, " See that thou make what thou wast caused to see, after their pattern shewed thee in the mount " (Exod. 25 : 40) ; which things, Paul says, are only " the image and shadow of heavenly things ", as God said to Moses : and elsewhere he says that " the Jews have the model of the knowledge and of the truth in the law ". From which, and other passages that can be adduced, it is evident that the following proposition is true, namely, That *the Mosaic System of Righteousness is symbolical of the Righteousness of God in Jesus Christ.*

Definition.—By " Mosaic System of Righteousness " is meant, *All that was necessary to sanctify to the purifying of the flesh,* but which could not free the conscience from sin. To impart this carnal purification to the worshipper a High Priest and his household, distinct from the other classes of the Jewish nation, legally inaugurated and sanctified, were necessary ; also a tabernacle, sacrifices, washings, etc.

Definition.—By the " *Righteousness of God* " is meant, *A justification from all past sins devised and enjoined by God*—a purification of the heart, or conscience, without the necessity of obeying the law of Moses (which since the destruction of Jerusalem cannot be kept) but attested by that law and the prophets—a justification through Jesus Christ's faith (*dia pisteōs Iēsou Christou*) : that is, through belief of what he and his apostles preached concerning the Kingdom of God and his Name (Acts 8 : 12) ; in other words, through belief of the Gospel to all that shall put on Christ (Gal. 3 : 27). The " Righteousness of God " is the " Gospel of the Kingdom ", sometimes called " the gospel of Christ ", and often simply " the gospel ", which Paul says, " is the power of God for salvation of every one that believeth, to the Jew first, and then to the Greek ", or Gentile. Nothing can save Jew or Gentile but " the power of God ". The power for that special purpose is the gospel only ; so that *saving power* and *the gospel* are but different phrases for the same thing.

Look into these sayings narrowly—" Jesus became the author of eternal salvation to all them that obey him " (Heb. 5 : 9) ; " If ye love me, keep my commandments " ; " If a

THE FAITH IN THE LAST DAYS

man love me, he will keep my words " ; " Ye are my friends if ye do whatsoever I command you " ; " He that rejecteth me, and keepeth not my words . . . the word that I have spoken, the same shall judge him in the last day " ; " Love is the fulfilling of the law ". Hence, *love* and *obedience* in scripture language are but two words for the same idea, or thing ; so that God in Jesus Christ admits of no love, or professions of devotion and attachment, that are unaccompanied with a child-like obedience to " whatsoever " He commands. Where obedience is not, there love does not exist ; and where there is no scriptural love there is no obedience in word or deed ; and where these are absent the spirit of love, which is " the spirit of Christ ", is wanting. " Love suffers long, and is kind ; it envieth not ; it boasts not itself (not full of wordy professions) : is not puffed up ; doth not behave itself unseemly ; seeketh not its own ; is not easily provoked ; thinketh no evil ; rejoiceth not in iniquity, but rejoiceth in the truth ; beareth all things, believeth all things, hopeth all things, endureth all things."

To persons in whom such a disposition has been created, the precepts of Jesus are, *He who believeth the Gospel of the kingdom, and is baptized, shall be saved ; and he that believeth it not shall be condemned.* Here the gospel is that proposed for faith ; and baptism, the thing prescribed for obedience, that the believer may show or prove whether that faith hath worked in him a true and genuine love to its author. Baptism is only for such believers ; for baptism is " the obedience of faith " ; so that where belief of " the truth " does not exist, there can be no true obedience.

When Jesus came to John he demanded to be buried in water that he might come out of it an immersed man. With a view to this he said, " Thus (in this way) it is proper for us to fulfil all righteousness " ; and the apostle adds, " When he was baptized, he went up straightway from the water " ; clearly evincing that he must first have gone down into it. And now, mark this well : *After he had done this*, God acknowledged him as His Son, and declared himself well pleased with him (Matt. 3 : 13-17). Jesus had been God's most excellent Son for thirty years, but He withheld His acknowledgment of him till he commenced a course of obedience in being baptized.

Jesus was a Jew under the law of Moses. When therefore he spoke of the " all righteousness " to be " fulfilled ", he spoke of the necessity of *doing what was signified* by the propheto-symbolic institutions of the Mosaic Law.

Jesus, being the Anointed Seed long promised of God, was therefore the High Priest who was to arise after the similitude, likeness, or order of Melchizedec, and to sit upon his throne as a priest upon his throne, and to bear the glory (Zech. 6). This being so, he would have at some future time to occupy the place formerly held by Aaron ; and as the Aaronic inauguration was representative of the Melchizedec, Jesus had to be consecrated after the same example or type, that in so doing he might antitypically fulfil the representation of the law.

Aaron was forbidden to enter into the Most Holy Place of the Tabernacle without being adorned with garments of holiness, and therefore styled, " Holy Garments ". Nor was he permitted to enter even when habited with these, *unless he had been previously baptized,* upon pain of death. The law said, " He shall wash his flesh in water, and so put them on ". He was not permitted to officiate as high priest in his ordinary attire. He must " put off " this, and " put on " the holy linen robe ; and had he put this on without bathing his flesh in water, and proceeded to officiate, this unbaptized High Priest of Israel would have been struck with death. When legally invested and arrayed the Aaronic High Priests were " Holiness to Jehovah ", and the representatives of the Holy and Just One in his character and priestly office ; though oftentimes, as in the case of Caiaphas, by practice unjust and wicked men. The symbolism relative to the high priest was the " righteousness " to be fulfilled by Jesus before he could enter upon his functions by " the power of an endless life " as High Priest, first over the Household of God, and afterwards over the Twelve Tribes of Israel.

John the baptizer, a greater prophet than Moses (Luke 7 : 28), but not so great as Jesus, preached and administered " the baptism of repentance for the remission of sins ". Jesus came to him to be baptized of this baptism ; for as Moses baptized Aaron and his sons, so the greatest of all the prophets was appointed to baptize Jesus and his brethren. But some may object that Jesus had no sins to be remitted, and had no need of repentance, and was therefore not a fit subject for such a baptism. It is admitted without reserve that he had no sins of his own, having never transgressed the law : nevertheless, as the Sin-Bearer of the Abrahamic Covenant through whom it was confirmed (Rom. 16 : 8), Jehovah made the iniquity of all " the children of that covenant " to meet upon him, that by his bruise they might be healed (Isa. 53 : 5, 6). He was not the Sin-Bearer of every son of Adam that ever lived ; but of the true believers from Abel to the Day of Pentecost, and of the obedient believers of the truth constituting his Household, separated by " the obedience of faith ", from Pentecost in the year of the crucifixion to his future appearing in Jerusalem ; and of the living Twelve Tribes when their transgressions shall be blotted out as a thick cloud at their ingrafting into their own Olive Tree ; and of that family of nations of which Abraham is the constituted father when they are made righteous ; so that the sins of the whole of that world, which shall dwell upon the earth in the postmillennial eternal ages, and which will all of it have been separated from Adam's race by " the obedience of faith "—will have met upon him, and been borne away into everlasting oblivion.

But to return. Jesus, with the sin of the world thus defined rankling in his flesh, where it was to be condemned to death when suspended on the cross (Rom. 8 : 3), came to John as the " Ram of Consecration ", that his inwards and his body might be washed according to the law (Exod. 29 : 17, 22). But these representations of the law and the prophets could not have found their antitype in Jesus, if in the days of his flesh he had possessed a holier or purer nature than those for whom he was bruised in the heel. His character was spotless ; but as being the Seed of the Woman, of whom no clean flesh can be born (Job 25 : 4), and Seed of Abraham, which is not immaculate, be it Virgin or Nazarite, his nature was flesh and blood (Heb. 2 : 14), which Paul styles " sinful flesh ", or flesh full of sin, a physical quality or principle which makes the flesh mortal ; and called " sin ", because this property of flesh became its law as the consequence of transgression. " God made Jesus sin for us who knew no sin ; that we might be made the righteousness of God in him " (2 Cor. 5 : 21).

In this view of the matter, the Sin-Bearer of the world indicated was a fit and proper subject of John's baptism of repentance for remission of sins. The holy and undefiled disposition of Mary's Son was *granted to him for repentance* in fulfilling the symbolical righteousness of the law when he descended into the Jordan to enter into the antitypical robe of righteousness with which he must of necessity be invested before he could enter into the Most Holy as High Priest after the order of Melchizedec. In being baptized he commenced the development of a character distinguished by perfect faith and obedience. This character was his holy raiment, and was without spot, or wrinkle, or any such thing. This was the " fine linen, clean and white " with which he arrayed himself ; or " the righteousness of the (king of) saints " (Rev. 19 : 8). It was the antitype in part of Aaron's holy garments ; and he had to put it on in the same way that Aaron did, " by washing his flesh in water, and so putting it on ". He was baptized of John into a holiness of his own, which began with obedience in the Jordan, and ended with obedience in death on the cross. " He was obedient unto death, even the death of the cross ; wherefore God hath highly exalted him, and given him a name which is above every name : that every tongue should confess that he is Lord to the glory of God the Father." Had Jesus yielded to John (supposing the thing to have been possible), he would have stood before his nation as the High Priest of Israel, claiming to officiate in the Most Holy Place without baptism, a spectacle it had never seen before, nor ever will while the world stands.

But the symbolic righteousness of the Mosaic law not only required the High Priest to put on the holy vestments by having his body baptized, but it also commanded his Household to be baptized into theirs also. The law reads thus : " This is the thing Jehovah commanded to be done : and Moses brought Aaron and his sons and washed them with water. And he put upon Aaron the coat . . . and he put coats upon his sons, and girded them with girdles, and put turbans upon them, as Jehovah commanded " (Lev. 8 : 5, 6, 13 ; 16 : 4). Here, as I have said, Moses performed the part of John the baptizer to Aaron and his sons, who were to be rulers and priests in Israel. Aaron and his family were their nation's priestly household ; and it was the office of the High, or Chief, Priest to make atonement, or reconciliation, first for himself, *then for his household*, and lastly, for all the congregation of Israel ; but admission into the Holy and Most Holy places was only permitted to the baptized ; they must bathe their flesh in water and so put on the holy garments. Hence, all Israel's priests were immersed persons ; and so also all that shall be their priests and kings in the Age to Come, and have power over the Gentiles, must be immersed likewise.

Jesus, the Melchizedec High Priest of Israel, has a Household as well as Aaron had. A proof of this is found in the words of Paul. In writing to certain Hebrews who had believed the gospel of the kingdom and name of Jesus, and had obeyed it in having their "bodies washed with pure water", he says, "Christ is a Son over his own house, whose house are we, if we hold fast the confidence and the rejoicing of the hope (Acts 28 : 20 ; 26 : 6, 7) firm unto the end" (Heb. 3 : 6, 14). Now, Jesus speaking for himself and others said, "*Thus* it becomes *us* to fulfil all righteousness". It is therefore necessary for all "his house" to do as he did, but with this modification of the significancy of the deed, namely,—he was baptized as the initiative of his own holiness, sacrificial and priestly ; they must be baptized into his *and* into a development of their own conformable to his ; and with this induction for a beginning, thenceforth "continue patiently in well doing" that they may be holy as he was holy in the days of his flesh ; as it is written, "Be ye holy, because I am holy".

Jesus and his Household are the future kings and priests prepared of God to rule Israel and the Nations for Him. The law and the prophets which attest the righteousness of God require them all to put on that righteousness by bathing. Jesus commands the same thing, and says, "Till heaven and earth pass, one jot or one tittle shall in no wise pass from the law, till all be fulfilled". Therefore he said to his apostles, "Go and preach the Gospel to every creature" ; and "teach them who receive your proclamation to observe whatsoever I command you".

By virtue of this saying the apostles became the depositaries of his commands ; so that in the words of Jesus, "He that heareth them, heareth him ; and he that despiseth them, despiseth him ; and he that despiseth him, despiseth Him that sent him". Now, Peter, who was one of these plenipotentiaries of Christ, commanded Cornelius, "a devout man, and one that feared God with all his house ; and gave much alms to the people (Israel), and prayed to God daily",— Peter, I say, "*commanded*" this company of pious Gentiles, who believed the word Jesus began to preach in Galilee, "to be baptized in the name of the Lord". The apostolic style of address was, "Children of the stock of Abraham, and whosoever among you feareth God, to you is the word of this salvation sent". A man's supposed piety did not exempt him from the necessity of believing and obeying the gospel of the kingdom, or, as Paul styles it, "the word of this salvation". Peter went to

Caesarea to tell pious, god-fearing men, " words whereby they should be saved ".

But, however pious they may be who are ignorant of these saving words, they are alienated from the life of God through that ignorance (Eph. 4 : 18). Piety in general has so little to do with an understanding of the word of the kingdom and the obedience it enjoins, that it has passed into a proverb that " ignorance is the mother of devotion ". In a certain sense this is true. The most ignorant are for the most part the most pious, and the most intolerant of the truth and its obedience. This is Pharisaism, whether it flourish in the first, or in the nineteenth century ; and in reference to which Jesus has said, " Except your righteousness exceed that of the Scribes and Pharisees, ye shall in no case enter into the kingdom of the heavens ". Pharisaists " appear to men to be righteous " ; but men uninstructed in the gospel of the kingdom are incompetent to distinguish the counterfeit from the true. A man in this century will have no more ability to enter the kingdom of the heavens, if his righteousness exceed not that of contemporary churchmen of the straitest sect, than would those addressed by Jesus whose righteousness might be on a par with the pietists of his age.

Shall it be said that it was necessary for the Melchizedec High Priest, who was innocent of transgression, and who for thirty years had enjoyed the favour of God and man, to be immersed in a baptism of repentance for the remission of sins ; but that it is not necessary for the pious who would compose his household, who are sinners by nature and practice ? Nay, if it were indispensable for Jesus to be buried in water that he might begin a career of holiness to Jehovah in coming up out of it, it is definitely more so that all should tread in his steps of perfect faith and obedience who would be invested with " robes washed white in the blood of the Lamb ", having their loins girt around with the girdle of truth, and having on the breast-plate of righteousness ; and their feet shod with the preparation of the Gospel of peace ; and on their heads the helmet of salvation. An immersed High Priest requires an immersed household. There is one law for both, as there was one baptism for Jesus and his apostles ; on whom as upon all others of the household, the necessity is imperative to fulfil all righteousness foreshadowed in Aaron and his sons. There is no discharge from this necessity for Jew c Gentile ; " for *thus* it behoveth *us* to fulfil all righteousness ".

14

" THE GOOD CONFESSION "

"ALL things must be fulfilled ", said the Lord Jesus, " that are written in the Law of Moses, and in the Prophets, and in the Psalms, concerning me." When these words were spoken, the writings known among us as the New Testament had no existence. When, therefore, Jesus said, " Search the Scriptures, for they are they which testify of me ", he exhorts us to search Moses, the Prophets, and the Psalms ; which is indispensable, for he adds elsewhere, " If ye believe not Moses' writings, how can ye believe my words ? " It was impossible ; for the words of Jesus were his preaching; and he preached the "gospel of the Kingdom ", and himself as its King—" the Gospel of God, which ", says Paul, " he had promised by his prophets in the Holy Scriptures ". He preached what they predicted ; disbelieve this, and his preaching is denied.

The Law of Moses, the Prophets, and the Psalms, are the testimony *for Christ* ; while the written testimony of the inspired Apostles is the testimony *for Jesus*, that he is the Christ " of whom Moses in the Law, and the Prophets, did write ". This being proved, he came to be styled Jesus Christ, as though that were his family name. But neither Jehovah, Joseph, nor Mary, were named Christ. Jesus did not, therefore, inherit the name by descent ; nor did he acquire the title till he began to be about thirty years old. The word designates a person who had been, or was to be, anointed with oil, or spirit represented by oil. Aaron, Saul, David, Solomon, etc., were anointed with holy oil by Jehovah's command, and were therefore " The Lord's Anointed Ones ", or Christs. Moses and the Prophets foretold the appearing of a Son of David who should be Son of God and anointed with spirit without measure. For about 4,000 years after the formation of Adam, the world had been unvisited by the personage who thirty years afterwards was to be thus anointed. At that time, Jesus emerged from the Jordan, and the Spirit, descending in the form of a dove, rested upon him, and thus poured out upon him, filled him, and so anointed him. This was the fulfilment of the prophecy in Daniel about sealing the prophet, and anointing the Most Holy. It was the christening of Jesus by which " he was made Christ ", as he has since been " made Lord ".

When John the baptizer was performing his mission, Priests and Levites were sent to him from Jerusalem to inquire if he were the Christ or not. He replied that he was not ; but that he was his forerunner. Soon after this, Jesus was publicly anointed ; and forthwith claimed to be the person of whom Moses and the Prophets wrote. This was nothing less than laying claim to the kingdom of Israel and throne of David for ever ; so that henceforth it became a great national question with all Jews, seeing that John repudiated all pretention to the dignity, " Is Jesus of Nazareth the Christ—the Prophet like unto Moses, or do we look for another ? " There were great debates among the people upon this question. Some favoured the claims of Jesus, while others from various reasons of state policy rejected them altogether. After his crucifixion the question was revived and enlarged. It was not now simply, " Was Jesus the Anointed King of Israel ? " But, " Is he the anointed King of Israel raised from the dead to sit upon David's throne for ever ? " Yea, said the apostles, this is our proclamation concerning him : " Nay ! " said their opponents, " we deny it." Upon this point, then, God and the apostles joined issue with the rulers of the nation. Wherever they went they maintained that Jesus is the Christ, and God hath raised him from the dead ; and so triumphantly did they establish its truth to the conviction of multitudes that " Jesus " and " Christ " became inseparable ideas ; and came at length to lose the form of a proposition, and to be merged into a name for the Lord of Israel and the world.

If a Gentile of our day be asked, " Do you believe in Jesus Christ ? "—it represents to his mind, with a simple change of person, about the same thing as, " Do you believe in Pontius Pilate ? " He thinks you are asking him if he believes that there ever were such persons as Jesus Christ and Pontius Pilate ? His reply is, " Yes ; I do not recollect when I did not believe it ". But ask an intelligent Jew of the first, nineteenth, or intermediate centuries, holding on to Judaism, and he would say, " No ". But he would not mean by " no " that he does not believe there ever was such a person as Jesus ; but that he does not believe that Jesus was the Christ to be raised up as a horn in David's house for the restoration of the kingdom and Throne of Israel. This restoration, termed by Peter, " the restitution of all things spoken of by all the prophets since the world began ", is Israel's hope ; but to sectarian Gentiles known only as something that obtains in the undiscovered realms of trans-solar space. When therefore they profess to believe in Jesus Christ, they do not make " the good confession " witnessed by all who confessed Jesus in apostolic times. It was not his existence, or mere sonship, that they confessed ; but the same confession he himself made before Pontius Pilate. He did not confess that he believed in his own existence ; or that he was the Son of God ; or that he was the saviour of the world ; or that he was an atonement for sin through the shedding of his blood : but that he was born to be the King of Israel.

Paul reminds Timothy that he had " confessed the good confession before many witnesses ", which Christ Jesus had " witnessed before Pontius Pilate ". Now the reader can easily satisfy himself what this confession was by turning to John's account of the trial of Jesus at the bar of the Little Horn of the Goat. Pontius Pilate, the representative of this power in Jerusalem, asked the accused, "Art thou the King of the Jews ? " Had Jesus denied it, he would have denied that he was the Christ ; and by denying the truth have saved himself from death by crucifixion, with the loss of " the joy set before him " in the gracious promises made to David. But he denied not ; for " he came unto the world that he should bear witness unto the truth ". The truth he witnessed in answer to Pilate's question was, " Thou sayest it, I am a King. To this end was I born ". Pilate understood him to say by this that he was king of the Jews ; for he afterwards asked the question of the clamorous people, " Will ye that I release unto you the King of the Jews ? " The same thing is evident also from the superscription he placed on the head piece of the cross.

But it may be inquired, " If Jesus witnessed that he was born to be king of the Jews, how could Pilate, Caesar's friend and representative, say, ' I find in him no fault at all ' ? " The answer to this is found in the statement Jesus made of the *time* and *origin* of his kingdom. As to the time of it, he said " My kingdom is not of this world " ; as to the origin of it, " My kingdom is not now from hence ". In regard to the time, Christ's kingdom did not belong to the Mosaic Kosmos constituted by the law, and contemporary with the Little Horn Power in its undivided form as represented by Pilate. Christ's kingdom belongs to a Kosmos characterized by the co-existence of Ten Kingdoms of the Roman earth, as known to exist at present. Had it belonged to the Mosaic era Christ's servants would have given battle to the enemy in his defence.

This is true of his kingdom to whatever epoch it may belong. Its establishment is sure to be opposed by " the Powers that be " ; because the earth is not large enough to contain Christ and them. His servants will therefore fight against them, and " grind them to powder ".

Then as to the origin of the kingdom. It was not to originate at that time from Jewish enterprise. It is to be set up by the God of Heaven, and the saints ; that is, by Christ, and his associates, who shall take the kingdom and the dominion under the whole heaven. The armies of Israel, and a mixed multitude of Gentiles, will be a great sword in their hands to execute upon the goat nations and their governments " the judgment written ". Pilate had sagacity enough to perceive that the royalty of Jesus would not disturb the existing government ; and therefore, leaving the future to take care of itself, he pronounced the prisoner at Caesar's bar faultless before the law—" I find in him no fault at all ". How wicked then his condemnation to the cross !

Of what value then, is the popular belief in Jesus Christ while it denies the truth he witnessed before Pontius Pilate ? " Theology ", or pulpit tradition, and collegiate divinity speculation, denies that Jesus was born to rule over Israel as king upon the throne of his father David on Mount Zion. It laughs to scorn so outrageous a supposition ! Yet no truth is more plainly taught in the Bible. Popular belief in Jesus is a mere matter of course assent to current opinions concerning him, and totally insufficient as a foundation for union to his name. It does not confess the truth, being ignorant of it ; and is therefore of no efficacy for the renewal of the heart, and purification of the soul.

15

THE APOSTLES JUSTIFIED BY FAITH BEFORE "THE FAITH" CAME

THE point of difficulty in a correspondent's mind is this—if the "defective faith" of the apostles did not necessitate their re-immersion, why should the defective faith of our contemporaries? In other words, if the ignorance of the apostles in regard to the death, burial, and resurrection of Jesus, and the things founded upon these facts, did not invalidate their baptism by John, why should men's ignorance of the kingdom of God and His righteousness, make invalid the immersion to which they have been subjected? Is not their immersion the "one baptism" although their "faith" is defective of many things embraced in the "one faith" and the "one hope of the calling"?

This appears to be the difficulty for us to consider. Let us see, then, if it be real and insuperable or not.

In the first place we remark that the case of the apostles is exceptional. They were Israelites under the law, which was then in full force, the Abrahamic covenant not having been confirmed by the blood of its Mediator, the Christ. They were not required to believe in the mystery of its confirmation any more than the prophets were until the confirmation was established. They were under a dispensation of "justification by faith", not of "justification through the faith"; because when they were justified "the faith" had not come (Rom. 3 : 30 ; Gal. 3 : 24). Until the resurrection of Jesus they were "under the law" as Jesus was himself under the law, which was the schoolmaster of Israel who were "shut up to the faith which should afterwards be revealed". This was a position which could only be occupied by Israelites previous to the revelation of the faith. After that faith came, they were no longer "shut up". The apostles were shut up as Daniel, Isaiah, Jeremiah, and Ezekiel were "shut up to the faith". Their faith was the faith of these prophets, with the addition that they believed that Jesus was the Son of David and Son of the Deity whom He had anointed with the Holy Spirit ; in other words, "the Christ the King of Israel" whom He had covenanted to Abraham and David to inherit the land and to occupy the throne.

This was their faith. They believed the things covenanted to Abraham and David, and that Jesus was the Christ ; but they did not understand nor believe, though it was told them, that Jesus should be put to death and rise again ; they did not know, in any sense of the word *know*, that there should be remission of sins to the prophets and themselves through the death and resurrection of Jesus ; that is, through the crucificial outpouring of his soul as the blood of the Abrahamic and Davidian covenants, in the promises of which they believed. This is evident from Luke 18 : 31, 34, where it is written that Jesus said to the twelve : " Behold, we go up to Jerusalem, and all things that are written by the prophets concerning the Son of man shall be accomplished. For he shall be delivered unto the Gentiles, and shall be mocked, and spitefully entreated, and spitted on ; and they shall scourge him, and put him to death ; and the third day he shall rise again. *And they understood none of these things ; and this saying was hid from them, neither knew they the things that were spoken* ". John tells us that their ignorance of this class of truths continued until Jesus was glorified (John 12 : 16). Then they received the Holy Spirit, the spirit of truth, which guided them into all the truth : and showed them many things which in the beginning of the week of confirmation, Daniel's seventieth week, they were not able to bear (John 16 : 4, 12, 13, 25).

The apostles, then, were justified by faith in the gospel of the kingdom, and in Jesus as its anointed king. This is positive. They were not justified by faith in a Christ who they believed would suffer death and rise again. This is negative. That they were justified before the death of Jesus is evident from John 15 : 3, where it is written, " Ye are clean through the word which I have spoken unto you ". This word which Jesus spoke to them was " the word of the kingdom ", also styled " the Gospel of the Kingdom ", and " the kingdom of God " (Luke 18 : 17 ; 9 : 60, 2, 6 ; 8 : 1 ; 4 : 43, 18 ; Matt. 9 : 35 ; 4 : 23). Faith in it and Jesus was justifying. It cleansed, or purified them all from sins, except Judas. He was excepted, and pronounced " unclean " ; for he had not received " the word " into an honest and good heart.

The apostles believed all they were required to believe. They were not required to believe what was purposely hidden from them. They had honoured God in accepting His counsel preached to them through John the baptizer. They had been baptized with " the baptism of repentance for the remission of sins ", predicated on faith in the promises covenanted to Israel's fathers, and the approaching manifestation of the Christ. When he appeared they recognized him. He preached the same gospel as John, but amplified in detail. They believed it, and Jesus completed what John had begun in washing their feet, and without which they could have no part with him in the joy that was set before him (John 13 : 8). They had washed in John's baptism, therefore they needed not save to have their feet washed by Jesus, who thus " shod them with the preparation of the gospel " and made them clean every whit (verse 10 ; Eph. 6 : 15). Things being thus ordered, it only remained " to redeem them from the curse of the law " ; to redeem them by the same act that should purchase Isaiah, Jeremiah, Daniel, and all the saints under the law, from its curse.

This redemption was effected by Jesus submitting to be made a curse for them. This was accomplished, not by his wilful violation of the law, but by his enemies nailing him to a tree, or cross ; and so forcibly bringing the curse of the Mosaic law upon him, which says, " Cursed is every one that hangeth on a tree ". Thus the nature crucified was cursed, eternally cursed ; and therefore can never occupy the kingdom of God and the earth for ever. The life of the nature that transgressed in the person of the first Adam, became a covering for sin in the sinless person of the second Adam. When glorified the crucified nature was transformed into holy spirit-nature, styled by Paul, " spiritual body ", or the body consubstantial with the Father. This is the nature Jesus now possesses, and to which he attained at the price of " the crucifixion of the flesh " in every sense of the phrase.

When the redemption price was thus paid the law of Moses had no more dominion over the apostles. Its curses had become ineffectual in their case. Every whit clean by the arrangement indicated, they could stand up on Pentecost, and under inspiration of Holy Spirit, could reveal to the astonished Israelites the new doctrine of God's system of justification in the name of Jesus, attested by the law that cursed him, and by the prophets. Being redeemed from the curse of the law they had received the adoption of sons ; and because they were sons He had sent forth the spirit of His Son into their hearts ; and they could stand up and proclaim without sin " justification through the faith ", independently of the sacrifices prescribed by the ritual of Moses. " The faith " had come, and they were no longer under the Mosaic schoolmaster.

The reader, then, will bear in mind the distinction subsisting between " justification by faith ", and " justification through the faith ". The apostles and prophets were justified, or cleansed from all their sins " by faith " ; but since the day of Pentecost no Jew or Gentile can obtain pardon or purification by the same formula as they. To believe the word of the kingdom, and that Jesus is Son of God, will, since that notable day, save no man apart from the revealed mystery ; nor would the belief that the Christ should die and be raised again, apart from the recognition of Jesus as the Christ, and the word of the kingdom, save a believer. The area of " faith " was enlarged by the apostolic proclamation into " the faith ", so that after the day of Pentecost the doctrine of the apostles presented people with more things to be believed for justification than were believed by Abraham, Moses, David, Daniel, or themselves. Till the glorification of Jesus they were " fools, and slow of heart to believe all that the prophets had spoken " ; for they did not understand that the Christ ought to have suffered the things Jesus suffered, and afterwards to enter upon his glory (Luke 24 : 25). But when Jesus was about to be taken up and received into glory, he opened their understanding that they might understand the scriptures of Moses, the Prophets, and the Psalms, concerning him ; and said unto them, " Thus it is written, and thus it behoved the Christ to suffer, and to rise from the dead on the third day ; and that repentance, and remission of sins should be preached in his name among all the nations, beginning at Jerusalem " (verse 44).

Such was the case of the apostles in regard to their personal justification, which resolved itself into :

1.—Their baptism of John's immersion of repentance for remission of sins through the word Jesus should preach to them.

2.—Their belief of that word of the kingdom in an honest and good heart.

3.—Their confession that he was the anointed Son of the Deity and King of Israel ; and,

4.—Their feet being washed by the personal ministry of the King himself.

Here was a work of the Spirit which occupied a much longer time to accomplish than a modern clerical religion-getting. This is the excitement of an instant which leaves the

179

proselyte as ignorant of the truth as it found him : whereas the cleansing of the apostles every whit was, like that of Abraham's justification, an affair of years.

The apostles were a practical illustration of the word in Dan. 9 : 27 concerning the transactions of the seventieth week, " He shall confirm a covenant for many one week, and in half of the week he shall cause to cease from sacrificing and offering ". They belonged to the Week of Confirmation, in which the Spirit was causing to cease from sin-offerings ; preparing a covering for iniquity ; introducing a righteousness for the hidden periods ; sealing the vision of the eighth chapter, and the prophecy ; and anointing the holiest of the holy ones, or saints. Their baptism of John did not cause them to cease from sacrificing and offering according to the Mosaic law ; nor did their feet-washing by Jesus. Till he put away sin-offerings by the sacrifice of himself, the immersed apostles were under the dominion of the law, and bound to attend to its requirements ; but when Jesus died " to redeem the transgressions under the law ", their iniquity and that of all the prophets was covered ; and in his resurrection their justification was complete. The righteousness they had acquired was such as the law could not give. This could only represent the taking away of sins, not actually and permanently abolish them ; while the state perfected by the death and resurrection of Jesus invested them with a purification which needed not to be renewed in all subsequent time, and would be found sufficient for the Millennial Period and beyond, in other words, " for ever ".

After Deity was " justified in spirit ", by the perfecting of Jesus, the apostles no longer offered sacrifices and offerings. They " ceased sacrificing and offering ", though sacrifices and offerings continued to be offered according to the law for nearly forty years after by all Israelites who did not submit to the Deity's system of righteousness exhibited in the gospel the apostles preached.

From these premises the reader will perceive that John's baptism was altogether wrong and out of place after the resurrection of Jesus. It was quite right in its right place ; but altogether wrong out of its place. A pre-pentecostal immersion is therefore impossible ; and the case of the apostles who are subjects of it, altogether irrelevant to any supposable among us. Their faith was according to the formula of the week of confirmation, which terminated with the cutting off of Messiah the prince at the crucifixion. It was not defective for " justification by faith ", though it was defective for " justifi-cation through the faith ", which, however, when they were cleansed was to them impossible, seeing that " the faith " had not then as yet come.

But " justification by faith " according to the import of the phrase under the law, is as impossible to us as " justification through the faith " before the resurrection of Jesus was to them. Jesus preached the coming faith, but his hearers none of them understood it, because it was hidden from them. For this cause, it was styled " the wisdom of the Deity in a mystery, even the hidden wisdom ". Their justification was not predicated upon what was purposely hidden from them ; for God is not an austere master reaping where he hath not sown, and gathering where he hath not scattered. Men's justification, whether Jews or Gentiles, is predicated on their belief of what He hath revealed. When the hidden wisdom was revealed, then " the faith came ", and men were required to believe it *in addition to what the apostles believed* when they were " justified by faith ", before the cutting off of the Prince of the Host. Our justification does not depend on our believing what will be revealed to the nations in the millennial dawn, when the law shall go forth from Zion, and the word of Jehovah from Jerusalem, as testified in Isaiah 2 : 3. This is to us " hidden wisdom ". Secret things belong to God, the things that are revealed to us, and to our children (Deut. 29 : 29). This was the rule for Israel, and the rule for us who would find the " righteousness of God ".

The revelation of the hidden wisdom or mystery of the Deity, styled in Acts 2 : 11 " the wonderful works of God ", was the grand distinctive peculiarity of the apostolic preaching on Pentecost and forward. Nothing less than the belief of the teaching of the apostles can now justify a single son or daughter of the first Adam. He that hears them so as to believe and do what they taught, hears the Deity ; and he that hears them not is not " taught of God ", and cannot therefore be saved, however pious he may be in his own estimation, and that of his contemporaries. This is evident from the words of Jesus, who said to the apostles, " It shall be given you what ye shall speak ; for it is not ye that speak, but the Spirit of your Father which speaketh by you : and he that heareth you heareth me ; and he that despiseth you, despiseth me " (Matt 10 : 19, 20 ; Luke 10 : 16). And speaking of those who come to him as the result of the attracting influence of the Father, Jesus said,

" It is written in the prophets, And they shall be all taught of God. Every man therefore that hath heard and hath learned of the Father, cometh unto me " (John 6 : 45). To hear the apostles, then, is to hear Jesus and the Father ; and consequently to be taught of God ; and all that are so taught have heard and learned of the Father, and are drawn or attracted by what they have heard and learned to Jesus.

None else " come to Jesus " in the scriptural sense of the word. All who come to him are intelligent in " the faith ". There are no ignoramuses among the genuine disciples, for these are " all taught of the Deity " ; and when the Deity teaches, His teaching " opens the eyes ", turns the taught " from darkness " " into the marvellous light " of the gospel of His glory (Acts 26 : 18 ; 1 Pet. 2 : 9). How different this from the result of clerical teaching, preaching, ministration, or by whatever name they may designate the wordy outpourings of their cracked and truly earthen vessels ! Those who " come to Jesus " in the clerical sense, are those who come to the clergy, and become members of their synagogues. They are brought to this, not by the teaching of the apostles, but by the " enticing words of man's wisdom ", which leave them in darkness as profound as the craftiest soul-dealer could possibly wish. Any intelligent believer conversing with such can easily discern that they are not taught of God, but only of the clergy ; for he will find them entirely ignorant of the first principles of the oracles of God. With the prophets they have nothing to do ; for the apostles they have as little use ; of the gospel of the kingdom they have never heard ; and the revelation of the mystery might as well have never been revealed, for any use they have for it in their system of " getting religion ", and saving immortal souls from the death that never dies !

In such a system " marvellous light " is out of the question ; for in every corner of it can be discovered only the murkiest gloom, and darkness that may be felt. The Father and Jesus are despised by the adherents of the clergy, because the apostles are not heard. The whole establishment is Laodicean, and the voice of the Deity finds no utterance within its pale. These are incontrovertible facts. The teaching and mandates of the apostles are not regarded in the kingdom of the clergy, and therefore, we know that the spirit of their establishments is not the Spirit of the Deity ; but " the Spirit of Error " and of " strong delusion ", which is the spirit of their revivals, and the spirit of which their " religion " comes (1 John 4 : 5, 6 ; 2 Thess. 2 : 11, 12).

The Pentecostian " truth as it is in Jesus " is " rightly divided " by that skilful workman, the apostle of the Gentiles, in Rom. 16 : 25. In ascribing glory to the only wise Deity, he refers to the word of truth in a three-fold relation of things which may be thus stated :

1.—" My Gospel ",

2.—" The preaching of Jesus Christ ", and

3.—" The revelation of the mystery concealed from the times of the ages "—the times of the law and of the periods that preceded it.

1.—These are the triple elements of the whole system of faith Jesus called " the gospel " and which he commanded the apostles to go forth and preach, and declared that whosoever believed it and was baptized should be saved, but whosoever believed it not should be condemned. The " one hope " of this system Paul styled " my gospel ", or " the gospel of me "— the gospel preached of me, Paul. In another place he terms it " the hope of Israel ", on account of which he was a prisoner in chains (Acts 28 : 20). Elsewhere he alludes to it as " the gospel preached to Abraham ", and which announced the justification of all the nations through faith, and the blessing of them in company with faithful Abraham. It was therefore his gospel in an especial sense, because he was separated by the Deity to declare and teach it authoritatively to the Gentiles ; and whoever taught any thing perversive or subversive of it, he pronounced " accursed " (Gal. 1 : 6-9 ; 3 : 8, 9). The clergy do not preach this gospel. Indeed, how can they ! For they are as ignorant of it as though it had never been apocalypsed or revealed. Paul, then, whose image they set in niches for the ornamentation of their bazaars, not we, though we approve his sentence, pronounces them " accursed ". Let the reader, then, renounce these men-pleasers whom the world hears and glorifies, and study diligently Paul's gospel of the approaching government of the habitable by the resurrected and anointed King of Israel (Acts 17 : 31).

2.—When Paul's contemporaries had come to comprehend the purpose of the Deity with respect to the nations existing in the age to come—that he intended to rule them by the Christ—he next proclaimed to them that Jesus was that Christ. This he styles " the preaching of Jesus Christ ". Their belief of the gospel of the kingdom and name of Christ abstractly from Jesus, would not have justified, or saved them from their sins, and given them a right to the life of the age, after Pentecost. They were required to recognize him as the Son of David, Son of the Deity, and King of the Jews ; for if they rejected, or did not accept him as Lord, and received not his words, their fate was to be " destroyed from among the people " (John 12 : 48 ; Acts 3 : 23). This arrangement has not been altered by the authority of heaven since Paul's day. The clergy have abolished or superseded it by their traditions ; but God has no respect for them or their institutions. They are elements of a power " that thinks to change times and laws " (Dan. 7 : 25), and which speaks great things, and blasphemies, and opens its mouth in blasphemy against the Deity, to blaspheme His name and His tabernacle, and them that dwell in the heaven (Rev. 13 : 5). The influence of this clerical power in all its Laodicean developments is self-deceptive, and destructive of the people who obey its behests. In relation to them " the times and laws " are changed, and a way of salvation which, in verity, is no salvation at all, established, that makes the truth of God of no effect. But all this with God is nothing. His plan of salvation is unchanged ; and if any man of this generation be saved, he can be saved only as men were saved in the days of the apostles. They must believe Paul's gospel, and the preaching of Jesus Christ.

3.—But a man may believe the hope Paul proclaims, and that Jesus is the Christ, and yet not believe enough to save him. He must believe, in addition, the revealed mystery in its facts and doctrine. Suppose he believe that all nations shall be blessed in Abraham and his seed ; that Abraham shall inherit with his seed, Jesus and the saints, the promised land for the millennial period and beyond ; that David's throne shall be established and exist in all that period ; that the twelve tribes, then an obedient and faithful nation, shall occupy the land ; that Jesus and his holy brethren shall possess the government of the world, as Jehovah's anointed kings and priests, incorruptible and deathless—suppose he believe all this, what benefit would it be to the man if he denied, or did not believe that Jesus died, was buried, and rose again—that he was delivered for the sins of his people, and raised again for their justification ? These facts, and the teaching predicated upon them, are indispensable elements of " the faith " through which men are justified. It was in the preaching of Jesus Christ and the revealed mystery, that Paul's Israelitish fellow-countrymen needed to be especially indoctrinated. The gospel preached to Abraham was well known to them, for it was " the hope of Israel ", and had been preached to them in the reading of the prophets for many centuries. Not so, however, with the Gentiles. These were ignorant of the whole subject, and had to be taught everything from the beginning.

The apostles, then were " justified by faith ", and preached " justification through the faith " to all who should " obey the truth ". " Ye have purified your souls ", says Peter, " in obeying the truth." The truth cannot be obeyed unless it be believed. In other words, if a man have not the faith in his understanding and affection, he cannot yield " the obedience of faith ", or obey " the law of faith ". The burial of a true believer with Christ in immersion is the act of faith which constitutes obedience. None but a true believer can enact it. The immersion of an ignorant sinner is altogether out of the premises of the gospel. He that does it knowingly is a wilful blasphemer of the name of the Deity ; and the person dipped only adds to his sins by his presumption. The one faith and the one hope of the calling must precede the immersion to constitute the " one baptism " ; if either, or both, be wanting, the immersion is invalid. Fifty immersions will not supply the want of the faith ; but, on the other hand, if the subject's faith be apostolic, one immersion is sufficient, and ought, on no account, to be repeated.

16

THE GOODNESS OF GOD

" Despisest thou the riches of his goodness . . . not knowing that the goodness of God leadeth thee to repentance ? "—PAUL.

THE phrase " the goodness of God " is found occurrent in various places of the Holy Scriptures. It is not peculiar to the New Testament, but common to it and the Old. It occurs first in the writings of Moses, who, speaking of the effect of his narrative of Jehovah's severity upon Egypt and deliverance of Israel upon the mind of his father-in-law, says : "And Jethro rejoiced for all the goodness which the Lord had done to Israel, whom he had delivered out of the hand of the Egyptian ". From this the reader will perceive that the Lord's goodness is comprehensive both of good and evil. It is not unmixed good—good, pure, and absolute—but mixed and relative. If His goodness had been pronounced upon by the Egyptians, they would have characterized it as pure evil ; because His goodness plagued them with grievous plagues, and destroyed their army with a terrific overthrow. But this pure and absolute evil upon Egypt was unqualified goodness to Israel ; for it delivered them from a sore and cruel bondage, and commenced the fulfilment of the " good thing " (Jer. 33 : 14) which Jehovah had promised to Abraham, Isaac, and to Jacob, and their seed. God's goodness, then, is good in act and promise to His people ; but only evil to them who afflict them, and blaspheme His name.

God's goodness to His people, and severity upon His enemies, are the necessary result of His peculiar character. Hence His goodness and character are inseparable ; so that to declare " THE NAME " of the Lord is at once to make known His character and goodness, which stand related as effect and cause. Because of this it is written, " I will make all *my goodness* pass before thee, and will proclaim *the name of the Lord* before thee ; and I will be gracious to whom I will be gracious, and I will show mercy on whom I will show mercy ". Jehovah, therefore, descended in a cloud, and stood with Moses on Mount Sinai, and proclaimed the attributes which constitute His character, saying, " Jehovah, Jehovah, a God merciful and gracious, long suffering, and abounding in goodness and truth, keeping mercy for thousands, forgiving iniquity, and transgression, and sin, and destroying not utterly the guilty ; visiting the iniquity of the fathers upon the children, and upon the children's children, unto the third and to the fourth generation " (Exod. 33 : 19 ; 34 : 6, 7).

Such a God is Jehovah in His character, or relations of goodness to those whom He chooses for His people ; but at the same time " a consuming fire " to His enemies (Heb. 12 : 29). He is a great and absolute sovereign in all His doings, having mercy upon whom He will, and hardening at His pleasure (Rom. 9 : 18). He chose Israel for His people, or nation, to whom He granted a constitution, laws, and institutions, burdensome to be borne, but most agreeable to Himself, and promotive of His purpose in the manifestation of His goodness concerning them in the latter days (Acts 15 : 16). All His promises emanate from the essential goodness of His nature, which is favour, forbearance, abounding in truth, faithfulness, pardoning, and corrective but not utterly destroying. His promises are made to Israel, and to Israel alone ; nevertheless He has condescended to invite those of all nations who believe His promises to share in them when the time shall arrive to perform them. To Israel He is gracious ; to Israel He is long-suffering ; to Israel He is abundant in goodness and truth ; for thousands of Israel He keeps mercy in store ; He forgives Israel's iniquity, transgression, and sin ; and He corrects Israel, but He does not utterly destroy him, as his history shows even to this day. He hath not dealt so with any other nation. " Jehovah found Israel in a desert land, and in the waste howling wilderness : he led him about, he instructed him, he kept him as the apple of his eye " (Deut. 32 : 10). There is no nation so dear to him as Israel ; for " Israel is beloved for the fathers' sake " (Rom. 11 : 28). So tenderly compassionate is He of His nation that He said by His prophet, " He that toucheth you, O Israel, toucheth the apple of Jehovah's eye " (Zech. 2 : 8). And all this mercy to Israel is shared by those Gentiles who believe the promises and obey the law of faith ; for *believing* Jews and Gentiles are all the children of God *through the faith* in Christ Jesus. For as many of these believers as have been baptized into Christ have put him on. They are therefore all one in Christ Jesus ; and if Christ's, then Abraham's seed or Israelites, and heirs according to the promise (Gal. 3 : 26, 29). Being thus adopted, the Gentiles who believe the gospel of the kingdom in the name of

Jesus are no more strangers and foreigners, or aliens from Israel's Commonwealth, and strangers from the covenants of promise, but fellow-citizens with the saints of Israel, and of the household of God, which for about seven years after the resurrection of Jesus consisted only of faithful Israelites (Eph. 2 : 12, 19).

It is an attribute of Jehovah's goodness to " keep mercy for thousands ". These thousands for whom mercy is kept are " those who love him, and keep his commandments " (Exod. 20 : 6)—the Israel of God in the higher import of the phrase. The mercy kept for them is the *chesed* styled the *berith olahm chasdai Dahwid*, or Age-covenant mercies of David, rendered by Lowth " an everlasting covenant, the gracious promise made to David ", which shall never fail (Isa. 55 : 3). These gracious promises, or loving-kindness, or mercy which Jehovah keeps for thousands, are based upon the *chesed* or mercy to Abraham, to which Mary and Zacharias refer in these words : " He hath holpen his servant Israel, in remembrance of his mercy, as he spake to our fathers, to Abraham, and to his seed for ever " : " Jehovah hath raised up a horn of salvation for us (Israel) in the house of his servant David ; as he spake by the mouth of his holy prophets, which have been from the beginning of the age : that we should be saved from our enemies, and from the hand of all that hate us : to perform the mercy promised to our fathers, and to remember his holy covenant ; the oath which he swore to our father Abraham, that he would grant us (Israel) that we being delivered out of the hand of our enemies might serve him without fear, in holiness and righteousness before him, all the days of our life " (Luke 1 : 54, 55, 69-75). The birth of Jesus was a proof that Jehovah remembered the mercy he had promised to Abraham and David. Jesus, the born king of the Jews, was the Horn or Power by which the nation is to be saved from all its enemies ; he is therefore styled " a horn of salvation for Israel ". He has not saved them yet. They are still subject to the Horns of the Gentiles, and have no part in their native land. So long as their condition remains as it is, the mercy promised to Abraham and David continues unfulfilled. The resurrection of Jesus, however, is the earnest that it will be accomplished in the appointed time ; and that he will certainly deliver them from the tyrants " who destroy the earth ". Hear this, ye who profess to love the Lord, but believe not what He saith : " Behold, saith he, the days come that I will perform the good thing which I have promised unto the house of Israel and to the house of Judah. In those days, and at that time, will I cause the Branch of Righteousness to grow up unto David ; and he shall execute judgment and righteousness in the land. In those days shall Judah be saved, and Jerusalem dwell safely : and this (is his name) which shall be proclaimed to her : The Lord our Righteousness. For thus saith Jehovah ; David shall never want a man to sit upon the throne of the House of Israel : neither shall the Priests the Levites want a man before me to offer burnt offering, and to kindle meat offerings, and to do sacrifice continually " (Jer. 33 : 14-18 ; 23 : 5, 6). This " good thing " is the subject-matter of the mercy promised to Abraham and David, which Jehovah, the fulfiller of promises, keepeth for thousands ; and which is as certain to be communicated as that He exists, for " He magnifies his word above all his name " (Psa. 138 : 2). That good thing in its details is abundantly spoken of by the mouth of all the Prophets through whom Jehovah hath kept alive the remembrance of it from the foundation of Israel's Commonwealth. It is Israel's Hope, and therefore the hope of the true Christian ; for " salvation is of the Jews ".

Behold, then, the promised goodness of God ! An Immortal King shall reign and prosper in the land of Israel, and shall execute judgment and justice there over the Twelve Tribes, and the obedient nations of the world, for a thousand years. This is the oath which Jehovah swore to Abraham, saying, " In thee and in thy Seed shall all the nations of the earth be blessed "—a blessedness in the establishment of which Israel will have been delivered out of the hand of all their enemies, and henceforth enjoy the privilege of serving Jehovah without fear, in holiness and righteousness before Him all the days of their mortal career. The nation of our adoption will then be the chief of all the nations dwelling safely in its own land. Gentiles by birth, but Jews by regeneration, the goodness of God promises us resurrection from among the dead, and exaltation to the highest honours of the State ; as it is written, " The saints of the Most High shall possess the Kingdom for ever, even for ever and ever ".

Such mercy Jehovah keeps for thousands of Israel and adopted Gentiles who believe the promises He has made to the fathers. But His goodness promises even more than eternal life and honour to the just. It promises them wisdom, and knowledge, and physical strength, the possession of the world

189

and the fulness thereof, glory, equality with the angels, and the high favour of God for ever. He keeps this mercy in store for them that love him, and obey His word. Who that believes these things would hesitate to respond, " Jehovah is good, for his mercy endureth for ever ? " Yea, it is even so : for " the mercy of Jehovah is from everlasting to everlasting upon them that fear him, and his righteousness unto children's children ; to such as keep his covenant, and to those who remember his commandments to do them ". Mark, dear reader, " to such as keep his covenant and obey him ". Dost thou know what it is to keep Jehovah's covenant and obey Him ? Know then that it is *to believe the gospel of the kingdom, and to be baptized, or united to the name of Jesus, and thenceforth to continue patiently in well-doing.* The covenant is the covenant concerning the kingdom of which the gospel treats—the oath of national blessedness through Abraham and his seed, which Jehovah swore to him when He brought him into the territory of the future kingdom. You must believe this same particular gospel or you cannot " keep the covenant ", or have any part in the kingdom it proclaims.

Now, beloved reader, " Despisest thou the riches of this goodness of God " ? Read, mark, learn, and inwardly digest the good things of His mercy we have brought up herein, and say if they are not of peerless import. Are not endless life and good days, boundless riches, honour, and eternal glory in a kingdom of God's establishment upon the earth, more to be desired than all the world can give you now ? Can you be of sane mind and despise all these riches of goodness ? Can you be rational and self-possessed ? But if you despise them not, but " *believe on God* ", that is, be fully persuaded that what He has promised He is able to perform, and will do it, will you not likewise be willing to make any sacrifice to obtain them ? If you were till a certain time devoted to the world and the enjoyment of the flesh, but came afterwards to believe in these promises with an honest and good heart, or as men say, " sincerely ", would not your views of things present and future have undergone a radical change ? Would you not cease to set your affections on earthly things ; would not your affection rather be transferred to the things contained in that " mercy kept for thousands " ? Yea, verily. And would you not have been led to this change of views, affection, and will by the goodness of God exhibited in the testimony of His holy prophets ? Even so ; and you would then be a practical illustration of the

Bible sentiment that " it is the goodness of God that leadeth to repentance ".

God's goodness leads to repentance. It leads believers to place themselves in such a relation to the truth that " repentance unto life " may be " *granted* unto them " (Acts 11 : 18). The goodness of God is like to choice and goodly wares exhibited in a bazaar for sale. Their *goodliness* attracts the attention of passengers, and *leads* them to desire to possess them. The merchant *grants* their desire on certain conditions. They accept the terms, and *receive* the right of property in them ; and he promises to put them in possession of them at an appointed time. The goodness of God which leads to repentance is exhibited in the gospel of the kingdom, and no-where else ; for this gospel is the grand theme of the word of God contained in the scriptures, old and new : and because it is displayed in that royal proclamation, therefore John the Baptist, Jesus, and the apostles before their Lord's crucifixion, went through the towns and cities, and country parts of Judea, " preaching the gospel of the kingdom of God, saying, Repent ; for the Majesty of the heavens is arrived " (Matt. 3 : 2 ; 4 : 17, 23 ; Mark 1 : 14, 15 ; Luke 4 : 18, 43 ; 9 : 2, 6). The kingdom and arrival of its king were preached to lead those who believed it to repentance. The goodness of God set forth in the doctrine of the kingdom was preached also after the Lord's resurrection, to lead men to repentance, that they might be made meet for its inheritance ; but the motive hereto, founded on the personal presence of the king, was not repeated. It could not be ; for " the Majesty of the heavens " had departed into a far country (Luke 19 : 11, 12). The apostles no longer said : " Repent ; for the kingdom of heaven is at hand " ; but, " Repent : because God hath appointed a day in which he will rule the world in righteousness by that man whom he hath ordained, whereof he hath given assurance to all in that he hath raised him from the dead " (Acts 17 : 30, 31) —in other words, " Repent ; because the Majesty of the heavens, who hath departed, will come again to rule the world in righteousness ". This is now the glad tidings of the kingdom for repentance unto life.

That " *the gospel* " and " *the goodness of God* " are phrases importing the same things, is clear from the use of them by Paul. He says : " the Jews became the enemies to the gospel for the sake of the Gentiles ". It was no good will to the

Gentiles on their part, that they refused to believe ; but their refusal was the result of hardness of heart : therefore, as a punishment God blinded and hardened them still more, so that, instead of filling His house or kingdom with believers who were " Jews by nature ", He determined to make up the complement of the redeemed by believers separated from " sinners of the Gentiles ", who should become Jews by adoption, through faith in His goodness. Judah, though still beloved for Abraham, Isaac, and Jacob's sake, fell from gospel favour through want of faith ; while faithful Gentiles were grafted into the stock of Israel's olive, and recognized as Israelites in every respect save the accident of birth. This was just severity towards Judah ; but gracious goodness towards Gentiles.

Thus it is apparent that the principle according to which the position of Judah and the Gentiles relative to Jehovah and His mercy was changed, was that of faith. To continue in the faith of the gospel was to continue in the goodness of God. Judah did not continue in that goodness because the Jews did not continue to believe it. They were therefore " cut off ". The offer was to be made to them no more. Judah would indeed be grafted in again to the national olive : that is, reorganized with the rest of the tribes as a nation and common-wealth, or kingdom, in their own land, under the sovereignty of " Jesus of Nazareth, the king of the Jews " ; but those of them contemporary with the national blindness should have no share in " the joy " of their king—in those good things offered to individuals in the gospel of the kingdom. This gospel announces that the God of heaven will set up a kingdom and dominion upon earth, under whose righteous administration Israel and the nations will be blessed with all temporal and spiritual blessings for a thousand years ; such as, that there shall be war no more ; that oppression and injustice shall cease ; that the earth shall give her increase ; that the earth shall be filled with the knowledge of the Lord's glory ; that the poor shall be comforted and protected ; that there shall be but one religion, and so forth—these are gospel blessings for the world, when by conquest it is brought into subjection to Israel's king ; but the gospel promises the glory, honour, majesty, and riches of the kingdom and dominion only to those persons who, *before the manifestation of them*, while they are yet a matter of faith, and not of sight, believe the promised goodness of it, and continue in it.

To Gentile people the apostle saith : " *If ye continue not in the goodness of God, ye also shall be cut off* ". In the same place, he saith : " *Thou, O Gentile, standest by faith* ". That is, so long as the Gentiles continue to believe the gospel of the kingdom, there shall be scope for repentance unto life, that they may inherit the kingdom ; but when they become faithless of the gospel, as Judah was before them, the door of mercy shall with like destructive violence be closed against them. " Be not high-minded, but fear ", saith Paul ; " for if God spared not the natural branches of the olive tree, beware lest he also spare not thee ". In the apostle's day there was a disposition in the Gentile mind to high-mindedness, and to boast against Judah, who had stumbled at the stone of stumbling and rock of offence. They do not seem to have entertained the idea of the re-engraftment of the broken-off branches, but concluded that God had cast Israel away as a people for whom He had no further use or affection. This was not the general idea ; but some seem to have held it, or the apostle would not have contradicted the supposition. " God forbid ", says he, " that such a thing should be; he hath not cast away his people, Israel, whom he knew before he received the Gentiles into favour ". But, though the apostle so promptly repudiated the notion, he did not succeed in repressing it. That Israel was finally rejected and cast away, took strong hold of the Gentile *professors* of Christianity, who in after times thought they were doing God service in persecuting the Jews. Even at the present day, after a lapse of eighteen centuries, the receiving of Israel into favour again is regarded as fabulous by " Christian professors ". Being " wise in their own conceits ", they boast themselves against the Jews, and denounce as " carnal Judaizers " those who, with Paul, affirm that " God hath not cast away his people, Israel, whom he foreknew ". Hear what Jehovah saith of Israel : " Thus saith the Lord, who giveth the sun for a light by day, and the ordinances of the moon and of the stars for a light by night ; who divideth the sea when the waves thereof roar—the Lord of hosts is his name ". " If those ordinances depart from before me ", saith the Lord, " then the seed of Israel also shall cease from being a nation before me forever." Mark the " if ", which is still further emphasized in the next verse, saying : " If the heaven above can be measured, and the foundations of the earth searched out beneath, I will cast off all the seed of Israel for all that they have done ", saith the Lord

(Jer. 31 : 35-37). This is equivalent to saying, Israel shall never cease from being a nation before Me though they have done grievously in My sight ; for the hypotheses upon which their casting away is predicated are absolute impossibilities. It is as impossible for their national existence to cease for ever, as it is for feeble-minded man to measure heaven, or to search out the centre of the earth.

We have said that the non-restoration of Israel was not the general idea entertained by Gentile believers in the apostle's day. To say that it was, would be to affirm that they did not generally believe the gospel ; for there can be no kingdom without the restoration of the Jews. There are those in our day who deny their restoration. This is proof-positive that they do not understand the gospel, which is the glad tidings of the restoration of the kingdom again to Israel, and the blessedness of all nations through their government ; for, we repeat it, " Salvation is of the Jews ".

The spiritual condition of the Gentiles at the present crisis in all countries of " Christendom " is the exact counterpart of Judah's at the period of the dissolution of their commonwealth. The Jews were without faith, and so are also the Gentiles of today. But thou wilt perhaps say, O reader, how can that be ? Are there not thousands upon thousands of holy men engaged in preaching Christ in every land ; and are not they sustained by millions of faithful men, who contribute immense sums for the propagation of the Christian faith ? We admit there are multitudes of preachers, and millions of sincere professors of religious faiths they call Christian ; but where are the preachers and believers of the gospel of the kingdom ; and rarer still, where are the believers thereof, who obey it ? " Faith ", such as it is, abounds, but " THE Faith " is known to very few, and preached by still fewer. The Jews believed the gospel of the kingdom, but they refused to obey it in the name of Jesus as king of Israel. They stumbled at him. They did not believe in him as Jehovah's Anointed One ; and therefore rejected " the mystery of the gospel " in his name. It is so likewise with the Gentiles at this day. They preach a character they call Jesus, whom Paul did not preach. Compare the popular notions of Jesus Christ with the Christ delineated in the old and new scriptures, and you will be astonished, O reader, at the want of congruity between them ! The Gentiles stumble at the character called Christ in the Bible, even as the Jews did at Jesus. These

194

repudiated a suffering Messiah ; the Gentiles reject a Christ who shall subdue the nations by the sword, replant Israel's olive in its native soil, restore the kingdom and throne of his father, David, sit upon it for a thousand years, and as sole monarch of the world rule all nations as Jehovah's vicegerent upon the earth. The Bible is at variance with them both, for it not only reveals a Christ who should be made perfect through sufferings, but one that should do all these things besides.

We repeat it with profound conviction, that the gospel is not preached, it is not believed, nor is it obeyed by the religionists of our day. The exceptions to this statement are so few that they do not affect the generality of its application. If, as in the days of Elijah, there be seven thousand in Christendom who believe the truth and have obeyed it, our statement is not at all invalidated thereby. They who believe in a gospel of kingdoms beyond the skies to be possessed with a Jesus who is to return to earth only to destroy it, believe a gospel that has no place in the Bible. How high minded and wise are professors in this day in their own conceit ! They plume themselves in their christianity and spiritual intelligence, saying " they are rich and increased in goods, and have need of nothing ; but know not that they are wretched, and miserable, and poor, and blind, and naked ". So Egyptian is the darkness which beclouds their minds that they discern not the awful crisis which is advancing upon them with gigantic strides. They are sporting themselves with their own deceiving, while destruction is at the door. Faithless of the gospel, high-minded, and wise in their own conceit ! This is itself a great sign of the times. By faith we stand ; by unbelief we fall. What then remains ? Nothing more, but that the Gentiles be cut off, and the process of their engraftment be terminated. Short will be the work when it is once fairly under weigh. The cutting off accomplished, the gathering in of Israel's tribes will then proceed, and shall not be intermitted until " all Israel shall be saved ". Hear, in conclusion, what Jehovah saith by the hand of Moses concerning this time of trouble coming upon the world : " The day of the calamity of Israel's foes is at hand, and the things that shall come upon them make haste. For the Lord shall judge his people, and repent himself for his servants, when he seeth that their power is gone, and there is none shut up or left. See now that I, even I, am he, and there is no god with me. I kill, and I make whole ; I wound, and I heal ; neither is there any that can deliver out of my hand. For I lift up my hand to heaven, and say, I live for ever. If I whet my glittering sword, and my hand take hold of judgment, I will render vengeance to mine enemies, and will reward them that hate me. I will make mine arrows drunk with blood, and my sword shall devour flesh ; with the blood of the slain and of the captives, from the beginning of revenges upon the enemy." When this shall be perfected, then " Rejoice, O ye nations, with his people ; for he will avenge the blood of his servants, and will render vengeance to his adversaries, and will be merciful unto his land, and to his people ".

17

CHRIST'S DISCOURSE WITH NICODEMUS

In John 3 : 3, Jesus states a truth in relation to God's kingdom over which he is to preside with the saints, which is unalterable and indispensable, and which the lapse of eighteen centuries has rendered no less imperative than at the moment he enunciated it : *Except a man be begotten from above, he is unable to see the Kingdom of God.* This is a great truth ; and to those who understand the nature of the kingdom, an obvious one. It is a truth of similar construction to this, that *except a man be begotten from beneath, he is not able to possess the things of Satan's kingdom.* And why ? Because he would have no existence at all ; but would be as his father **Adam,** before the Lord of the Elohim formed him from the ground, by the Spirit of the Invisible God. A man must be begotten of sinful flesh, or he cannot see the things of the flesh ; and this begettal is the being begotten " from beneath " to which Jesus refers, in saying, " Ye are from beneath ; I am from above : ye are of this world ; I am not of this world ". The Jews sprung *ek tōn katō,* " out of things below "—that is, of blood, of the impulse of the flesh, and of the will of man ; while he originated *ek tōn anō,* " from things above "—that is, of the Spirit, and the will of God.

Jesus, then, who is " the Heir of All Things ", was " begotten from above ". He was thus begotten to the days of his flesh ; for he was not the Son of Joseph, but of God. Nevertheless, " the flesh profiteth nothing ; it is the Spirit that makes alive ". Jesus was crowned with glory and honour, not because he had been begotten from above of God's spirit before he was born of Mary ; but because he was obedient unto death, and made perfect through sufferings. Having attained to moral perfection (not that he was ever immoral for he was " without sin " ; but until " the temptation " he was simply innocent, his virtue, or obedience to the Father, not having been tested by his sufferings), he was made alive by the Spirit, or from above, and so became " the Son of God with power, according to the spirit of holiness, by resurrection from the dead ".

The Lord Jesus was the subject of two spirit-begettals and two births—the former were both of the Spirit ; and the latter its consequents. His fleshly birth was of Mary, which we are not now considering. His first spiritual birth was on being " born of water ", and so fulfilling the righteousness of God ; which multitudes think was quite necessary for the sinless Jesus, but not for them ! After this birth his trials commenced ; and his " patient continuance in well doing " prepared him, or rather became the premises upon which was predicated his second birth ; that, namely, from the dark and gravid womb of the grave where all his brethren lie. Thus he was " born of the Spirit " and became " the Lord, the Spirit " ; or as Paul has it, *eis pneuma zōopoioun*, " the last Adam was made into a spirit which shall make alive " ; for *zōopoioun* is the second future participle whose sign is *going to make alive*. Thus, " that which is born of the flesh is flesh ", like all the sons of the first Adam ; " and that which is born of the spirit is spirit ", like the second Adam, the Elder Brother and captain of the saints.

" Flesh and blood ", says Paul, " cannot inherit ", or possess " the kingdom of God." And why ? Because, as he says, " corruption cannot inherit incorruption ". The kingdom of God is the incorruptible, undefiled and unfading inheritance of the saints—the kingdom preparing for the blessed of their Father. It is " that which shall never be destroyed ", and which " shall not be left to other people ". That is, when it is given to the Father's blessed ones, it shall henceforth be possessed by them, and by them only : " it shall not be left to other people " ; but " the saints shall possess it for ever, even for ever and ever ". Now, that which is born of the flesh is flesh and blood, and " dead " or mortal and corruptible. How true this must be of mankind in general, in view of what Paul says to saints in the present life—" Ye are dead ", *apethanete*, says he : a word which signifies to become putrescent, or dry as a withered tree. This was the new law of their being relatively to " earthly things ", on which they were forbidden to set their affections. Their bodies were " dead because of sin " ; and their affections were dead to earthly things ; so that as far as flesh and blood and world were concerned, they were mortal and corruptible, and only so. But they had a hidden life. It was not a physical principle within them. All that was there was the word of life, assuredly believed ; in which sense Christ the word, was there, dwelling in their hearts by faith. By holding on to this word, they held on to eternal life—on to the Lord the spirit, who is to give them life in his day. They were dead ; but " your life ", continued the apostle, " is hid with Christ in God ; and when Christ, your life shall appear, then shall ye also appear with him in glory ". This being the condition of saints, unresurrected and unchanged it is clear that they are physically incapacitated for possessing the kingdom of God. However worthy and acceptable before him, they cannot, being mortal, " enter the kingdom of God ", and possess it for ever, until born of the spirit, for till then they are not spirit, but flesh only.

The saints must become " spiritual bodies ", or spirits, before they can " see " so as to possess the kingdom. Now, as a begettal of blood, or of the flesh, or of the will of man, cannot produce spirit-body, there is no ground for marvel that a second birth should be a necessary preliminary to the inheriting the kingdom of God. Hence the Lord Jesus said to Nicodemus, " Marvel not that I said unto thee, Ye must be born from above ". He then went on to say, " The Spirit breathes where he pleases, and thou hearest his voice, but thou knowest not whence he comes, and whither he leads ; in like manner is every one being begotten of the Spirit ". Thus are men begotten from above—by the voice of the Spirit breathing forth the truth, when, where, and how, He pleases. In some places, He will not breathe it at all ; and on occasion positively forbids its utterance (Acts 16 : 7).

But the inability of man to possess, or to enter, the kingdom of God, is twofold ; for while corruptible flesh and blood cannot inherit it, neither can the unrighteous. " Be not deceived ", says Paul ; " the unrighteous shall not inherit the kingdom of God." The unrighteous are as putrescent of heart as they are of flesh. The saints cannot inherit the kingdom until they cease to be flesh and blood ; and sinners cannot inherit it, until they cease to be unrighteous as well : thus, there is but one hindrance to saints, but two obstacles in the way of sinners—for " sinners shall not stand in the congregation of the righteous ". The being begotten from above, therefore, has relation to the begettal of a sinner to God's righteousness, that, like Jesus, the great exemplar of the faith, he may fulfil that righteousness in being born of water. " Of his own will the Father of lights begat us by the word of truth, that we might be a kind of first-fruits of his creatures." In these words, James teaches us that God is the begetter ; and " the word of truth " the means by which He begets the first-fruits of His creatures—the first-fruits who are to attain to eternal life and glory, before the general harvest of the sons of Adam. This word of truth is " the word of the kingdom ", which, as good seed, is sown into honest and good hearts. Referring to this, Peter says, " begotten again of incorruptible seed through the word of the living God, abiding even unto the age, and preached as gospel unto you ". Now, every one that believes this gospel with full assurance of faith, is begotten of the Father of lights ; that is, " from above " : and in proof of it, they " purify their souls in the obedience of the truth through the Spirit ". " The words I speak unto you are spirit and are life ", says Jesus ; and it is such words that bring honest hearts to " the obedience of the faith ", for which purpose the gospel was ordered to be preached. A man found in the obedience of the truth is one who believes the gospel of the kingdom, and has been baptized, according to the wholesome words of the Lord Jesus. The apostle addressed such a one as washed, sanctified, and justified. Thus, " Know ye not that the unrighteous shall not inherit the kingdom of God ? Be not deceived : neither fornicators, idolators, adulterers, effeminate, abusers of themselves with mankind, thieves, covetous, drunkards, revilers, nor extortioners, shall inherit the kingdom of God. And such were some of you ; but ye are washed, but ye are sanctified, but ye are justified in the name of the Lord Jesus, and by the spirit of our God ". This is equivalent to saying they had been born of water and of spirit ; for in the days of the apostles, believers in the kingdom were baptized into the name of the Lord Jesus, and so found in him and in his name ; and I find no place in God's book where this old-fashioned custom has been abolished.

This being begotten from above, then, leads to a twofold birth from below—first, from water ; and secondly, from the grave : and the one is as necessary as the other to the entering of the kingdom of God. " He that believes the gospel and is baptized shall be saved." He that spake these words also said, " Except a man be born out of water and spirit he cannot enter into the kingdom of God "—and he that enters not into that kingdom is- a lost man. A man not begotten from above is " alienated from the life of God through the ignorance that is in him " ; he is " dead in trespasses and in sins " ; he is not in Christ : he is (even though an immersed man) unwashed, unsanctified, and unjustified. The first thing is to believe the gospel of the kingdom ; and then to put on Christ by being introduced into his name. This is the first effectual move towards glory, honour, incorruptibility, and life in the kingdom of God. What remains is, " Be faithful unto death, and Christ will give thee a crown of life ", when he unlocks the gates of the unseen, and wakes his sleeping brethren from the dust. Their regeneration then will be complete, but not before. Awake, they once more stand upon the earth ; no longer, however, flesh and blood, but flesh, bones and spirit, as the Lord the spirit, and " equal to the angels ", and therefore deathless, and fit for the kingdom of God.

" Consider Christ Jesus ", says Paul, " the Apostle and High Priest of our confession." He is the heir of all things terrestrial ; and the saints are joint-heirs with him of all God has covenanted to him. He is the way and the truth, as well as the resurrection and the life. Would we know the true way to the kingdom ? Consider the narrow way in which Jesus walked, and follow in his foot-steps ; for he left us an example that we should follow in them. The members of Christ's house are with him the children of a common father, even God. They have all therefore since the proclamation of " the mystery " to follow him through the water and the grave. I speak not of those who remain at his appearing. These saints, washed and justified, will not pass through the grave ; but will become spiritual bodies, or spirits, being begotten to this from above in the twinkling of an eye. All else follow Jesus through the water and the grave ; and, after his example, rising from the dead, " are the children of God, being the children of the resurrection " ; so that it can be said to them in the prophetic words addressed to the Lord's Anointed : " Ye are my sons, this day (of your resurrection) have I begotten you ".

The kingdom of God is a spiritual institution. I do not mean by this that it is a mere aura, or gaseous afflation, like Plato's " immortal soul " ; but spiritual in the sense of its being incorruptible and indestructible ; and founded by the power of God, who is spirit ; and governed by a king who is spirit ; and everything relating to it divinely appointed. Such an institution as this is pre-eminently spiritual ; and because it is so every son of Adam who would inherit it must be spiritualized in heart and substance ; or, as the phrase is, " in body, soul, and spirit, the whole person ". The principle laid down by the royal teacher in John 3 : 5 may be termed the law of spiritualization, unsubject to which no man can possibly in the nature of things enter upon the possession of the glory, honour, life, power, and emoluments of " the kingdom of Christ and of God ". This law is to the kingdom what naturalization is to the kingdoms and republics of the world. The governments of these, " the rulers of the darkness of this age ", will not permit the natives of foreign states to inherit or possess the honours and emoluments of their institutions, unless they first abjure to all princes and potentates but themselves. They say, " Except ye be naturalized ye can in no wise enter any department of our State ". It would be very remarkable if all the kingdoms of the world had an alien law, and the kingdom of God none. All the sons and daughters of Adam are by nature aliens to the kingdom of heaven ; hence they have no more natural right to it than the Portuguese have to the privileges, immunities, and emoluments, of the throne, hierarchy, and aristocracy, of the British Empire. " The flesh profiteth nothing." Even a natural Israelite, to whose nation the kingdom belongs, has no right to the glory, honour, incorruptibility, life, power and wealth of it ; how much less right, or rather none at all, has he who is not even a descendant from Jacob according to the flesh. Even a natural born Israelite must " be born from above ", or he cannot inherit the kingdom when restored again to Israel. The character defined in the scriptures as " the Jew "—" an Israelite indeed in whom is no guile "—is the pattern to which they must conform who would " inherit all things ". Jesus is this Jew in manifestation. He claimed nothing promised to Abraham, Isaac and Jacob, because he was born of their daughter Mary, because " the flesh profiteth nothing " : but because he pleased God. Truth, and not sight, begets " the Jew "—faith in the word of the kingdom, the promised kingdom. Hence, it is " the children of the promise who are counted for the seed " that shall inherit all things. The whole Jewish nation will be grafted into its own olive tree when God shall have overcome their unbelief. They shall possess their native land no more to be expelled by the horns of the Gentiles, above whom they will be exalted as a nation very high. But it is only those Jews and Gentiles, who, by spiritualization, answer to " the Jew " walking in the steps of that faith of Abraham, which he had being yet uncircumcised, who will inherit the kingdom with eternal glory. For, " he is not the Jew in the appearance ; but he is the Jew who is such in the inner man ".

The king says that no alien shall inherit his kingdom unless he be spiritualized in mind and body. He has a perfect right

to say so, and no alien has any right to complain ; for citizeniza-
tion is a principle of their legislation. If you would inherit
the good things promised to Israel, become citizens of Israel's
commonwealth, and of its royal household, styled " the household of God ". Now, as there is but one alien law to a state,
so there is but one for the adoption of aliens into the kingdom
of God. The first step is the declaration of the intention ;
or confession with the mouth, as the result of believing the
things of the kingdom and name with the heart ; " for with the
heart man believeth unto righteousness ; and with the mouth
confession is made unto salvation ". Next comes obedience to
" the Law of Faith ", which commands the confessor to " be
baptized in the name of the Lord Jesus ". He is now in mind,
body and estate, " the purchased possession " of the King of
Israel. He is in mind and heart " begotten from above ",
and in body " washed with pure water ". Thus he is
intellectually and morally begotten of the spirit-truth ; and
corporeally washed with water, made " pure " by the special
use to which it is appropriated, in connection with the subject's
faith in the things of the kingdom and name. Thus being
begotten of the word and born of water, he is scripturally
responsive to the exhortation of the apostle, who says to all
such, " Let us draw near with a true heart in full assurance of
faith, having our hearts sprinkled from an evil conscience
(by the blood of sprinkling in the obedience), and our bodies
washed with pure water : let us hold fast the confession of the
hope unwaveringly ". And now, what waits he for ? For the
Son of God from heaven, to change the body of his humiliation
into a like form with the body of his exaltation and glory,
through that spirit-energy by which he is able, and at that
time prepared, to subdue all things to himself. This
accomplished, and he is corporeally begotten of the spirit, and
an actual inheritor of the then established, glorious, and all
conquering kingdom of God.

18

THE GOSPEL IN MACEDONIA

" THE Jailor and other untaught Gentiles heard, believed, and obeyed the Gospel in the short time of an hour. Therefore, a correct understanding of the Gospel must have been obtained by them in that brief space of time."—(*Prophetic Expositor*, p. 104.)

Luke informs us in Acts 16, that in a vision Paul had, there stood before him a man of Macedonia, who entreated him to come over to that country, and help them. This was regarded by Paul and his companions as a vision from the Lord, calling upon them to announce the glad tidings in Macedonia. They had essayed to " preach the Word " to the idolators in the provinces of Anatolia, called Asia and Bithynia, but had been forbidden by the Holy Spirit. The cause of this interdict is not stated. The province of Asia contained the seven apocalyptic churches which were, doubtless, already existing there (Acts 2 : 9) ; and Bithynia, also, was not destitute of the truth. But the time and circumstances were not yet quite appropriate for the annunciation of " The Fellowship of the Mystery " among them ; importing " that the Gentiles (or pagans) should be fellow heirs (of the kingdom with the saints of Israel), and of the same body (that is, of the ' One Body '), and partakers of God's promise concerning the Anointed through the glad tidings ". Having proclaimed the Christian fellowship of Jew and Gentile in the Syrian Antioch, Seleucia, Cyprus, Perga, Antioch in Pisidia, Iconium, Lystra, Derbe, and Attalia, they were directed to visit the country west of Constantinople, and north of the Ægean Sea, where, it is probable, Christian-Jewish prejudices were not so strong as in Asia and Bithynia.

In the region of country indicated, and not far from the sea, stood the City of Philippi, so called after Philip, King of Macedon, and father of Alexander the Great, " the great horn of the rough goat " of Dan. 8 : 21. This region was *Macedonia Prima*, and Philippi was a Roman colony ; so that the Philippians, though Macedonian born, were Roman citizens as they declared (verse 21).

In his letter to the Philippians, Paul styles his labours among them at this time, " the beginning of the Gospel "

(4 : 15), that is, that the glad tidings of the Fellowship began
to be proclaimed to the " untaught Gentiles " of Macedonia
when he responded to the prayer, " Come over to Macedonia
and help us ! " Now, Macedonia contained many cities,
among which were Amphipolis, Apollonia, Thessalonica, and
Berea. All these Paul visited as well as Philippi, *announcing
in one those same glad tidings as in all the rest.* No one, we presume,
will dispute this. Thus, when he visited Thessalonica, he gave
them to understand that he was the bearer of an invitation to
them from the living and true God of Israel, who had commanded him to invite them to His kingdom and glory (1 Thess.
2 : 12). Many of the idolatrous Macedonians there accepted
the invitation joyfully (1 Thess. 1 : 6) when they discovered
that it was genuine—that it was no fiction, but *a word sent to
them from heaven,* and therefore styled " *the Word of God* ",
in deed and in truth, being confirmed by the power of God
(1 Thess. 1 : 5). This created in them a hope which was the
" one hope of the calling ", or invitation ; so that he could
address them as he could not address their idolatrous friends,
saying, " Be not as the others, who have no hope ".

The hope formed in them by the apostle's preaching
looked forward to the coming of the day of the Lord in which
Jesus should re-appear upon the earth. But so well had he
instructed them that they did not expect that day to arrive
until there had first been an APOSTASY FROM THE FAITH,
acuminating in a power styled " *the Man of Sin* ", whose
revelation would be preceded by the removal of the power
then existing. " *Remember ye not* ", says he, " *that when I was
yet with you, I told you these things ?* and what witholds now for his
being revealed in his appointed time, ye know." Yea, so
conspicuous a place had these things in his preaching that
an outcry was soon raised against him, accusing him, in the
city of the Philippian jailor, of " teaching precepts which were
not lawful for them to receive, neither to observe, being
Romans " ; and in Thessalonica, of " doing contrary to the
decrees of Caesar, saying there is another king—one Jesus ".

Referring to " the beginning of the Gospel ", the apostle
says to the Thessalonians, " God hath from the beginning
chosen you for deliverance by a separation of spirit and belief
of truth ; for which he called you through our glad tidings
for the obtaining of the glory of our Lord Jesus Christ "
(2 Thess. 2 : 13, 14). In this he tells them that by a separation
of spirit and faith, that is, by a holy disposition created in

them through the truth believed, they had been chosen of God for deliverance from the wrath to come upon those who know not God, and hearken not to the glad tidings of the Lord Jesus Christ, and for sharing with him in the things covered by the phrase, " his kingdom and glory ". They were separated or sanctified by faith, and " called ", or invited, to their high destiny through the glad tidings they believed. The sanctification of spirit, or heart-purification, referred to by Paul, was " righteousness, and peace, and joy, in the Holy Spirit ", resulting from belief of the glad tidings of the kingdom ; wherefore he saith that " the kingdom of God is not meat and drink ", that is, the doctrine concerning it does not teach believers to concern themselves about distinctions of meats and drinks, saying, " touch not, taste not, handle not " ; but it inculcates and develops in them who embrace it with honest and good hearts, righteousness and peace, and joy in a holy spirit. This fruit of faith is the " *Divine Nature* ", and essentially diverse from the nature common to pagans and all others ignorant of the truth. It is only produceable by " the exceeding great and precious promises believed ". Belief that Jesus is the Son of God, in the modern Gentile sense, neither hath nor will produce it. The fruit of this believed is not righteousness, peace, and joy in a holy spirit ; but, on the contrary, resistance to the righteousness of God, doubts and fears, and despondency in a faithless, perverse, and sordid spirit. " By their fruits ye shall know them."

Having indoctrinated the Macedonians in Thessalonica with the glad tidings he announced to them, in writing to them he informs the reader that they " received the word with joy of a holy spirit " ; and that in consequence they " turned to God from idols to serve the living and true God ; and to wait for his Son from the heavens, whom he raised from among the dead, even Jesus delivering us from the wrath to come ". Before Paul went over to help them, they knew nothing about the God, and the Son of the God, whom Paul preached ; they knew not that there was any wrath to come upon the world, nor of any deliverance from it through a resurrected man, coming from the heavens ; nor did they know that those delivered from it would share in the glory and dominion of the Deliverer. Will any reasonable man, then, pretend to impose upon us the notion that all that was submitted to these " untaught Gentiles ", to turn them from their vanities, was that a certain Jew, who had been crucified as a malefactor about 1,100 miles off, was the son of the God of the Jews, and raised from the dead by His power ? What moral power is there in such a statement as this to cause a Macedonian idolater to cast his idols to the moles and the bats ? None. It had no more power to produce this result than it now has to cause papists to turn from their image worship, and the adoration of dead men's bones ; or sectarian devotees to renounce the systems of foolishness and impiety they profess. It is evident from the nature of the case that the first thing Paul essayed to do was to reason the Macedonians out of their idolatry, as he did the Athenians ; then to acquaint them with the living and true God ; after that to announce to them *the purpose of God*, or " secret of his will which he had purposed in himself according to his own good pleasure " ; then, that " one Jesus " was he by whom he intended to execute that purpose, whereof he had given assurance in raising him from the dead ; that he was to return from the heavens to perform the work assigned to him ; and lastly, that whosoever believed these things, and became obedient, should receive repentance and forgiveness of sins, and a right to eternal glory in the kingdom, " *through his name* ". To instruct them in these things was for Paul to fulfil his mission, which was " to open their eyes, to turn them from darkness to light, and from the power of Satan unto God, that they might receive forgiveness of sins, and inheritance among them (of Judah) who are sanctified by faith that leads into Jesus ". The Macedonians were in darkness, and in Satan's power, and unable to help themselves. They were " Gentiles in the flesh ", whose moral destitution is well described by the apostle who went over to help them. "At that time ", says he, " ye were without Christ, being aliens from the Commonwealth of Israel, and strangers from the covenants of the promise, having no hope, and atheists (*atheoi*) in the world " ; " walking in the vanity of your mind, having the understanding darkened, being alienated from the life of God through the ignorance that was in you, because of the blindness of your heart ". But from this state they were happily delivered by Paul's preaching ; so that he could say to them, " Ye who were formerly afar off are now *in* the anointed Jesus, made nigh by the blood of the anointed one ". They were " *made nigh* " by the blood of the anointed one ; that is, instead of being " aliens from Israel's commonwealth, and strangers from the covenants of the promise ", they had become " fellow-citizens of the saints (of Israel) and of the household of God " ; instead of " having no hope ", they hoped in the kingdom and glory of God, of which they were invited to become " HEIRS " by the preaching of Paul ; and instead of being " without Christ ", and " atheists ", they were " IN the anointed Jesus ", and worshippers of his Father, the God of the Jews, for the return of whose Son from the heavens they were patiently waiting (2 Thess. 3 : 5). These originally " untaught ", but now instructed, " Gentiles " had become " light in the Lord " ; " the sons of God without rebuke, shining as lights in the world " ; " children of light and of the day ", and " not of the night, nor of darkness " (1 Thes. 5 : 5) ; invested with " the armour of light " ; so that, " the eyes of their understanding being enlightened ", the apostle could now say to them, " Ye are all the sons of God in the anointed Jesus through the faith ; because as many as are baptized into the Anointed have put on the Anointed ; and if ye be the Anointed's then are ye Abraham's seed, and heirs according to the promise ".

What soul-stirring tidings must they have been which constituted the subject matter of Paul's preaching, and that could have effected so wonderful a change on the understandings, affections, and conduct of the idolaters of Macedonia Prima, and of " untaught Gentiles " in sundry other places ! In what did the power of his preaching consist ? In the teaching of God, called " the truth in Jesus "—" *the light of the glad tidings of the glory of the Anointed,* who is the image of God ". " Of his own will ", says James, " the Father of lights begat us by the word of truth, that we should be a kind of firstfruits of his creatures ", of whom " it is written in the prophets, They shall be all taught of God. Every man, therefore, that hath *heard* and *learned* of the Father ", says Jesus, " cometh unto me ". Paul, as God's messenger, taught the word of God, which he did not handle deceitfully ; " but by manifestation of the truth, commended himself to every man's conscience in the sight of God " (2 Cor. 4 : 2-4). This was the secret of his power—his doctrine was God's teaching, confirmed by God's power, through the mighty deeds with which he astonished the world. Who need wonder at the results with such an instrumentality ? " We ", said Paul, " are ambassadors in the Anointed's stead, as if God did invite you by us " ; which invitation was expressed in the glad tidings of the kingdom and glory he preached. The joyous character of the tidings miraculously confirmed, commended them to the hearts of the people, and kindled a joyousness in them, that energized them to accept the divine invitation in the face of ruin, imprisonment, torture, and death ; so that, in writing to the Macedonians, he says, " Ye became followers of us and of the Lord, having received *the word* in much affliction with joy of a holy spirit ".

But in opening the eyes of Macedonian Jews his method was somewhat different. He had not to turn them from idols, nor to bring them to wait for the Son of Israel's God : nor yet to instruct them in the purpose of God to rule the habitable in righteousness by him, for they were not idolaters ; and they were waiting for the appearing of the Son promised them in Isa. 9 : 6, 7 ; and were fully in the belief of his sitting upon the throne of his father David, and reigning over Israel and the nations for ever. All that was necessary in their case was to convince them that Jesus was that Son of David and of God, Jehovah had covenanted to resurrect for them in the house of David (1 Chron. 17 : 11-14 ; Acts 2 : 30 ; 1 Cor. 3 : 4, 5). Thus, in his preaching to " the Jews he became as a Jew, that he might gain the Jews " ; in other words, " to them that are under the law, he became as under the law, that he might gain them that are under the law ". If he had gone to the Macedonian idolaters " as a Jew ", he would not have gained them ; he therefore went to them as a Roman, which is evident from his reply to the magistrates at Philippi, saying, " They have beaten us openly uncondemned, being Romans, and have cast us into prison, and now do they thrust us out privily ? Nay, verily ; but let them come themselves and fetch us out ". Now, Romans were not under the Law of Moses ; so that in relation to that law they were " without law " ; therefore in approaching the Romans as a Roman citizen, he says that " to them without law, he became as without law, that he might gain them that are without law ". He addressed the Greeks, Romans and barbarians, as an ambassador, sent to them direct from a God whom they knew not, but who had made the universe, and continued to uphold all things by His power. It was not necessary for such a person to do more before such an audience, ignorant of all things pertaining to the God, prophets, and hope of the Jews, than to state the truth confirmed by divine power, and to persuade them to receive it. Thus, as he says, " My word and my preaching was by indubitable proof of Spirit and power, that your faith might not stand in men's wisdom, but in God's power ". And again, " Our glad tidings came not to you *in word only*, but also in power, and in holy spirit, and in much assurance ". This course, however, would not answer with believers in the prophets. He could not approach Jews as a Gentile citizen of Rome, and expect them to believe on authority without appeal to the prophets. Idolaters might be built upon apostles, but a Jew required to be built upon the prophets ; for they would receive no testimony of apostles, though confirmed by miracle, unless it could be shown to be in accordance with the Oracles of God, read in their synagogues every sabbath day. When, therefore, idolaters built upon the apostles, testifying the same things as the prophets, and Jews built upon the prophets illustrated by the apostles, came together into the " one body ", Paul could say to them, " Ye are built upon the foundation of the apostles and prophets, Jesus the Anointed himself being the chief corner stone ". They were all, both Jews and Gentiles, brought to acquiesce joyously in the " One Faith " ; the *method* only of bringing them to that acquiescence so as to prepare them for the " One Baptism ", differed.

The reader, then, will readily perceive that the apostolic preaching was very much simplified in regard to the Jews. All that was necessary was to show them what their prophets taught, and then to prove that to a certain extent their predictions were accomplished in Jesus, as an earnest that what remained would be fulfilled in and by him likewise. This was the course pursued by Paul in Thessalonica. He went into their synagogue, and reasoned with them out of the Scriptures of the prophets, opening and alleging, *firstly*, that the Messiah they were looking for must needs have suffered, and *secondly*, that he must needs stand up from among the dead. These were among the *first things* (*en prōtois*, 1 Cor. 15 : 3) he delivered to the Jews ; how that their Messiah was to die for their sins, according to the prophets ; be buried, or "make his grave with the wicked, and with the rich in his death ", and arise on the third day, according to the scriptures. If he could convince them of these things, their minds were then prepared for his *third* proposition, which was, " that this is the Messiah, even Jesus, whom I announce to you ".

They err greatly who imagine that one method of preaching " the glad tidings of the glory of Christ " would have been suitable for idol-worshippers, and the members of the synagogue. The proposition that " Jesus is the Anointed, the Son of the living God ", would have been meaningless and unintelligible to idolaters. To have comprehended it they must have been made previously acquainted with the existence of that living

God, and with the doctrine concerning the Anointed One. And this the apostle set himself to do in laying before them the glad tidings of the kingdom, as exhibited in the revelation of His will, which God had purposed to Himself. When they came to understand this part of the subject, they would very naturally desire to know, *Who should be the King by whom the world should be ruled in righteousness, when the appointed time for the manifestation of the divine purpose should arrive?* Paul told them that it was a certain Jew, named Jesus, who was dead, but came to life again, and is alive for evermore, who is to be king of the whole earth. This answer to the question very naturally prompted another, namely, " *If the Jesus he proclaimed were to be king of all nations, what would become of Caesar's throne?* " Nor did Paul hesitate to answer this inquiry, as we have seen in the second epistle to the Macedonians of Thessalonica. " He shall be taken out of the way ", and then a power, embodying the Mystery of Iniquity already working, shall take his place, which shall also be utterly abolished by the manifestation of the Lord's presence from the heavens. Such questions and answers as these created a great stir among the multitude, many of whom renounced their idols, and declared themselves, not only willing, but earnestly desirous to become heirs of that kingdom and glory, that they might reign with Jesus when he should receive the dominion, glory, and kingdom at his return from the right hand of power. But the Jews who rejected the claims of Jesus to the Davidian throne of universal empire on earth were moved with envy at this revolution in the pagan mind, and determined to put a stop to it, if possible. They excited the lowest of the people against Paul and his friends, both in Thessalonica and Berea. As Paul was preaching politics, which had been forbidden by the emperor, they assailed him as a transgressor of the imperial decrees, saying, that *there is another king than Caesar, one Jesus.* The same outcry was raised in Philippi with the same result— proclaiming principles unlawful for loyal Romans to receive and do, and thereby exceedingly troubling the cities of Macedonia Prima.

Philippi, Thessalonica, Berea, etc., were *thrown into an uproar by Paul's preaching the glad tidings of the glory and kingdom of God.* Let not this fact be overlooked. Was it done by a sixty minutes' discourse, the burden of which was that Jesus, whom perhaps no Macedonian pagan had ever heard of before, was the Son of the unknown God of the despised Jews, and sacrificed for sin ? What would they have thought of the doctrine that the blood of a murdered Jew, in some mysterious way, was to save them from wrath to come, of which they knew nothing ? Instead of such preaching as this (of which the world has a surfeiting in these superficial times) exceedingly troubling cities, and turning the community upside down, the apostles would not have obtained a second hearing. No ; they might have preached the divine sonship of Jesus *in the modern Gentile sense of it*, not for an hour only, but until this day, and have never made a Christian, or agitated a single family, That Jesus is the Son of the God of Israel, and not the Son of Mary's husband, is most true, and a very important truth in its proper place ; it is a genealogical truth upon which all his claims are founded ; but in the Gentile sense of it, there is no good news in it. His blood cleansed from all sin ; true, but what then ? If that be all it leaves without hope, and the future is a blank. Such a Gospel never came from heaven to Jew, Macedonian, or Italian, or to any other Gentile family of man.

Paul's preaching was the same in all the cities of Macedonia. It planted the same hope in the hearts of the people at Philippi, as at Thessalonica. Here, it taught them to turn from idols to serve the God of Israel, and to wait for His Son from the heavens, when they should receive the kingdom of God, for which they suffered persecution ; there, it taught them to be like-minded with the apostle in pressing toward the mark for the prize of the high calling of God by the anointed Jesus (2 Thess. 1 : 5). This " mark " was the resurrection that Paul desired by any means to attain to, because the prize could not be obtained until that mark were reached. The prize was the subject of the glad tidings he preached to them. It was for the obtaining of this prize that they entered the lists by being baptized, that they might from that time start in the race, and press onward to the goal. Did they begin to run without knowing what they were running for ? No indeed. When men, as in Paul's day, entered upon a race which exposed to torment, imprisonment, and death, they were very careful to know what they were to gain by the risks they encountered. " I so run, not as uncertainly ", saith the apostle ; " so run, that ye may obtain " ; obtain what ? That which God sent Jesus to invite men to in the glad tidings of the kingdom which he preached, and therefore styled " the high calling of God by the anointed Jesus ".

An everlasting kingdom is the prize set before us as " untaught Gentiles ", connected with which are glory, honour, riches, and life eternal. Hence, James says to them who are taught of God, " he has chosen the poor of this world, rich in faith, as heirs of the kingdom which he has promised to them that love him " ; and Jesus saith, " Fear not, little flock, it is your Father's good pleasure to give you the kingdom ", and when they that love him stand in his presence after rising from the dead, he saith to them, " Come, ye blessed of my Father, possess the kingdom prepared for you from the foundation of the world ". Were these blessed ones baptized in ignorance of the kingdom and glory they were called to ? In darkness plunged into water, not dreaming that the God of Israel purposed to set up a glorious kingdom in Palestine for Jesus and his brethren, which was to rule over all ? Was their faith so meagre, so death-stricken in its birth, that it could only faintly whisper an assent to a leading question about the genealogy of Jesus, before they descended into water ? Were their eyes so blind that they could see nothing in the future ? No, no ; before they were baptized they took care to know what they were baptized for. *They were baptized that they might become Abraham's seed, and heirs according to the promise, which they understood and believed with joyous and faithful hearts.* Hence, the apostle could write to the Roman citizens of Philippi, who believed, and the jailer and his house among their number, saying, " Brethren, be followers together of me, and mark them who walk, so as ye have Paul and Timotheus, servants of Jesus Christ, for an example, for our citizenship begins in the heavens ; out of which also we earnestly expect the Saviour, the anointed Lord Jesus ; who shall transform the body of our humiliation, that it may be conformed to the body of his glory, through the power whereby he is able to subdue all things to himself ". And afterwards he adds, " Those things which ye have both learned, and received, and heard, and seen with me, do ". This covered the whole ground of his teaching, which was effective to their illumination as lights in the midst of a crooked and perverse nation.

19

BAPTISM OF SPIRIT

(i) *IN APOSTOLIC TIMES*

BAPTISM of spirit, in all the subjects of it, was known to all observers *by the effects produced*. There could be no mistake in this. A Christian who said, " I have been baptized with spirit ", could prove his assertion to the conviction of all reasonable persons. He never undertook to prove such a baptism by an appeal to his own feelings ; for what he might feel in himself was no demonstration to his contemporaries. Baptism of spirit was an inpouring of power until the believer's vessel was filled. Being full of power, " *powers* " were manifested, which Paul styles " the powers of the *future course* ", or *Mellontos aiōnos*, termed in the Common Version, " the world to come " (Heb. 6 : 5), and of which he says in the same place, his brethren had " tasted ". These spirit-baptismal effects are also by him styled " powers ", *dunameis*, in 1 Cor. 12 : 29, but here rather restricted to a particular class of manifestations.

The Hebrew brethren were said to have " tasted of the powers of the future course of things ", or AIŌN, in possessing spirit-gifts, because when that course of things, commonly called the Millennium, or Age to Come, should be introduced, they would possess the same powers, but without limitation ; not that they will exercise them without limitation, but that they will possess the ability so to do. In the apostolic age they tasted of the powers, but in the future they will drink in a full draught of spirit-power. " Be not drunk with wine ; but be filled with spirit." Though they might be filled to overflowing, the fullness would be but a taste of the powers of the coming AIŌN. Their vessels, like ours, were but earthen, and of limited capacity ; but in the future Aiōn of a thousand years, the bodies of the saints will be consubstantial and conformed to that of Christ's ; and therefore of vastly greater capacity and susceptibility of manifestation and enjoyment than the " vile bodies " they now possess. The nature of the body through which the powers are displayed makes the great difference between the tasting and the fullness, when the Deity shall be " the all things in all "—*ta panta en pasin*. " Now, concerning spirit gifts (*pneumatika*), brethren, I would not that ye be ignorant." Thus speaks Paul in 1 Cor. 12 : 1. By *pneumatika* he means spirit manifestations resulting from the working of God's power in those who confess the lordship of Jesus consequent upon their understanding and belief of the divine testimony concerning him. These spirit-manifestations, given to the intelligent and obedient in Paul's day, in 1 Cor. 14 : 12, he terms *pneumata* or *spirits*. He did not wish the brethren in Corinth to be ignorant concerning spirits, which were not the ghosts of dead men, women and babes, as the heathen around us imagine in the blindness of their heart ; not many separate and independent disembodied " immortal souls " of a " spirit world " ; but a diverse operation and manifold manifestation of one and the same deity by His own abstract and independent power. The " spirits " were spirit-powers radiated from the divine presence into the saints, who were thereby enabled to do wonders, and signs, and powers, according to the will of the Deity. Every wonder, every sign, every power, was a spirit, visible to all who beheld the extraordinary phenomena. They did not mutter, and rap, or move tables ; nor did they give forth dubious and lying oracles through unclean and ignorant pretenders ; they uttered divine wisdom and knowledge, which was in harmony with what the Deity had moved holy men of old to write in " the law and the prophets " thousands of years before. They raised the dead, discerned spirits, spoke the languages of men intuitively, and interpreted them intelligibly. All these spirits worked that one and the self-same spirit, dividing to every believer severally as he willed (1 Cor. 12 : 2).

There were some in Paul's day, as in ours, who pretended to speak by the spirit of the Deity, yet did not possess it. Because of this pretence, the Apostle John exhorted the brethren, saying : " Beloved, believe not every spirit (or manifestation), but try the spirits, whether they be of God " (1 John 4 : 1). This was addressed to those of the saints who possessed " the spirit " called " discerning of spirits ", which was common to all the presbyteries, or elderships, of the flock. All the apostles had this gift, so that it was not possible to impose spurious, or counterfeit spirits upon them. Being thus qualified they were competent to give their brethren a rule by which they might distinguish the true from the false. There were some spirits in their day who taught false doctrines in the name of Christ. The same class of spirits exists now ; only that, whereas they were in the minority in apostolic times, they are now almost universal, nearly to the entire suppression of the true. These " spirits " are styled by John " false prophets ", because their teaching was false and subversive " of the truth as it is in Jesus ". Hence, every teacher, or one who does not teach the truth, is one of these spirits, no matter what age or generation, name or denomination, he may belong to. Nor is it difficult to discern these spirits by the apostolic rule. *All spirits are of the world, which are inspired of the world, and which the world gives heed to and glorifies.* This is an infallible rule, and demonstrates that the clergy, ministers, parsons, or preachers (it matters not by what name the spirits are called), are all false prophets or spirits . . .

The apostles used to say of themselves, " *We are of God* ". And this was a true testimony : for Jesus said to them, " It shall be given you what ye shall speak. For it is not ye that speak, but the spirit of your Father which speaketh in you ". Well might he say, therefore, " He that heareth you heareth me ; and he that despiseth me, despiseth Him that sent me ". The apostle John was therefore perfectly justified in saying, " He that knoweth God heareth us ; he that is not of God heareth not us ". Do the spirits of Rome, Wittenberg, Geneva, Oxford, Bethany, etc., hear the apostles, or do they not ? No intelligent believer of the truth can honestly affirm that they do. There is but one thing such can truly affirm, and that is, that they do not give heed to the teaching of the apostles. They are then false prophets or spirits ; and all their pretensions to holy spirit, to baptism of spirit other than the spirit of the flesh, to getting religion by the operation of the spirit of God, and so forth, is mere twaddle and blasphemy ; false and only false, and that continually. This hearing of the apostles is an unerring rule for the " discerning of spirits ". A man may be as pious as the pagan Aeneas ; or as devout as a Turk who prays to Allah five times a day ; or as earnest as the Jews who had " a zeal of God, but not according to knowledge "—he may be all this, and as well skilled in Plato as Dr. Lewis ; and as holy toned and grimacious as a pulpitarian—it matters not ; all this goes for vanity and vexation of spirit ; he is a false spirit if he believe not the teachings of the apostles ; if he be not mindful of the words spoken before by the holy prophets, and of the commandment of the apostles of the Lord and Saviour (2 Peter 3 : 2). " Hereby know we ", saith John, " the spirit of truth, and the spirit of error."

Having, then, obtained a divine rule, and therefore an infallible one, by which to discern spirits, we are not to be imposed upon by pretenders to spirit, and what they call baptism of spirit. They know nothing correctly about the subject, because they do not give heed to the apostolic teaching. They only tasted of the powers of the future course of things who had been guided into the truth ; and so now, if any man say he hath the spirit in its powers or manifestations ; or that he has been converted or born of the spirit ; try him by conversing with him about what the apostles taught for faith and practice ; and if you find that he is ignorant, you may then certainly know that he is an impostor, deceiving or deceived, or both ; he is a false spirit, having never drunk into the spirit of God. A man truly and scripturally enlightened would never claim to be baptized of spirit in the dry time that intervenes between the early and latter rains. He claims only to have been begotten of the truth which is spirit, not to be indued with any of its baptismal powers.

" Spirits ", then, is a word apostolically used to designate the gifts of the spirit of God : and those who undertook to teach by the spirit. Of the former, there were " diversities ", and of the latter, two classes. The diversities in the aggregate made up the baptism of holy spirit, which was given for administrations and operations. These exhibitions of power were styled collectively " The manifestation of the Spirit ". The powers were not given to any one for his own private benefit, but for the general use and benefit of the Body of Christ ; as it is written, " to every one is given the manifestation of the Spirit for the collective good "—*pros to sympheron*. This is an important feature in the case. People who pretend to be the subjects of spirit baptism can adduce nothing else but their feelings which all terminate in themselves. No one is profited by any thing they pretend to have received. Not a single scriptural idea do they possess more than before their pretended baptism ; nor have they a single power they had not before. They are as ignorant and perverse as ever, and as hostile to the truth when laid before them as pagans. Not so with the apostolic believer. When he was baptized with holy spirit, he acquired wisdom and knowledge which was advantageous to all who lacked them ; he had the gift of faith by which he could remove mountains, if the good of the body collectively required it ; he could heal the sick ; inwork powers ; speak to the brethren to edification, exhortation, and comfort, no mean accomplishment in an apostolic community. He could discern spirits, and so protect and warn the unlearned against the imposition of the false apostles that would certainly arise. He could speak the languages of the nations without previous study, and in them make known the wonderful works of the Deity : all these things the spiritually baptized could do for the benefit of those who were not so baptized, and of the Jews and heathen round about. Such a baptism as this nowhere exists upon earth in these times ; yet every congregation of believers could glory in such an indwelling of the Deity among them by His Spirit in the days of Paul (Eph. 2 : 22). The want of this baptism is practically acknowledged by all " the names and denominations ".

In the days of the apostles, the belief and obedience of the truth simply, constituted believers " saints " ; but did not perfect them " for the edifying of the Body of Christ ". The saints in general " occupied the room of the private *idiōtou* " (1 Cor. 14 : 16) ; until certain of them came to occupy the room of the public men by the gift of holy spirit. This division of class resulted from baptism of spirit, which all were not permitted to receive . . .

The case of the Samaritan brethren (Acts 8 : 14-24) clearly shows the prerequisites to a baptism of spirit in all cases save that of the apostles and the house of Cornelius. Before receiving the spirit it was necessary for the candidate

1.—To believe the things of the kingdom of God, and the name of Jesus Christ (Acts 8 : 12) ;

2.—To be buried with Christ by baptism into death (*ibid*) ; and,

3.—That the Apostles, or some inworker of powers like them, pray for the believer that he may receive it, and lay their hands on them (verses 15, 17 ; 1 Tim. 4 : 14 ; 5 : 22 ; 2 Tim. 1 : 6).

On the day of Pentecost the gift of holy spirit was promised to those who were added to the name of Jesus Christ by baptism. As they were about to return to remote places, where they would carry the gospel to Israel there, it is probable all the visitors to Jerusalem so returning would receive it, that through them God might confirm the word when they preached it. But though promised to all such, the cases of the seven chosen to serve tables (Acts 6 : 7) ; of the Samaritans ; of Saul (Acts 9 : 17) ; and of the twelve at Ephesus (Acts 19 : 6), show that the divine appointment for imparting the spirit was prayer and the imposition of the hands of the Apostles, or of a presbytery of inspired men, or of an inspired individual believer, as Timothy. These elements of the appointment do not now exist among men. We have no apostles but false ones ; and all the presbyteries, or leaderships, are uninspired ; and there is no individual on earth the imposition of whose hands is of any value in the premises. A man must be a saint, and must have the gifts with himself before he can impart them ; and then even if he had gifts, if among them he was deficient of the " *inworking of powers* ", he could not transmit what he possessed to others. Philip could expel unclean spirits, and heal the palsied and the lame ; but he could not impart spirit-gifts to the baptized. The apostles had to be sent for to accomplish this.

Baptism of spirit, then, was only partially bestowed even upon the saints in the apostolic age. It was an outpouring of divine power upon certain of the saints having natural and moral qualifications fitting them for the administrative use of it. They were not only to be " faithful men ", but " apt to teach ", " able to teach others ", " holding firmly according to the teaching of the faithful word, that by sound instruction they might be able both to exhort and to convince opponents " ; and good rulers of their own houses (1 Tim. 3 : 2, 4 ; 2 Tim. 2 : 1 ; Titus 1 : 9). Having these and certain other qualifications, they were considered eligible for baptism of spirit by prayer and imposition of hands. They must be saints first ; for no apostle nor presbytery, nor inworker of powers, would lay hands upon sinners to impart divine power to them " for the work of the ministry ". When the Laodicean Apostasy which now fills all " Christendom ", as the heathen call their Babylonish system, came to be established, sinners laid hands upon sinners, as at this day, but notwithstanding all their prayers for the gifts and graces of the spirit, no other spirit comes into manifestation but " the spirit of error " which strongly works in all " the children of disobedience "—the spirit of their own nature, " sin's flesh ", in which " dwells no good thing " . . .

Saints, and saints only whose hearts have been prepared by faith, are eligible to the baptism of spirit. Christ ascended to the right hand of power that he might receive the gifts for his own brethren to whom alone he promised them. Paul, addressing the saints thus spiritually endowed, says concerning the gifts, " Unto every one of us is given the grace according to the measure of the gift of Christ " ; the grace which John says came by Jesus Christ : " The law was given through Moses, the grace and the truth came through Jesus Christ ". In Paul's quotation from the sixty-eighth Psalm, he shows that by " *grace* " he has reference to the *gifts* of the spirit ; for in the next sentence to that above quoted, he says, " Wherefore he saith, Ascending into heaven he led captive captivity, and bestowed gifts upon men ". He then indicates the " grace " or gifts bestowed by designating the saints who had received them by the official names they then bore (Eph. 4 : 7-12). He styled these saints apostles, prophets, evangelists, pastors, and teachers ; and referring to these well known *spiritual*, or spiritually endowed official brethren, found in all the assemblies of the saints, he says that the ascended and glorified Jesus " gave indeed the apostles, and the prophets, and the evangelists and the pastors and teachers " ; that is, he gave to these who were first saints, the gifts he had received from the Father on his ascension to glory, called in Acts 1 : 4, " the promise of the Father ", which he had said he would send the apostles while they waited for it in Jerusalem (verse 5 ; John 16 : 7)—he gave these gifts, I say, to qualify them for apostles, prophets, evangelists, pastors and teachers. Now, were all apostles, prophets, evangelists, pastors, and teachers ? Did all the saints sustain these offices in the body of Christ ? No person intelligent in the word will affirm that they did. It is then certain that all the saints were not baptized with holy spirit ; for Paul teaches that the grace was given " for the perfecting of the saints for a work of service for a building of the body of the Christ ". The saints thus qualified were the builders Paul refers to in 1 Cor. 3 : 10. In this place he styles himself " a wise architect ", who had laid the foundation for an edifice upon which others were building ; to whom he saith, " Let every one take heed how he buildeth thereon ". The saints in the aggregate were the building—the temple built for the Deity to dwell in through or by the spirit. The spirituals among the saints were the builders of this holy temple ; nevertheless the temple was " a building of God ", " a house not made with hands ", because all the power of these spirituals for the work of building was from the Deity, and consisted in the truth they taught which was from God, and which He confirmed through the gifts He had bestowed upon them ; so that they " were labourers together with God ".

We may remark here by the way that the holy temple these co labourers with the Deity were engaged in building in the apostolic age, has its holy and its most holy, after the pattern of the Tabernacle in the wilderness, which was " a house made with hands ". The building of " *the holy* " resulted in the Body of Christ as manifested in Paul's day. This was " *the heavenly* " constituted of the holy ones, or saints, collectively. But " *the most holy* " is not yet manifested, nor will it be until the apocalypse of Jesus Christ in his glory. This most holy is " a house not made with hands, *aiōnion* in the heavens ". *Aiōnion*, that is, *belonging to the course* to which the things which are not seen pertain. When this house is built (and the builder of all things is God), it will be constituted of those saints only who in the " present evil world " walk in the truth. Those saints, who since they became saints, " walk after the flesh ", will be purged out of the flock, and will never be reckoned among " the most holy ". Concerning these the apostle says, " If ye walk after the flesh ye shall die ". This is the death they shall be subject to after their resurrection. They shall die out from among the most holy, and be swallowed up of mortality, being found naked. These are " the wood, hay, and stubble", which builders even in Paul's day built upon the foundation he had laid. The saints who shall constitute the most holy are " the gold and silver and the precious stones " of Zion, who, when the kingdom comes to her, shall be her foundations, windows, and borders (Isa. 54 : 11-13 ; Micah 4 : 8). The present house not made with hands is a mingled people, in which the faithful " groan being burdened ; not for that they would be unclothed ", or reduced to dust and ashes ; " but clothed upon that mortality might be swallowed up of life ".

But " the Day shall declare it " : the day when the manifestation of the work of the builders shall be made. " The spirits of the prophets were subject to the prophets " (1 Cor. 14 : 32). That is, the gifts called " spirits " could be used or abused by those on whom they were bestowed. If they were abused, or misused, in disorder and the confirmation of error, the Holy Spirit would be grieved. Therefore, because of this property, Paul exhorted the spirituals, saying, " Grieve not the Holy Spirit of the Deity by which ye are sealed for a day of redemption " (Eph. 4 : 30). But some did greatly grieve it, and went out from the apostolic community, and became " false prophets " or spirits. These became builders of wood, hay, and stubble upon the foundation ; while other builders, whose teaching was scriptural, sometimes unwillingly placed on the foundation " false brethren ", who " crept in at unawares ". All this building work is unprofitable for the Master's use, who, when the day of declaration shall arrive, will be " as a refiner's fire and like fuller's soap " ; for the prophet saith, " He shall sit as a refiner and purifier of silver . . . But who may abide the day of his coming ? And who shall stand when he appeareth ? " This day, now near at hand, will declare the work of all ; because it shall be revealed by fire, and the fire shall try every one's work of what sort it is. " If any one's work abide which he hath built thereupon, he shall receive a reward. If any one's work shall be burned, he shall suffer loss ; but he himself shall be saved ; yet so as by fire." Builders and the built will all be subjected to the fiery ordeal of the Divine scrutiny ; and those only who can stand the searching examination will be saved. If a spiritual, or teacher endowed with the gifts, have built a thousand upon the foundation, and seven hundred and fifty of them turn out to be mere wood, hay, and stubble, he will only receive a reward for the two hundred and fifty jewels fit for the Master's use in the most holy " *in the heavens* " of the Millennial Age. This loss of his work, however, will not affect his salvation, if he be found to have held fast the name and not to have denied the faith of Jesus ; holding on to the truth, and walking in it, in the love of it. " He shall be saved, yet so as by fire."

(ii) *IN THE RESURRECTION ERA*

" The grace " designed for the saints, and purposed to come through Jesus Christ, was not intended to be revealed all at one time. The grace, or gift of holy spirit, was to be rained upon the saints at two different periods. The spirit in Joel shows this. " Be glad ", saith he, " ye children of Zion, and rejoice in Yahweh your Elohim ; for he hath given you the former rain moderately, and he will cause to come down for you the rain, the former rain, and the latter rain in the first month " (Joel 2 : 23). The original of this text is quite remarkable. The Hebrew reads, " For he hath given to you the Teacher of Righteousness, and he shall cause to descend for you a rain ; a teacher and a latter rain in the first month ". This teacher hath been given in the person of Jesus ; and the Father who gave him caused to descend upon the children of Zion, the saints, " a rain " when on Pentecost He poured out His spirit upon the apostles and their brethren. This as the substitute for Jesus guided them into all the truth, and showed them things to come. Christ is " the Lord the Spirit ", " a quickening spirit " ; and from him Holy spirit-rain came in the third month, or fifty days after the passover and cruci-fixion. But there is to be " a teacher and a latter rain in the first month ". That is in the month Nisan, or when the passover shall be fulfilled in the kingdom of God (Ezek. 45 : 21 ; Luke 22 : 15-18). The result of the appearing of this teacher in the time of the latter rain will be that the sons of Zion will " eat in plenty and be satisfied, and praise the name of Yahweh your Elohim that hath dealt wondrously with them ; and *his people shall never be ashamed*. And they shall know that I am in the midst of Israel ; and that I "—the Spirit made flesh, and glorified, and so both Lord and Christ personal and mystical—" am Yahweh your Elohim, and none else ; and *my people shall never be ashamed* " (Joel 2 : 26). But the people of Yahweh, political and spiritual, are now put to shame. Israel after the flesh is a by-word and a proverb ; and so is Israel after the spirit, or the saints, who have been, are, and will be prevailed against by the enemy until the Ancient of Days shall be revealed in power and great glory. Joel's prediction, then, has not been yet fulfilled, and the latter rain of spirit in the first month is yet in future.

Now when it shall have come to pass that Israel and the saints are no more put to shame by their enemies, " the latter rain in the first month " will descend. For immediately after predicting that His people shall never be put to shame, the Spirit in Joel saith, " and it shall come to pass *afterward* I will pour out my spirit upon all flesh ". Peter referred to this prophecy of the baptism of spirit and said of the out-pouring on Pentecost, " This is that which was spoken by the Prophet Joel ". It was " the *earnest* of the spirit ", not the full measure of it ; " the *earnest* of the inheritance ", not the inheritance itself. Thus Paul saith to the spirituals, " He that hath anointed us (or christened us with spirit) is the Deity, who hath also sealed us and given the earnest of the spirit in our hearts " (2 Cor. 1 : 21) ; and again, " In Christ also after that ye believed, ye were sealed with that holy spirit of promise, which is the earnest of our inheritance for a redemption of the purchased possession unto the praise of his glory " (Eph. 1 : 13). The remarks of Peter by no means limited Joel's prophecy to the third month of the year of the ascension of Jesus. Peter referred more especially to the Teacher or the Comforter, not to " the latter rain in the first month ". Joel's prophecy covers the whole ground in saying " he will cause to come down for you a rain " ; not a continuing rain for eighteen hundred or more years from the descent on Pentecost to the second advent of Christ, but a copious shower in the Apostolic age, followed by a long, dry time in which everything is parched up : and then, when this drought shall end, the " latter rain in the first month ".

The spirit-rain of the Pentecostian era was bestowed upon certain of the saints to qualify them officially, that they might exercise the gifts for the public benefit—" for the building up of the body of the Christ ". Paul tells us how long this arrangement was to continue. " Till ", says he, " we shall come into the unity of the faith and of the knowledge of the Son of God— into a perfect man ; into a measure of the stature of the fulness of the Christ." This limits the gifts to the above apostolic saints ; that is to those contemporary with the apostles, but who may have nevertheless outlived them many years. He testifies to this effect very plainly in 1 Cor. 13 : 8, where he speaks of the cessation of the baptismal gifts of prophesying, of tongues, and of the word of knowledge ; " Prophecies ", says he, " shall be brought to an end ; tongues shall be caused to cease ; knowledge shall pass away ". This was finally accomplished when the spirit spued the Laodicean community out of his mouth. The spirit-baptism was withheld because its gifts were abused, as every other good has been that has been committed to the guardianship of flesh and blood.

The body of Christ, whether considered under the figure of a man or a house, belongs to two states ; to that before the resurrection, and to that after it. In its former state it has its infancy and manhood. In the days of the apostles the institution was in its infancy, childhood, and, in the time of John's old age and exile, manhood, being three score years and ten. During these years its administrations were in part, that part consisting of apostles, prophets, evangelists, pastors and teachers ; so that the knowledge and the prophesyings were in part and not distributed to every member of the body. But in process of time that perfection came by which the body could sustain itself without baptismal gifts ; and then " that which was in part was done away ". The manifestation of the spirit being withheld, all that remained to the body was " faith,

hope, and love ; these three ; the greatest of which is love ",
as defined by Paul in 1 Cor. 13 : 4-7. There was a manhood
when the baptismal gifts ceased ; and there shall be a manhood
when we shall know experimentally even as we have known
theoretically. This is the post-resurrectional maturity of the
" perfect man ", or body of Christ, every member of which
will see " face to face ". That which is perfect will have come
in the full sense ; and the members of the body will be none of
them any more " children tossed to and fro, and carried about
with every wind of doctrine, by the sleight of men and cunning
craftiness, whereby they lie in wait to deceive ". They will
all then be baptismally imbued with " the latter rain in the
first month ". They will be spirit, and filled with spirit—a
God-manifestation of eternal power ; and thus they will have
" grown up into him in all things, who is the Head, even unto
the Christ ".

The baptism of the Spirit, then, is peculiar to certain
seasons or epochs, and not common to all times from the first
to the second advent. These epochs are :

1.—The apostolic age ;

2.—The resurrection era.

Between these two periods is a long interval occupied
by " the times of the Gentiles ", during which the Laodicean
Apostasy prevails to the almost entire suppression of " the
faith ". These constitute a DRY TIME—a time of drought,
in which spirit is withheld. In all this long series of ages and
generations there are no gifts and no other baptism than that
of water. The gifts answered their purpose, and then ceased ;
and nothing remained but " faith, hope, and love ", the
product of the word read and studied by the honest and good-
hearted. Baptism of spirit was for confirmation of the word
preached by the apostles ; and for the perfecting of the saints
who were to do public service. It was only promised to genuine
believers, and they only received it ; though afterwards some,
turning out to be like Demas, betrayed their trust, and misused
it.

When a believer was baptized with spirit he did not
necessarily possess all the gifts. There were diversities of gifts
which were bestowed distributively. That is, one might speak
foreign languages by inspiration, but he could not therefore
work miracles : still another might be able to work miracles,
but could not therefore speak other tongues than his own.
The grace was distributed according to the will of the Deity

who worked or operated the all (all the gifts) in all who received them ; while those saints to whom no gifts were distributed were benefited by the labours of those who possessed them. Thus, " prophesying served for them who believed " ; for " he that prophesieth speaketh unto men to edification, and exhortation, and comfort " ; and " he that prophesieth, edifieth the church ". Therefore, in another place Paul saith, " despise not prophesying ".

Baptismal grace seems to have been distributed into nine gifts : 1—The word of wisdom ; 2—The word of knowledge ; 3—Faith that removes mountains ; 4—The gifts of healing ; 5—The inworking of powers ; 6—Prophesy, or the gift of prophesying ; 7—Discerning of spirits ; 8—Kinds of tongues ; 9—The interpretation of tongues.

"All these worked that one and the self same spirit, distributing to every one severally as he would." The body was one thing, the members or organs of the body, another. To the organs of the body these nine gifts were distributed for the benefit of all the atoms of the body. The number of the organs in each ecclesia would depend on the size and necessities of it. The organs of a congregation of saints constituted collectively " the presbytery ", or " eldership ". They might be relatively many or few. By way of example, one congregation might have an eldership of nine, another of eighteen, and a third of twenty-seven. If the last, three saints might be endowed with the same gift ; and three others with another ; and so on. Or in another case, one saint might have a plurality of gifts, and thus fewer organs would suffice for a small church. Each of the thirteen apostles probably possessed all the gifts.

Baptism of spirit, then, developed the elderships of the churches in the apostolic age ; so that Paul could with great propriety address those who were constituents of them, and say, " Take heed, therefore, to yourselves, and to all the flock, in the which the Holy Spirit hath made you overseers, to feed the ecclesia of the Deity which he purchased with his own blood ". The spirit made them elders through baptism of spirit, and distributed them into orders according to the following ranks : 1—Apostles ; 2—Prophets ; 3—Teachers ; 4—Powers ; 5—Healers ; 6—Helps ; 7—Governors ; 8—Linguists ; 9—Interpreters.

These were those who had the rule *by divine authority*, and to whom the private saints, *hoi idiōtai*, were exhorted to yield obedience, as to those who watched for their souls and would have to give an account. These were they to whom Paul wrote in Gal. 6 : 1, saying, " If any man be overtaken in a fault, *ye who are the spirituals (hoi pneumatikoi)*, restore such an one in the spirit of meekness ". These also were they who taught the brethren in the word, and were by them to be supplied with all good things ; " Let him that is taught in the word communicate unto him that teacheth in all good things ". And concerning them he says in another place, " We beseech you, brethren, to acknowledge them who labour among you, and are over you in the Lord, and admonish you ; and esteem them very highly in love for their work's sake ". " Let the elders who rule well be counted worthy of double honour, especially they who labour in the word and teaching. For the Scripture saith, Thou shalt not muzzle the ox that treadeth out the corn. And, The labourer is worthy of his reward ". They were not to be lightly accused, nor rebuked. No accusation was to be received against them but under two or three witnesses. They were not to be rebuked by their brethren, but entreated as fathers ; but if they sinned, and the offence was proved, they were to be rebuked before all by the proper authority, and not by every one that chose to be impertinent.

Collectively, these orders were the lightstand of a congregation, through which the Holy Spirit shone into the surrounding darkness of Judaism and Gentilism. They are, therefore, apocalyptically symbolized by " a star ", the angel or messenger star, whose mission was to illuminate by making known the manifold wisdom of the Deity.

Such were the members, or official organs, of the Body of which Christ was the Head in the apostolic age, styled by Paul, or rather likened to, the foot, the hand, the ear, the eye, and the organ of smell, in the body natural . . .

Peter says, " the elders that are among you, the elect (1 Peter 1 : 2), I exhort, who am also an elder . . . feed the flock of the deity, which is with you, overseeing it, not constrainedly, but willingly ; not for filthy lucre, but of a ready mind ; neither as being lords over The Heritages, but being examples of the flock. And when the Chief Shepherd shall appear, ye shall receive a crown of glory that fadeth not away " (1 Peter 5 : 1-4). The flock was composed of " the heritages ", each congregation being a heritage or clergy. The holy orders were forbidden to usurp lordship over these clergies ; but when the apostles passed away, they disregarded their interdict, reduced the clergies to abject vassalage, and arrogated to themselves the title of " the clergy, or heritage of God " !

From these premises, then, it is manifest that the only real clergy of the Deity among the Gentiles extant at present are those possessed of " *the more excellent way* " than the best of baptismal gifts (1 Cor. 12 : 31)—those in whom " now abideth faith, hope and love ". Those who being in Christ walk in the truth are the only clergy among men recognized of heaven. All others are usurpers, impostors, and deceivers of the people ; and to be stripped of the woollen garment they have stolen to conceal their wolfishness, by all who are loyal to the throne of the spirit of God. If the reader comprehend the spiritual constitution of the One Body in the apostolic age, he will scarcely be astonished at what he beholds in antichristendom. The Laodicean Apostasy of the third and fourth centuries was familiar with, and almost an eye witness of, the apostolic constitution of the body of Christ. The gifts and the orders which went together, were as household words with its leaders. When the Spirit " spued them out of his mouth " by withdrawing spirit-baptism, they still retained the scripture-phraseology in speaking of them, and claimed to be as much the holy orders as ever. But this is characteristic of apostasy and superstition . . .

Then from the premises before us the reader may perceive the utter impossibility of an apostolic organization of the saints at this time. There are no spirituals among them as in the beginning. By " spirituals " is meant true believers distinguished from other believers by being baptized with holy spirit as proved by its manifestations. In a certain sense, all the saints are spiritual as opposed to carnal, in so far as the word dwells in them with all wisdom. What we would express may be comprehended by comparing a saint with an unenlightened sinner. The former understands the truth, loves it, rejoices in it, walks in it, and thinks in harmony with it, and is therefore spiritual, or spiritually minded. The unenlightened sinner, be he " divine ", " supervisor ", " inventor ", or " patentee ", of human systems, crotchets, or institutions, is the reverse of all this. He is carnal, or carnally-minded—which is death ; a mere " natural man who receives not the things of the spirit of God, for they are foolishness unto him. Neither can he know, for they are spiritually discerned ". A congregation of saints may exist as the result of the word intellectually believed and obeyed. Such is " a perfect man ", relatively to this imperfect state. There is no need of baptizing him with the Holy Spirit for the confirmation of the word of reconciliation which was sufficiently confirmed for the purpose of God when He co-operated with the apostles. Neither is there any necessity for holy orders for his edification, exhortation, and comfort. This any saint intelligent in Moses and the prophets can now do. All that he needs in his sphere is order, not orders. A few unpretending, wise and intelligent brethren who have no by-ends and interests to promote other than the truth, are sufficient for the preservation of order, and the conducting of his affairs in the church. These are his five senses, which it does not require any special spirit-baptism to develop. As to those without, as he is presumed to be intelligent in all his elements, these are entitled all of them according to the rules and regulations, to say " Come ", and to show men how to come to repentance and remission of sins, and to immortality in the kingdom of God. Thus, the means in existence are adequate for all the necessities of the saints congregationally ; and for the taking out of those who remain yet unadded to the name designed to be for a people who shall execute judgment and establish righteousness in the earth.

20

AGE TO COME, PARADISE, ABSENT FROM THE BODY

(2 Cor. 5 : 8)

THE BIBLE reveals, or rather treats of the two states, the present and the future. We may almost say of the past and future, for the present is no sooner here than it is gone ; so that the past becomes as it were a completive present. Of the future state we know nothing but as it is revealed in the scriptures. What do they testify as to this state ? That like the past, and present, it has to do with the living and not the dead. State is organization, individual and physical, or national ; but death is dissolution and the reverse in everything. The scriptures also testify that the future state is a constitution of things upon earth growing out of those that now exist as the elements thereof ; and that is subdivisible into two eras, the Millennium, or "Age to Come ", and that which succeeds it, called " the Ages of the Ages ". The Age to Come is styled " the economy of the fulness of times " by Paul, and " the New Heavens and New Earth wherein dwelleth righteousness " by Peter, as contrasted with the Mosaic economy in which ungodly men and scoffers, walking after their own lusts, had rule over Israel. The Age to Come is intermediate between " the times of the Gentiles " and the Ages of the Ages ; and is the only " intermediate state " treated of in the word of the truth of the gospel. The Age to Come is the New Heavens and Earth of Isaiah 65 : 17, and 66 : 22 ; the era contemporary with the kingdom of God, when his son Jesus Christ our Lord shall sit upon the throne of his father David as king of Israel and Emperor of the world.

The Ages of the Ages are the New Heavens and New Earth spoken of by John in the Revelation 21 : 1. They are also the third Heavens, or Paradise in full development, beheld by Paul in vision. The earth undergoes great changes at their introduction, for when established there is " no more sea ". They commence with the folding up of the heavens of the Age to Come like a vesture ; for these shall be changed, having then waxed old as doth a garment. The constitution of the kingdom is changed at that epoch ; for sin being taken away from among men, and death its punishment abolished, the element of priesthood must be removed. Then the end will have come when the Son shall deliver up the kingdom to the Father that God may be all in all. From this end the Ages of the Ages take their rise, and things on earth are changed no more.

A resurrection from among the dead marks the introduction of a future state. It precedes the Age to Come ; and it precedes the Ages of the Ages ; the former being the resurrection of the Firstfruits of God's creatures, and therefore termed the First Resurrection ; the latter, a thousand years after at " the End ". " Blessed and holy is he that hath part in the first resurrection : on such the Second Death hath no power, but they shall be priests of God and of Christ, and shall reign with him a thousand years."

Now the subject matter of the " great salvation " is the Kingdom and Age to Come to which believers are introduced by a resurrection from among the dead. We affirm this on the authority of Paul in his letter to the Hebrews. " How shall we escape ", says he, " if we neglect so great salvation, which at the first began to be spoken by the Lord ? " " For unto the Angels he has not put into subjection the future habitable concerning which we speak." Here then we learn that when the Lord Jesus began to preach he spoke about the future habitable.

But what is the future habitable ? The answer is found in the testimony of Luke concerning what Jesus preached. He informs us that when the people of Capernaum besought him to remain among them, he refused, saying, " I must preach the kingdom of God to other cities also, for therefore am I sent ". Mark also says that " after John was put in prison, Jesus came into Galilee, preaching the gospel of the kingdom of God, and saying, The time is fulfilled, and the kingdom of God draws near ; repent ye, and believe the gospel " (Luke 4 : 43 ; Mark 1 : 14, 15). *In preaching about the future habitable, then, Jesus preached the gospel of the kingdom.* Now a " habitable ", is a place or country capable of being inhabited ; a " future habitable", a country uninhabitable in the present, but habitable hereafter. This is true of the Land of Israel, called the Land of Promise, because God promised it to Abraham and Christ (Gen. 12 : 7 ; 13 : 15 ; 15 : 7, 8, 18 ; Gal. 3 : 16-19). At present, it is uninhabitable by Jesus and those who neglect not the " great salvation ", for " the uncircumcised and the unclean " possess it : but when it becomes the area on which is erected the kingdom of God—upon which David's tabernacle and throne are existing in their glory—the enemy will have been expelled from the country ; and it will be inhabited by the Twelve Tribes of Israel, " a kingdom of priests, and a holy nation " (Exod. 19 : 4-6), the subjects of the kingdom ; and by Jesus and the Saints, his co-heirs and brethren, the inheritors of its glory, honour, immortality, and dominion. The Land will then be the *habitable land*, concerning which, says Paul, we speak.

This condition of the Land of Promise will be manifested in the Age to Come, of which " the Son given " to Israel is the " father " or " founder " (Isa. 9 : 6-7). Concerning the country, then become " a heavenly country ", Jehovah saith to the Saints, and to his people Israel, by the mouth of the prophet, " Hearken unto me, ye that follow after righteousness, ye that seek the Lord : look unto Abraham your father, for I called him alone, and blessed him. For the Lord shall comfort Zion : he will comfort all her waste places ; and he will make her wilderness like Eden, and her desert like the garden (Paradise) of the Lord : joy and gladness shall be found therein, thanksgiving and the voice of melody " (Isa. 51 : 1-3). No one who understands this testimony (and before he gives his opinion he should read the whole chapter to the tenth verse of the next) can be at a loss to answer the question, " *What and where is Paradise ?* " It is the Land of Israel made like Eden and the garden of the Lord, when Jerusalem, the holy city, puts on her beautiful garments, being henceforth " no more " the habitation of the uncircumcised and unclean.

This is Paradise—the Land of Israel with the Kingdom of God established upon it in the Age to Come. Paradise is neither the grave, nor in Hades ; but the Holy Land converted into the garden of the Lord. It is a word that signifies the same thing as the kingdom of God ; and when the Lord Jesus sits upon the throne of his father David on Mount Zion, he will then and there be " the Tree of Life in the midst of the Paradise of God " (Rev. 2 : 7 ; 22 : 2, 14). We must eat of this tree if we would live for ever ; for it is " our life ". It is a Vine-Tree, with Twelve Branches, and " Twelve Fruits " ; and the unwithering " leaves are for the healing of the nations " (John 15 : 1, 5 ; Psa. 1 : 3). In other words, the work of healing the nations of their spiritual and political maladies is assigned to Jesus on the throne of David ; to the apostles on the twelve thrones of the house of David ; and to the Saints associated with them in the kingdom. These things are the topics of the great salvation which began to be spoken by the Lord, and was confirmed unto their contemporaries by the apostles that heard him, God also bearing them witness.

Now the righteous dead can only attain to this hope by a resurrection from among the dead ; and the righteous living who may witness its manifestation, by being changed, or immortalized in the twinkling of an eye. " The dead praise not the Lord, neither any that go down into silence " ; " the dead know not any thing " ; " in death there is no remembrance of thee, O Lord ; in the grave none can give thee thanks " ; " the grave cannot praise thee, death cannot celebrate thee : they that go down into the pit cannot hope for thy truth : the living, the living, he shall praise thee, as I, Hezekiah, do this day " ; " whatsoever thy hand findeth to do, do it with thy might ; for there is no work, nor device, nor knowledge, nor wisdom, in the grave whither thou goest ". These testimonies are true, and entirely set aside the foolish speculations of " the learned " with respect to the dead while in the power of death. If a man would praise the Lord ; if he would remember Him ; if he would celebrate His name and give Him thanks ; if he would hope in His truth ; if he would do any thing, and have any knowledge and wisdom after he departs this life, he must rise from the dead. Paul was thoroughly convinced of this ; hence his anxiety as expressed in his letter to the Philippians that " he might know Christ and the power of his resurrection, and the fellowship of his sufferings, being made conformable to his death : if by any means he might attain to the resurrection from among the dead " (Phil. 3 : 10, 11). Does the reader imagine in the face of these testimonies that Paul had " a desire to depart " into the death-state ; that he thought there was anything to gain in that region of darkness and silence by dying ; or that he considered that when dead he should be " present with the Lord " ? No, Paul said none other things, and believed none other things than what Moses and the prophets testified ; and these writers are in entire harmony with himself and all that is written in the New Testament, and this men would soon discover if they understood the Old.

Paul knew that as a living man in any sense he stood related only to two states, the present and the future ; and that as a dead man he would know nothing, he could offer no praise, he could have no recollection of the past and no hope for the future. The interval between dying and rising again he well knew was a perfect blank—an interval of which he would have no consciousness. Being therefore unconscious of it (and it is only the living that are conscious that such an interval exists), dying and rising became to him, though really centuries apart, but two successive acts, following each other in the twinkling of an eye. This must be of necessity, for there is no account taken of time by the dead. The testimony says they know nothing ; consequently they know no more about time than they do about anything else. If we understand this we are delivered from the perverting influence of the heathen philosophy, or mythology of " spirit worlds " (which have no existence save in the mesmerized imaginations of clairvoyant familiars and those who deal with them) which constitutes the mysticism of sectarianism, the flesh-eating " canker " that destroys the truth.

Paul then knew only of presence with the body, and presence with the Lord, both of them, however, bodily states ; for, he says, speaking of presence with the Lord, " we must all appear before the judgment seat of Christ, that every one may receive the things in body, according to that he hath done, whether good or bad ". " The things " are the things promised and threatened. He hopes to receive " the things " promised, such as glory, honour, immortality, and the kingdom ; and he hoped to receive them also " in body ". He knew he could not receive them if he were not existing bodily ; for as disorganized dust and ashes he could possess nothing. Presence with the Lord, then, is bodily presence ; and this is absence from the body of mortal flesh : for when the faithful are " present with the Lord ", their bodies have suffered transformation, being then incorruptible and deathlessly living, having put on immortality ; which putting on is their being " clothed upon by their house from heaven ", or being built up of God from the ruins of their mortal body, or former house, which had been dissolved or reduced to dust. This " building of God " is erected in the rising from the dead.

So long as believers are flesh and blood they are " at home in the body ", and absent from the Lord ; for " flesh and blood cannot inherit the kingdom of God ", because it is corruptible and mortal ; and until they do inherit the kingdom, they cannot be present with him : for it is in the kingdom he appears and meets them. They walk by faith now ; they walk by sight then ; but in the death-state there is no walking at all, for they walk neither by faith nor sight there, no knowledge nor wisdom existing in the grave whither they go. The apostle evidently did not expect to be present with the Lord in the death-state. He leaves us without a doubt on this subject ; for he tells the Saints in Corinth that " God who raised up the Lord Jesus, shall also raise them up by Jesus, and shall present him and Timothy with them ". He did not expect his own presentation to precede theirs ; but that he with them and the rest of the Saints should all be ushered into the Lord's presence together at his coming, when those of them turned to righteousness by him should be his glory, and joy, and crown of rejoicing evermore (1 Thess. 2 : 19).

The apostle's mind was fixed on the Age to Come, its kingdom, honour, glory and immortality, and not upon the dark, loathsome, and gloomy grave in which he was to moulder in unconsciousness till the trump of God awaked him. The things of the kingdom and Age to Come are " the things which are not seen ", and are enduring. They are not yet seen by the natural eye ; but are discerned by the eye of faith by the light of the divine testimony. These unseen, and as yet unrevealed things, existing only in promise, are the subject of the faith which justifies, and by which the ancients obtained a good report. Paul's faith agreed with his definition of it, as " the assured expectation of things hoped for, the evidence of things not seen " ; for says he in relation to the " far more exceeding and eternal weight of glory ", " we look at the things which are not seen ; for the things which are seen are temporal ; but the things which are not seen are eternal " : therefore he saith in another place, " If then ye be risen with Christ (by faith of his resurrection, and by being baptized in hope of being planted in its likeness), seek those things which are above, where Christ sitteth on the right hand of God. Set your affections on things above, not on things on the earth. For ye are dead (to earthly things) and your life is hid with Christ in God. When Christ, who is our life, shall appear, then shall ye also appear with him in glory " (Col. 3 : 1-4).

Was Paul's hope and expectation different from that he set before the Colossians and others ? Assuredly not. He sought for those things which are from above, and his affections were upon them. He walked in the belief of them, and hoped to realize them at the appearance of the Lord in glory. He would then be present with him, and not a moment before. He expected life and glory to be brought to him when the Lord shall depart from God's right hand on his return to Olivet. Walk so as ye have us for an example ; for our citizenship, says he, belongs to the heavens ; from whence also we wait for the Saviour, the Lord Jesus Christ ; who shall change the body of our humiliation, in order that it may become of a like form to the body of his glory according to the power whereby he is able also to subdue all things to himself (Phil. 3 : 17, 20, 21). After this who can scripturally affirm that Paul expected life, glory, and incorruptibility, and to be present with the Lord, at the instant of death ; or who is so blind that he cannot see that he looked for all these things when he should appear before the judgment seat of Christ in company with the Saints at the epoch of their resurrection ? He took no account of the period of his unconsciousness in the grave ; but connected the present with the future as continuous, which they are in fact to the generations of the living, by whom alone any interval is perceived at all, and that only in relation to the dead. The living perceive the lapse of time between dying and rising again ; but the dead do not.

We shall now conclude this exegesis of the passage before us by the following paraphrase of the text : For we know that if our mortal body be dissolved in the dust, we are to receive a new body and a new habitation, a building from God, a house not made with hands, enduring in the New Heavens. For in the midst of the things which are seen we groan, earnestly desiring that our habitation which is from heaven may be clothed upon us : if so be that being raised and appearing before the tribunal of Christ we shall not be found naked or destitute of the wedding garment. For we that are surrounded by the things seen and temporal do groan, being burdened : not that we desire to enter the death state by being unclothed or divested even of mortal life, but clothed upon by putting on immortality, that mortality may be swallowed up of life. Now he that has begotten in us this earnest desire and hope is God, who has given us the spirit as the earnest of what we shall receive at the coming of the Lord. We are therefore always confident, having full assurance of faith, knowing that whilst we who believe are mortal, we are absent from the Lord (for while absent we walk by faith, not by sight) ; we are full of hope, I say, and rejoice rather to be delivered from mortality, and to be present with the Lord. Wherefore we labour, that whether present at his tribunal or absent from it, we may be accepted of him. For we must all appear before the judgment-seat of Christ : that everyone may receive the things in body, according to that he hath done, good or bad.

CHRISTIAN DISCIPLES

THIS term Disciple is derived from the latin noun *discipulus*, which signifies a learner or scholar. He then who styles himself a Disciple announces to mankind that he is a student whose object is to learn. If he adopt the term as a sectarian distinction, it then imports that he is a student of the system of theology approved by his denomination, that he may learn all its mysteries. There are innumerable disciples of this class, subdivided also into a multitude of orders. In this sense they are as followers and adherents to the doctrine of another, who is therefore always more or less in advance of themselves ; and therefore their leader. But there is a non-sectarian sense in which men are styled disciples, namely, when they are students of the Word, " proving all things ", that they may be able to comprehend with all saints what is the breadth, and length, and depth, and height ; and to know the love of Christ, which passeth knowledge, that they might be filled with the fulness of God ; and so understanding what the will of the Lord is. Hence a church of disciples is an assembly of learners ; and a church of Christian disciples is an assembly of persons who believe the things of the Kingdom of God, and of the Name of the Lord Jesus, and, thus believing, have been immersed into Christ and patiently continue in the faith and well doing of their vocation, reading, marking, learning and inwardly digesting all things revealed in the scriptures of truth. Such were the disciples first called Christian at Antioch. These Christian disciples shone as lights in the world, holding forth the Word of Life. They counted not their lives dear unto them : but hazarded everything, reputation, liberty, wealth and friends, for the Word's sake. Their treasure was in heaven ; therefore their anchor was within the veil. The icy coldness of their old nature was thawed into the genial sympathies of the new man by the benevolence of God. Heart clung to heart, and hand joined in hand, the expressive symbol of unity and love. We want to behold a Church of Christian Disciples such as these ; we fear that such an one is yet a stranger in our world. When such a community of churches is restored, we shall glory in it as a Reformation in verity and deed.

" BEWARE OF COVETOUSNESS "

IN 2 Cor. 8 the Apostle informs the Corinthian brethren that
the Macedonian congregations had been subjected to great
persecution ; and that while thus suffering, their joy, notwithstanding their " deep poverty ", abounded so exceedingly that
the munificence of their contributions for the afflicted saints
transcended their power of giving without personal sacrifice.
The sum total of these donations, he terms " the gift of God
bestowed on them ", because this " fellowship " resulted
from an intense sympathy with those who were suffering and
enduring for the Truth's sake ; and will therefore redound
to their great recompense from God in the approaching day of
the Lord Jesus. They began well and ended well. " They
first gave their own selves unto the Lord " ; then to the
Apostle and his co-labourers ; and consummated the whole in
cheerfully giving to the necessities of the Truth more than their
extreme poverty justified.

This is a noble example of the devotedness and liberality
of the poor to the suffering Truth. The Holy Oracles abound
in such examples. We say, " the riches of their liberality
abounded " for the Truth's sake ; and this is the same thing
as if we had said, " for the Lord's sake ". The saints of
Macedonia were suffering shame, reproach, imprisonment, and
death " for the gospel's sake ", " for the Kingdom of God's
sake ", " for the name of Jesus' sake ", " for his sake ", " for
the word's sake "—all parallel expressions found in Matthew,
Mark and Luke. They were encouraged thus to suffer by the
precepts and example of Jesus, who had said, " There is no
man that hath left house, or parents, or brethren, or wife or
children, for the kingdom of God's sake, who shall not receive
manifold more in the present time, and in the future age
unending life " ; so also " for the joy that was set before him "
he embraced a life of poverty, affliction and reproach : " he
endured the cross, despised the shame ". Hence, because the
saints were suffering for the gospel of the Son of God, they were
suffering for Jesus' sake ; and the congregations of Macedonia
in communicating to their necessities served the Truth, and
proved their love and devotion to the King of Saints ; for
what is done to them for the gospel's sake is as if ministered
personally to him.

The Corinthian brethren were rich, as well in temporalities as in spiritual gifts. At this crisis, Titus was among them and engaged in stirring up their liberality. In order, therefore, that they might not fall short, and by contrast with the munificence of the poor Macedonian brethren, render Paul's boasting concerning them vain, he writes to them that as they " abound in every thing " they " abound in this grace (of liberality) also "—" to prove the sincerity of their love ".

Here, then, is a great principle set before us by the Apostle, namely, that to prove the sincerity of our love to the Lord Jesus, we must be liberal in our contribution to the Truth. From this there is no exemption—for rich or poor, " If there be first a willing mind, the contribution is accepted according to that a man hath " ; " deep poverty " is no excuse for not doing ; and riches only lay an increased obligation to excel in munificence. In giving her mite, the widow gave all that she had ; and in so doing, gave more than all the rich, who contributed of their abundance without experiencing the least inconvenience. Think of that, ye who are rich, " she gave all her living " ; think that ye can behold her generous countenance in the judgment and not remorsefully cry, " Shame upon us, for our not having been rich towards God ! " Aye indeed, you will then feel the force of the Master's warning, " *Beware of covetousness* ! " " Ye know the grace of our Lord Jesus Christ, that though he was rich, yet for your sakes he became poor, that ye through his poverty might be rich " ; yet ye have not the heart to part with the Mammon of unrighteousness to aid the Truth in its arduous combat with error and sin.

The Apostle brings to light another principle, namely, that of equality. " I mean not ", says he, " that other men be eased, and you burdened." The rich have no right to monopolize the privilege of doing all for the Truth, nor the poor to the exclusion of the rich, " that there may be equality ".

Lastly he teaches us that *we shall be recompensed in the age to come according to our liberality to the Truth in this*. Hear this, ye rich men ; " When thou makest a dinner, or a supper, call not thy friends, nor thy brethren, neither thy kinsmen, nor thy rich neighbours ; lest they also bid thee again, and a recompense be made thee. But when thou makest a feast, call the poor, the maimed, the lame, the blind ; and thou shalt be blessed ; for they cannot recompense thee ; for thou shalt be recompensed at the resurrection of the just " (Luke 14 : 12). And the Apostle says, " He which soweth sparingly shall reap also sparingly ; and he which soweth bountifully, shall reap also bountifully. Every man according as he purposeth in his heart, so let him give ; not grudgingly, nor of necessity ; for God loveth a cheerful giver ".

The profession of apostolic Christianity has made many a rich man poor ; but we have never heard, or read, of the poor man who has been enriched by it as pertaining to the good things of the present life. We are not placed here to accumulate riches for those who may come after us ; but to labour for the truth, in doing the truth ourselves, and in contributing to its establishment in our own day and generation. In occupying our time thus, we labour for the meat which endures to everlasting life. We do not believe that in the midst of so much ignorance, superstition, unbelief and woe as now prevails in the nominal household of faith, that a Christian can die rich, and possess the kingdom. It is easier for a camel to pass through a needle's eye.

23

BE NOT DISCOURAGED

WE need not be discouraged because of the stolid indifference of the people to the truth. Flesh and blood is naturally swinish and unimpressible by the thoughts of God. The world, which is choked with religion, such as it is, is made of this stiff-necked material. It is in the state of an inebriate who has caroused himself into *delirium tremens*, or a snoring apoplexy. Its excitation or brain-congestion can only be relieved by copious depletion. To preach the truth to it is like telling fables to a deaf man ; putting a jewel in a swine's snout ; or casting things holy to dogs. This is the nature of the flesh and blood world—it is only evil, and that continually. But all the *individuals* of this perverse *race* are not so absolutely controlled by the evil thereof as to be incapable of sobriety in word and deed. The race has some " honest and good hearts " yet, which are as salt, preserving it from total and irretrievable corruption. They require, however, to be salted with wisdom, and persecution, or fire, for the truth's sake, to make them fit for the Master's use (Mark 9 : 49, 50 ; Col. 4 : 6). It is for the salting of these hearts that those who are already salted have to labour with a right good will. They must " contend earnestly for the faith once delivered to the saints ", with the conviction all the time that a Paul may plant, and an Apollos water, but God only gives the increase. All we have to do is to dig, plough, sow, work, as men do who leave it to the sun by day and moon by night, and to the air, earth, and rain, to give the increase from that begotten in the soil. We as day labourers need not be discouraged, if we do our duty, be there increase or not. All that we have to do in the premises is that we be " workman who rightly divide the word of truth " (2 Tim. 2 : 15), and not as those who handle the word of God deceitfully ; and fear to affirm His principles boldly lest some one whose corns were pinched by the gospel-shoe (feet shod with the preparation of the good news of peace, Eph. 6 : 15) should cry out " Sectarianism ! " and threaten you with the rebuke of Jesus and the apostle Paul ! The word, where properly put into the right kind of soil, will yield just such an increase as God has predetermined. He has sent it as the rain and snow of heaven for the fructification of the earth, that sowers, and reapers, and eaters, may all rejoice together at harvest-home. Read Isaiah 55 : 10, 11, where Jehovah says, "As the rain cometh down, and the snow, from heaven, and returneth not thither, but watereth the earth, and maketh it bring forth and bud, that it may give seed to the sower, and bread to the eater ; so shall my word be that goeth forth out of my mouth : it shall not return unto me void, but *it shall accomplish that which I please*, and it shall prosper in the thing *whereto I sent it.*"

What hath He pleased, and what hath He sent His word to do ? " To take out of the Gentiles a people for his name " (Acts 15 : 14). He is going to set up a kingdom which is to rule over all the earth and sea ; and He requires a people sufficiently numerous to administer its affairs to His praise, honour, and glory. This being His purpose, He does not need as great a multitude as is generally supposed when men entangle themselves in speculations about the number of the saved. " Many are called ", says the King, " but few are chosen " ; " Strait is the gate, and narrow is the way which leadeth unto life, and few there be that find it " ; " Many will seek to enter in, and shall not be able " (Matt. 7 : 14 ; 20 : 16 ; Luke 13 : 23). These are not our words ; but they are his who spake the words of God.

Jehovah then requires a chosen few for His kingdom— " a *chosen* generation ", " from the beginning *chosen* of God to salvation through sanctification of the Spirit and belief of the truth ", called thereunto by Paul's gospel " unto obedience and sprinkling of the blood of Jesus Christ ", " to the obtaining of his glory " (1 Pet. 2 : 9 ; 2 Thess. 2 : 13, 14 ; 1 Pet. 1 : 2). John saw this company, this " little flock ", as Jesus styles them in Luke 12 : 32, to whom the Father will give the kingdom ; John, we say, saw them in military panoply and array, surrounding their Generalissimo in his wars upon the kings of the earth ; and he says they were " called, and *chosen*, and faithful " (Rev. 17 : 14).

But though relatively few, they are absolutely " a great multitude which no man can number " (Rev. 7 : 9). They are few compared with all the human race that ever fretted and stewed out their brief existence on the earth. A few taken out of each of the generations of the Old Man of the flesh ; a few out of Enoch's generation, and a few out of Noah's, and a few out of Moses', and so on ; until these parcels of the few, separated from the solid mass during 6,000 years, being gathered into ONE GLORIOUS COMPANY OF ANCIENTS, become absolutely a great multitude, and numerous enough to establish the will of God upon earth, and to cause it to be respected for a thousand years.

The Father hath given this company of the redeemed ones to the Son for his brethren and associates in all his future enterprises upon earth. " They follow the Lamb ", saith John, " whithersoever he goeth." They are " redeemed *from among* men, firstfruits to God and to the Lamb " (Rev. 14 : 4). "All that the Father giveth me ", says Jesus, " shall come to me ; and him that cometh to me I will in no wise cast out. And this is the Father's will, that of all he hath given me I should lose nothing, but should raise it up again at the last day." And again, " No man can come to me, except the Father who hath sent me draw him ; and I will raise him up at the last day. It is written in the prophets, *And they* (who attain to the resurrection he was speaking of) *shall be all taught of God*. Every man, therefore, that hath *heard*, and hath *learned* of the Father, cometh unto me " (John 6 : 37-45). " He that is of God heareth God's words ; ye therefore hear them not, because ye are not of God " (John 8 : 47). And again, he saith to these goats, " Ye believe not, *because* ye are not of my sheep, as I said unto you. My sheep hear my voice, and I know them, and *they* follow me ; and I give *unto them* the life of the Aion (*zoē aiōnian*), and they shall not be destroyed in the Aion (*eis ton aiōna*), neither shall any one wrest them out of my hand " (John 10 : 26).

Men have been commanded to preach the word, to be instant in season and out of season, to contend earnestly for the faith and so forth, as *the means* appointed for the separation of this people. *Testimony and reasoning,* or Scripture and reasoning out of the Scripture, are the spiritual elements constituting the *spiritual agency* for their " sanctification of the Spirit ". This spiritual agency is just adequate to the numerical completion of this people, termed " the fulness of the Gentiles " in Rom. 11 : 25, and no more. It is adequate to the accomplishment of this, for this result is that for which the word was given ; and Jehovah saith it shall accomplish it. It is not adequate to the conversion of all the world. This is a result never contemplated in the premises. If God had designed the conversion of all nations as such in the absence of His Son from the earth, He would have instituted a system of means adequate to such a result. The spiritual agency was more potent in the days of the Apostles in that it consisted not only of *a declaration of the testimony,* and a *reasoning out* of its points, but a *confirmation* also of the reasoning by signs, wonders, miracles, and gifts. Here were God and man visibly co-working in the separation of this people for His name. Yet with this more potent spiritual agency the world could not be converted ; nay, a multitude even of those who were primarily turned to God turned from Him again ; and that too while the apostles lived, and while the gifts of the Holy Spirit continued to be bestowed. The gifts were discontinued for two reasons ; first, because they had answered the purpose for which they were originally given ; and secondly, because through the working of the Mystery of Iniquity Christians proved themselves unworthy of the glorious indwelling of the Holy Spirit in their midst. The testimony was confirmed ; but the *confirmation of the reasoning* has been withdrawn, and the spiritual agency for the completion of the work begun at the house of Cornelius, reduced to what we see.

Now the nearer we approach to the apocalypse of Jesus, the less influence will the word be found to exercise over the mind of the general public. We ought not to be discouraged at the fact. The time is fast approaching for the Gentile branch to be broken off.; and for Israel to be grafted in. The branches of Israel and Judah were broken off because of unbelief—because they did not fear the name of Jehovah their Elohim—the Jehovah-Spirit manifested through David's Son—nor believe the gospel of the kingdom preached in his name. For this cause the brotherhood of Israel and Judah was broken by the Roman power ; and a day of grace granted to the Gentiles. But these have proved as faithless of the truth as Israel. There were many Jews in Jerusalem and Palestine who believed with unexceptionable fidelity the things apostolically delivered ; still their faith was only enough for their own salvation ; and altogether inadequate to avert the judgment of God from the nation.

24

" PREACH THE WORD "

In writing to Timothy the apostle said, " I charge thee before God, and the Lord Jesus Christ, preach the Word " : and in another place, he says, " Study, O Timothy, to show thyself approved unto God, a workman that needeth not to be ashamed, rightly dividing the word of truth " (2 Tim. 4 : 1, 2 ; 2 : 15). This was a solemn charge—a charge before the two most exalted, wise, intelligent, holy, glorious and powerful beings in the boundless universe : an apostolic charge, uttered in the presence of God's Spirit, imparted to Paul and Timothy by Jesus Christ, to preach and rightly divide the Word of Truth, so that God might approve him as a good workman. Here, then the thing to be preached and " rightly divided " is the Word of Truth. But what is that Word ?

Will the reader accept the definition offered by one of the prophets of Jehovah ? Isaiah says it is " the law and the testimony ", and that there is no light, or knowledge, in those who speak not according to it (Isa. 8 : 10). The law of Moses is a part of " The Word ", because it is the form, or " representation of the truth ", by which believers of the promises made to the fathers of Israel were instructed as by a schoolmaster into the faith (Rom. 2 : 18-20 ; Gal. 3 : 24). Paul preached the law when he preached the word ; not, indeed, as theologists preach the word, raining down fire and brimstone upon sinners ; but as declaring the things contained in the law representative and affirmative of the sufferings of the Christ and the glory that shall follow his resurrection : thus he said before Agrippa, " I continue unto this day, witnessing both to small and great, *saying none other things than those which the prophets and Moses did say would come* ". Men cannot preach " the Word of the Truth of the Gospel " without preaching Moses and the prophets ; for " the testimony for Jesus is the spirit of prophecy ", and Moses was a great prophet. Paul declared nothing else. The exposition of the writings of Israel's prophets as partially and limitedly fulfilled in Jesus, and hereafter wholly to be accomplished in his second advent mission, constituted the apostolic preaching of the word. They were predicants of the law and testimony of God concerning His kingdom and the name of Jesus His anointed.

245

Therefore, saith Paul, in addition to what he said before Agrippa, " I come to you in Corinth *declaring the testimony of God* " (1 Cor. 2 : 1). He says, he did not come to them " with excellency of speech or of wisdom "—such wisdom and oratory as the Greeks delighted in, whose wisdom " is foolishness with God ",—he did not blend their foolish wisdom with God's testimony, as some were beginning to do ; " for ", says he, " I determined to take notice of nothing among you, except Jesus Christ, and him a crucified one ". He paid no regard to their wisdom or its dogmas, but introduced an entirely new system of doctrine among them, which it had not entered the heart of their " philosophy and vain deceit " to dream of— a doctrine which taught the setting up of an imperishable kingdom and empire on earth, which is to rule all nations under the administration of the King of the Jews, even Jesus, and of those Jews and Gentiles associated with him, who shall believe what God has promised concerning it, recognize his right to the throne, believe the things concerning his name, be baptized into him, and thenceforth be faithful unto death. He taught this ; and that this indestructible dominion under which all nations shall be blessed, shall not pass from one generation of rulers to another, but shall be held for ever by those promoted to its glory, honour, and power, as its establishment, thereby necessitating their resurrection from among the dead to immortality.

Dit it ever enter into the heart of Socrates, Plato, or any other of the Greeks, to conceive of immortality of body on such principles as these ? Nay, it was foolishness to them, and derided as the ignorant speculation of a wandering Jew. It was " new doctrine "—entirely new—more new to them than the gospel of the kingdom and age to come advocated by us by speech and pen, is to this generation to which it is almost unknown, though as old as the heavenly oracles of the Blessed God.

" Preach the Word ", then, because it contains the testimony which God has given concerning the kingdom, and all things related to it—preach the law and the testimony, for if men believe not Moses and the prophet's writings, how can they understandingly believe the words of Jesus ; for " all things must be fulfilled which were written in the law of Moses, and in the prophets, and in the Psalms, concerning him ". But little comparatively has been fulfilled that is written in those records respecting the Christ. The Jews, blind as they are, see this ; and, therefore, it is because the Gentiles in their ignorance claim more for Jesus than is yet accomplished in him, that they become a cause of the rejection of his Messiahship by Israel. Thus a counsellor who knows not the law is worse than none.

But the workman who preaches the word is to divide it rightly. No workman is approved of God who doth not do this. He is to " study " to divide the word of truth rightly. It requires study, and much study, too, or its right division cannot be discerned. If this be neglected, the preaching or writing will be mere confusion, and the word quoted unintelligible. The hearer or reader must study as well as the speaker or writer, or the subject will be obscure to him, no matter how lucidly presented. There is a right division, and a wrong division of the word ; and no division at all. The absence of division is the almost universal characteristic of popular preaching. Textualizing under " three heads " is not dividing the word of truth at all, because it is not preaching the word. In fact, it has nothing to do with it. Neither is itemizing dividing the word. By itemizing, we mean the reduction of a theory to items ; such as when an " evangelist " says, " The gospel consists of three items—facts to be believed ; commands to be obeyed, and promises to be enjoyed ". This is true neither in theory nor division. It doth not touch the word ; therefore, the workman is not approved.

To rightly divide the word of truth is, first to study it without bias, or subjection to uninspired authority, or antiquity. Attend to what is written, as a child listens to a story. Study history, and ask questions, and be thankful for all the information you can get, even if you have to pay for it. While you are engaged in this pursuit, do not imagine that you are a workman. It is not easy to become a workman in such an age as this. The great names in theology, so much applauded by the world—a world that has been " wondering after the Beast " for more than twelve centuries—were not even apprentices ; they were students of the classics and systems of divinity, not students of the word. If they had been, they would never have written such foolishness as passes current with their names. No ; it is the result of much time and labour to become adequately proficient for a right division of the word. Men who do not understand the prophets, have no scriptural pretensions to workmanship in the word. They can neither preach it, nor divide it. When a man comes to understand the gospel of the kingdom, believing and obeying it, he has then qualified himself to lay the foundation in others. Let him go on to perfection. Let him dive into the testimony, and let it dwell richly in him, with all wisdom. If he have ability to state intelligibly what he understands, then let him work away, as unto God, and not to man. Let him search out, and apply the testimony to the Covenants of Promise ; to the territory ; to the subjects ; to the inheritors of the kingdom ; to its throne and king ; to his humiliation and exaltation ; to the nations ; to the mystery of the Name ; to the Gentile fellowship of the mystery ; to the identification of his majesty, and so forth. Here are topics to which the Word of Truth must be distributed, or " rightly divided ", and he who can do this work most efficiently is the workman that has least reason to be ashamed before God, however much he may be slighted or reproached by men.

Now, where are we to find such preachers and dividers of the word of truth ? They are like comets in our heavens for multitude ! Let the reader choose a clear dark night, and go forth and count them.

25

" BLASPHEMY " AND " NAMES OF BLASPHEMY "

(i) *BLASPHEMY SCRIPTURALLY DEFINED*

" *I have heard all thy blasphemies which thou hast spoken against the mountains of Israel, saying, They are laid desolate, they are given to us to consume. Thus with your mouth ye have spoken great things against me, and have multiplied your words against me : I have heard them* " (Ezek. 35 : 12, 13).

IN the above passage of Ezekiel's prophecy the word " blasphemies " in the original text is *nĕahtzoth*, reproaches, contumelies, or, in the words of the prophet, " great things spoken with the mouth against " an object.

In the Greek, *nĕahtzoth* is expressed by the noun *blasphēmiai*, which the English or Anglo-Saxon reader will readily perceive is the anglicized word blasphemies in its Greek dress. It is derived from the verb *blasphēmeō*, which is itself derived from the phrase *blaptein tēn phēmēn*, to injure the reputation or fame of any object ; which, if undeservedly done, is to calumniate, rail against, revile, reproach it, etc.

In scripture the objects of blasphemy are various, such as " God, his name, his tabernacle, them that dwell in the heaven ", the Jews, the mountains of Israel, the Holy Spirit, the doctrine of God, the word of God, the sanctified of the Father, the king of Israel.

The following passages will sufficiently establish this. In Rev. 13 : 5, 6 it is said that a mouth was given to the Gentile Beast, or System of Powers, " speaking great things and blasphemies. And he opened his mouth (papal) in blasphemy against God, to blaspheme his Name and his tabernacle, and those dwelling in the heaven " ; that is, to the injury of the reputation of all these in the estimation of society.

" The Jews " are blasphemed by pretenders to that honourable community who cannot establish their claim to citizenship in the commonwealth of Israel. Thus in Rev. 2 : 9, the king of the Jews says, " I know the blasphemy of those who say they are Jews, and are not, but are the synagogue of Satan " : and in chapter 3 : 9, he styles them liars.

The text at the head of this article shows that the mountains of Israel may be blasphemed, and that in blaspheming them Jehovah is Himself blasphemed.

Mark testifies to the Holy Spirit being an object of blasphemy in his day, in 3 : 29, 30 ; and Paul exhorts or commands that Christians, who are servants and wives, be respectful and obedient to their masters and husbands, that the name, doctrine and word of God be not blasphemed (1 Tim. 6 : 1 ; Titus 2 : 5).

To blaspheme is, therefore, in a scriptural sense, to bring divine things into disrepute ; so that whatever words or doings tend to, or really do accomplish this, are blasphemies.

The punishment of blasphemy, by divine law, is death. " He that blasphemeth the name of Jehovah shall surely be put to death, as well the stranger as he that is born in the land " (Lev. 24 : 16).

For men to say they are Jews, while yet they are not, is blasphemy, because it is a lie, whether they intend to lie or not. The intention does not alter the fact. Lying is the *hypostasis* or substance of blasphemy ; for no good thing can be injured by the truth. When Gentiles, who are neither Jews outwardly nor inwardly, pretend to be Jews, they calumniate that society of which the King of Jews is the chief; and in so doing they calumniate or blaspheme him ; the change of object from the less to the greater only enhances its iniquity. Verbal and practical lying are both mortal sins ; but their iniquity is aggravated when the lie is against God, His name, and His doctrine or word. Practical lying is profession contradicted by practice. Thus, " If we say we have fellowship with God and *walk in darkness*, we lie, and *do not the truth* ". " If a man say I love God, and hateth his brother, he is a liar " (1 John 1 : 6 ; 4 : 20), and, " If ye love me, keep my commandments " ; for " Ye are my friends *if ye do* whatsoever I command you ". Thus, the truth of men's professions is made to turn upon the conformity of their actions to the words of God. When those actions are a denial of His doctrine or word they make God a liar, so far as their influence extends. If their words and actions agree, and both give the lie to God or His word, which is the same thing, though less hypocritical, they are not less impious ; and the impiety is itself blasphemy.

No greater offence can be committed against God than not to believe what He has promised. The reason of this is because he " HAS MAGNIFIED HIS WORD ABOVE ALL HIS NAME " ;

and not to believe that word is to treat Him as a liar, which is blasphemy ; and " he that blasphemeth the name of Jehovah shall surely be put to death ", whether Gentile or Jew : this is the reason why it is decreed that " he who believeth not (the gospel) shall be condemned ". When we do not believe we walk in darkness ; and walking in darkness, or unbelief, we do not the truth ; for in relation to the truth no man can walk in the light of what he does not see, or do that in which he does not believe.

There is another form of lying or blasphemy against God which is brought out in the text from Ezekiel. It is this ; *If men in their ignorance or impiety affirm a thing, which in its logical or practical bearing contravenes the promises of Jehovah, they blaspheme, or speak evil of the subjects of those promises ; and in so doing speak words against, or blasphemies against the promiser.*

If the reader peruse Ezek. 35 in the light of God's covenanted promises to Abraham, Isaac, Jacob, David and their seed, he cannot, we think, fail readily to perceive the truth of our statement. In that writing, Mount Seir, the seat of Edom's dominion, is addressed as a Power having perpetual hatred against the descendants of Jacob ; rejoicing in their calamities, and in actual occupation of their country, commonly styled THE HOLY LAND. While thus possessed of Palestine as the fruit of conquest, Seir is represented as saying of the kingdoms of Israel and Judah, " These two nations and these two countries shall be mine, and *we will possess it* though Jehovah were there ". Upon this the prophet forewarns them that Idumea shall be recompensed according to its hatred of Israel, who shall be delivered after Idumea is destroyed ; " I will make myself known among Israel when I have judged thee, O Mount Seir, saith Jehovah ; and thou shalt know that I am Jehovah, and that I have heard all thy blasphemies which thou hast spoken against the mountains of Israel, saying, They are laid desolate, they are given us to consume ; thus with your mouth ye have boasted against me, and have multiplied your words against me ; I have heard them ".

The reader will observe that *Jehovah regards blasphemies, or false statements, concerning the destiny of the mountains of Israel, as great words or boastings against Himself*; the Idumean Seir declares that those mountains, even though Jehovah were there, would never belong to Israel, but to Edom ; for it says, " they are mine, and we will possess it though the I-Shall-Be were there ". But why is this declaration a blasphemy against the Holy Land ? and why, if a blasphemy against that land, is it a boast and multiplication of words against Jehovah ? Because it states falsely the destiny of Palestine. At present the two nations of Israel and Judah, and their special divisions of the Holy Land, are in the hands of Esau, Edom, or Idumea, synonyms of the power that in the latter days inherits the hatred of Isaac's eldest son against Jacob ; " for ", says Adonai Jehovah (the Old Testament title rendered Lord Jesus in the New), " *when the whole earth rejoices* I will make thee desolate. As thou didst rejoice at the inheritance of the House of Israel because it was desolate, so will I do unto thee ; thou shalt be desolate, O Mount Seir, and all Idumea, even all of it ".

Idumea, then, represents a power to be made desolate when the whole earth rejoices with God's people, Israel, as Moses has predicted. Idumea now triumphs over Israel and their land, and blasphemes them both ; the Idumeans decree that Judah's and Israel's two territories shall for ever constitute integral parts of the Ottoman Empire* ; and, consequently, that the two nations or twelve tribes of Jacob shall never constitute one independent kingdom and nation in the land ; this is pronouncing a sore evil against Israel and their native mountains ; but being a lie against their destiny it is a blasphemy against them all.

But why are these blasphemies against the Jews and their inheritance, boastings or calumnies against Jehovah ? Because, if it should so happen that Idumea, in this controversy concerning Zion, were to establish its power in the Holy Land, to the final exclusion and suppression of the kingdom and throne of David there, it would make the promises of Jehovah, which He has sworn by His own life and holiness to fulfil, of none effect. It is impossible that such a result should come to pass ; but to attempt to establish it, or to declare such a result, or to believe the declaration, *is equivalent to denying and rejecting the contrary,* and in effect declaring that Jehovah is a deceiver and a liar.

Now let us see what Jehovah has said—whether He has given the inheritance to Esau or to Jacob. Read the next chapter of Ezekiel ; this portion of his prophecy contains a testimony of God in direct opposition to the blasphemies of the Idumean nations, concerning Israel and their mountains ; the prophecy is addressed to these—a prophecy of good things.

*i.e., in 1857.

" Because, saith Adonai Jehovah, *the enemy* (a term which stands for the Desolater who triumphs while the land enjoys its Sabbaths) hath said against you, Aha ! even the ancient high places are ours in possession "—thus they boast at this day—" therefore prophesy and say, Thus saith Adonai Jehovah, Because they have made you desolate and swallowed you up on every side, that ye might be a possession to *the residue* of the nations, and *ye are taken up in the lips of talkers*, and are an infamy of the people ; therefore, ye mountains of Israel, hear the words of Adonai Jehovah : Thus saith Adonai Jehovah to the mountains and to the hills, to the lowlands and to the valleys, to the desolate wastes and to the cities that are forsaken, which became a prey and a derision to *the residue* of the nations that are round about : therefore thus saith Adonai Jehovah : Surely in the fire of my jealousy have I spoken against *the residue* of the nations (that " residue " to be stamped with the feet of the fourth beast—Dan. 7 : 19), and against all Idumea which have appointed MY *land* for their possession with the joy of all their heart, with despiteful minds, to cast it out for a prey.

" Prophesy therefore concerning the land of Israel, and say unto the mountains, and to the hills, to the lowlands and to the valleys, Thus saith Adonai Jehovah, I have spoken in my jealousy and in my fury, because ye have borne the shame of the nations ; therefore thus saith Adonai Jehovah ; I have lifted up my hand (that is, I have sworn), surely the nations that are about you, they shall bear their shame. But ye, O mountains of Israel, ye shall shoot forth your branches, and yield your fruit to my people of Israel, for they are at hand to come. For behold, I am for you, and will turn unto you, and ye shall be tilled and sown ; and I will multiply men upon you, *all the house of Israel*, even all of it : and the cities shall be inhabited, and the wastes shall be builded ; and I will multiply upon you man and beast ; and they shall increase and bring fruit ; and I will settle you after your old estates, and do better for you than at your beginnings ; and ye shall know that I (Adonai) am the I-SHALL-BE. Yea, I will cause men to walk upon you, even my people Israel ; and they shall possess thee, and thou shalt be their inheritance, and thou shalt no more henceforth bereave them ; thus saith Adonai Jehovah, Because they say unto thee, Thou land devourest up men, and hast bereaved thy nations ; therefore thou shalt devour men no more, nor cause thy nations to fall any more ; neither will I cause men to hear in thee the shame of the nations any more, neither shalt thou bear the reproach of the people any more, neither shalt thou cause thy nations to fall any more, saith Adonai Jehovah " (Ezek. 36 : 2-15).

Here is a time indicated which has manifestly not come ; for the Jews and their country are still subject to all these things, which at a " set time " of their history shall be no more.

There is another testimony in Ezekiel which convicts " the talkers " of the Gentiles of blasphemy against the two nations and their two territories which they claim for themselves, and of calumny against God. In chap. 37 : 21-28, Adonai Jehovah saith, " Behold, I will take the children of Israel from among the nations whither they be gone, and I will gather them on every side, and *bring them into their own land* ; and I will make them one nation in the land upon the mountains of Israel ; and *one king shall be king to them all* ; and they shall be no more two nations, neither shall they be divided into two kingdoms any more at all ; neither shall they defile themselves any more with their idols, nor with their detestable things, *nor with any of their transgressions* : but I will save them out of all their dwelling-places wherein they have sinned, and will cleanse them ; so shall they be my people, and I will be to them for Elohim. And David my servant (David II) shall be king over them, and they all (the twelve tribes) shall have one shepherd : they shall also walk in my judgments and observe my statutes, and do them. And they shall dwell *in the land that I have given unto Jacob* my servant wherein your fathers have dwelt ; and they shall dwell therein, even they and their children, and their children's children during the age (*ăd-ōlām*) ; and my servant David shall be prince over them for the age (*lĕ-ōlām*) ; moreover, I will make a covenant of peace with them, it shall be *an everlasting covenant* with them ; and I will place them and multiply them, and I will set my temple in the midst of them for the age (*lĕ-ōlām*). My dwelling-place also shall be with them : yea, I will be to them for Elohim, and they shall be to me for a people. And the Gentiles shall know that I, Jehovah, do sanctify Israel, when my temple shall be in the midst of them for the age (*lĕ-ōlām*)."

From these testimonies, then, we learn that the following things are decreed :

1.—That " the two countries ", or territories of the Holy Land formerly occupied by the " two nations " of the Jews, that is, the kingdom of the Ten Tribes and the kingdom of

Judah, are to be exalted to a better condition than when possessed by the Israelites in the beginning ;

2. That the Gentile Power in possession of Adonai Jehovah's land is to be finally dispossessed when He makes himself known among Israel's tribes ;

3.—That " *all the house of Israel, even all of it* " are to take possession of the land, and to be settled upon its mountains, and hills, and lowlands, and valleys, and desolate wastes, and forsaken cities, after the old estates of their realm, in peace, plenty, security, and great perpetual prosperity :

4.—That the nations and kingdoms of Israel and Judah shall be one united nation and kingdom upon the mountains of Israel ; so that " Ephraim shall not envy Judah, and Judah shall not vex Ephraim " any more : but as a bird of prey, " they shall fly upon the shoulders of the Philistines toward the west (the western powers) ; they shall spoil them in the east together ; they shall lay their hand upon Edom and Moab ; and the children of Ammon shall obey them " (Isa. 11 : 13, 14).

5.—That when finally resettled in Adonai Jehovah's land (his, by covenant made with Abraham and his seed, " who is the Christ ", says Paul), the whole twelve tribes will be under one supreme head or king ;

6.—That they will then be a purified and sanctified people—" *they shall defile themselves no more with any of their transgressions* " ; this implies that all their past national offences will have been blotted out ;

7.—That their Shepherd-King will be a David, and immortal ; and reign over them *during the age* of their national glory, however long its continuance may be predetermined by Jehovah (*ăd-ōlām*).

8.—That all these benefits will be guaranteed to the nation by the " covenant of the age " ; styled also the " covenant of peace " (*bĕrith shālom, bĕrith olām*) ; *the Constitution of the Kingdom*, in the phraseology of the Gentiles :

9.—That during the age, and for the purposes thereof, *a Temple* will be placed in the midst of the nation. Ezekiel described it, chapters 40-42. The mystery of the temple is set forth by Paul, Peter and John :

10.—That Adonai Jehovah, Israel's Shepherd-King, will dwell with them, and be to them for Elohim, or Gods—for all the saints or future kings and priests of Israel and the nations are consitutionally or federally " in him " ; HE is for *Gods*.

Now, these ten items, deduced from the foregoing testimonies, are the intelligible and obvious purpose of Jehovah with respect to Canaan and its heirs national. No language could have been devised to make His intentions plainer or more easy to be understood. He has not said that these things may come to pass if fortuitous circumstances favour their development ; but He has declared that *He will create the situation* that shall necessitate the results ; and that He will accomplish them, not for the sake of the generation of Israel existing at the crisis, but for their fathers' sake, on whose account they are beloved, and for the honour of His own character. " I have pity for *my holy name*, which the house of Israel have profaned among the nations whither they went ; therefore say unto the house of Israel : Thus saith Adonai Jehovah ; I do not for your sakes, O house of Israel, but for my holy name's sake, *which ye have profaned among the nations* whither ye went. And I will sanctify MY GREAT NAME which was profaned among the nations, which ye have profaned in the midst of them ; and the nations shall know that I am the Jehovah, saith Adonai Jehovah, when I shall be sanctified in you before their eyes. For I will take you from among the nations, and gather you out of all countries, and will bring you into your own land " (Ezek. 36 : 21, 24).

How easy to be understood, how devoid of mystification ! Is it not astonishing that any man professing to believe and study the scriptures should affirm that God has utterly and for ever cast off the Jews ; that there will be no restoration of them to Palestine ; and that God has no more use for them than for the gypsies ! To affirm this is to speak blasphemies, or lies, against the mountains and people of Israel ; and in so doing to speak great things against God with the mouth, and to multiply words against Him. This is the wickedness of all the children of Esau. *Nationally* they seize upon Jacob's inheritance, slay his seed with the sword, and proclaim the independence and integrity of a dominion that incorporates the land of Adonai Jehovah and His people in its domains. " These two nations and these two territories ", say they, " shall be mine, and we will possess it though Jehovah were there ", " they are laid desolate, they are given to us to consume ". Individually, they endorse the truth of this ; they preach it from their " sacred desks " ; they publish it in their creeds ; ignoring Israel and Israel's land in all the plentitude and folly of their traditions. But the issue is briefly and simply this : *If the doctrine of Esau's progeny be true, then the promises of Jehovah, covenanted with an oath, and confirmed by the blood of Adonai Jehovah, are a deceit and a bald imposition on the credulity of the Jewish nation and their friends.* To AFFIRM THE DOCTRINE OF ESAU IS TO GIVE THE LIE TO GOD.

But with the apostles, we say, " Let God be true, but every man a liar ; as it is written, That thou mightest overcome when thou art judged ". The sentence of God stands firm, though over thirty-eight hundred years have elapsed since it was uttered—" *The elder shall serve the younger* ". Edom shall be subject to Jacob ; therefore Edom shall not always triumph in the land. He that doctrinally reverses this decree belongs to the family of Esau, sets himself against the promises of God, and becomes the enemy of Jacob. Can the reader possibly have any difficulty in discerning this principle ? *We blaspheme God when we affirm the contrary of what He decrees.* It is an oblique method of telling Him that He has not decreed the truth. It is taking sides against him in " THE CONTROVERSY OF ZION " (Isa. 34 : 8), a controversy to be decided in favour of them that believe truth.

This great controversy it is that in reality defines the seeds— the seed of the woman, and the seed of her enemy. The seed of the woman are all on the side of Zion. They believe all " the glorious things " that Jehovah hath spoken concerning her. They love Jerusalem, and rejoice in all the good Jehovah hath sworn to do unto her ; while they repudiate with indigna- tion all traditions which reduce the promises to a nullity. This is right in every view ; for to make void the future glory of Zion is to rob the faithful of their inheritance ; for " Salvation ", saith Adonai Jehovah, " is of the Jews ", and when men are robbed of their rights, they do not feel very charitable towards the thieves.

All systems of religion, or forms of faith, are blasphemies or " abominations ", which uphold dogmas subversive of the promises of Jehovah. Piety of disposition in the worshippers, or moral precepts commingled in their ethics, will not transform blasphemies or indignities into things worthy of God. His doctrine and word are blasphemed when they are brought into disrepute, and contempt is generated in men's minds respecting the things they set forth. This is characteristic of the thing called " orthodoxy " among the Gentiles ; which assigns all the curses of God to the Jews, and all His blessings to their enemies. But all Gentilisms that do this, whether orthodox or heterodox, are blasphemies against God, His name, His tabernacle, and them that dwell in heaven. They constitute the darkness of this world, and they who walk in them " walk in darkness ", and neither believe nor do the truth. Such persons are very apt to " say they have fellowship with God ", because they appear to one another to be righteous in talking piety, and making long prayers ; and because, under the influence of human applause, they " feel good ", profess to be " at peace with God ", and are on excellent terms with themselves. But it is easy to show that their peace with God and their conscience is all on one side.

(ii) *THE BLASPHEMY OF THE CHURCHES*

Blasphemy against the mountains and people of Israel, and consequently of the covenanted promises of Jehovah, is the mortal sin of all who believe not " the gospel of the kingdom ", which is *the said promises evangelized.* He that directly denies the restoration of the Jews, and the reign of Jesus over them in the Holy Land " during the age ", or indirectly denies this by affirming that his hope, and consequently his *only* hope (for scripturally, there is but " one hope of the calling "), is the translation of his immortal soul to transkykingdomia at death, and its return for reunion with the mortal dust it left when it comes with Jesus to burn up the earth and world ; he who thus directly or indirectly denies this great and divinely attested purpose of the Most High One, is under the condemnation of the sentence which reads, " *He that believes not shall be condemned* ". This infidelity is the sin of all the ecclesiastical factions of the Gentiles. They content themselves with the creed prepared for them by the Apostasy, called " the Apostles' Creed ", which ignores the Hope of Israel, for which Paul was a prisoner in Rome, as completely as if earth had no Holy Land, no Jewish inhabitants, and no destiny involved in their glory and independence ! This credal version of what the apostles believed recognizes a resurrection of the body and a judgment ; but such a resurrection and judgment as never entered into their heads to conceive of. This resurrection dogma of Gentilism is *the reunion of a fictitious celestial soul from the skies with certain grains of dust in the earth's crust!* This is not the resurrection the apostles believed in. To admit the Gentile dogma is to admit " the immortality of the soul ", which is Paganism, and not Christianity. Their " judgment " is akin to it—a judgment invented by the fleshly mind for " immortal souls " ; *the judgment of nonentities!* It is a libel upon the apostles, a defamation of their Christian fame, a blasphemy of their glorious faith, to dignify such nonsense with their official name. They believed in God the Father Almighty, and in Jesus Christ, His son, *their* Lord ; they believed that he was born of a virgin, but not of an " immaculate " one, nor that his nature was immaculate, as Protestants do ; they believed that he was condemned by Pilate, and crucified unto death, and buried, and rose again the third day, and ascended to heaven afterwards ; and that he will come from thence again to judge the world, but not to burn it up ; they believed in remission of sins, the resurrection of the body, and in life everlasting ; but not in the sense imposed upon the words by Gentile theology. The Gentile " Names and Denominations ", styled apocalyptically " NAMES OF BLASPHEMY ", do not believe the things the apostles believed and taught, and interpretations of some of those things approved by their blind leaders of the blind. These interpretations, which are anti-scriptural discords, constitute their theology, which, making of none effect the promises of God, as the leaven of the old Pharisees did, generates a vain worship, and blasphemies against Him and His doctrine.

The popish and sectarian interpretation of " the Apostles' Creed " is the gospel believed by all " Christendom ". The apostles, however, did not preach the Gentile interpretation of their creed, which is therefore " another gospel ". This the Papal and Protestant, or sectarian world, now believes. The world's gospel is that Jesus, a person of immaculate nature, is Son of God, who died for sins, was buried, and rose again ; and that whosoever believes this, and believes that he died for him, and repents, his immortal soul shall be saved from eternal torment in liquid fire and brimstone ! Some sects may modify this statement somewhat ; nevertheless, as a general definition, it is the Gospel according to " the Mother of Harlots and of all the Abominations of the Earth ", and of those Harlots and Abominations too. This is a gospel that has nothing to do with the promises covenanted to the fathers. When a man professes this gospel and presents himself to the old Roman Mother, or to any of the State-Harlots, or to any of the innumerable sectarian-Abominations, or "Names of Blasphemy", all styled "Churches", from the Mother to the most insignificant of her rebellious progeny : when such a one makes application for admission within their pale, no member thereof, lay or clerical, ever thinks of inviting his confession of faith in the things promised to Abraham, David, and their seed ! The unlucky zealot, or bigot (by whatsoever name they might reproach him matters not), who should presume to make inquiry as to whether the candidate's "faith" embraced "*the substance of things hoped for*", "unto which hope the twelve tribes of Israel, constantly serving night and day, hoped to come ", and on account of which Paul was accused of the Jews : if such should be his inquisition that he might assure himself if the candidate's faith were justifying faith ; and, finding that he knew nothing about the good things God had promised to Israel, nationally and individually in Christ, he were to object to his fitness for admission to church-fellowship— were he clergyman or layman, who does not know that he would immediately become a marked man, an object of suspicion, and be regarded as an uncharitable disturber of the peace, a presumptuous and conceited fellow ? It is well known that such is the fact. What has Gentile church-fellowship to do with God's promises to Abraham, David, and their seed, national or individual ? Nothing ! Only "believe in Jesus ", as they define it, and a fig for Israel, their mountains, and the promises. It is enough, say they, that you believe that Jesus is the Christ, the Son of God. But the demons believed this, and trembled.

This is enough for them who endorse the blasphemies of Edom. Believe a barren proposition, and be pious, and make a bonfire of the promises. I say, a barren proposition ; for the confession that " Jesus is the Christ ", in the Gentile sense of it, is the mere acknowledgment of " a fact ", irrespective of the promises evangelized concerning the kingdom by the apostles and himself. What more natural than that the sons of Edom should delight in a gospel that ignores the promises ? Is it likely that they would rejoice in the blessing of Isaac upon their brother Jacob—that he " shall be as the smell of a field which Jehovah hath blessed " ? Would they, pluming themselves on having the birthright, rejoice that God should give Jacob " of the dew of heaven, and the fatness of the earth, and plenty of corn and wine "? Is it to be expected that, they being

Gentiles, and rejoicing in Gentilism, would respond " Amen " !
to the eulogy, " Let people serve thee, O Jacob, and nations
bow down to thee ; be thou lord over thy brethren, and let
thy mother's sons bow down to thee : cursed be every one that
curseth thee, and blessed be he that blesseth thee " ? (Gen.
27 : 28). It is expecting too much of reckless Edom that he
should delight in such promises as these. " Thou shalt serve
thy brother Jacob ", to a man that lives by his sword (verse 40),
is a galling and bitter humiliation. No wonder that Edom hates
Jacob, and repudiates all the promises concerning him—that
having acquired dominion by his sword, and for the time,
broken Jacob's yoke, he should seek to persuade himself that
Jehovah hath indeed cast off his people, Israel, for ever !
For, if this be so, then Edom shall not serve Jacob, and the
word of God becomes a lie !

Such is the blasphemy of Edom, the name used in Scripture
for the enemies of the Jews ; and surely they are their enemies
who assign all God's curses to them, and monopolize the
blessings for themselves. Upon this principle, then, all the
sects of Edom are incorporations of blasphemy against God ;
an idea apocalyptically set forth in the words, " Upon the
seven heads of the beast THE NAME OF BLASPHEMY " ; and in
Rev. 17 : 3, where the beast is said to be " full of names of
blasphemy ", and commented on above ; a gospel-nullifying
fraternity, denying the truth *in ignorantly maintaining the
opposite* ; or, in mixing it up with their traditions ; or, in
rejecting it without qualification or reserve. The disciples of
these systems are the " talkers " on whose lips Jewish affairs
are taken up reproachfully. They prate against the truth with
volubility inexhaustible ; being " unruly and vain talkers and
deceivers, whose mouths ", says Paul, " must be stopped.
Wherefore rebuke them sharply, *that they may be sound in the
faith* ".

The same apostle says, " There is one faith ". Now this
is the faith which justifies ; but not the faith of Christendom.
Justifying faith, and the faith of the unruly talkers of Edom,
are antagonist and mutually destructive systems of belief.
The latter has no soundness ; and in the former, soundness
can only be attained by an intelligent belief of the " covenants
of promise ". Men are justified by an enlightened and hearty
faith in the gospel of the kingdom of God preached by Jesus
and the apostles. This is evident from the consideration that
when the Lord Jesus sent Paul to preach the faith that justifies,

he sent him to " *open the eyes of the Gentiles, and to turn them from darkness to light,* and from the power of Satan to God, that they might receive remission of sins (or be justified) and inheritance among them (the saints of Israel) who are sanctified by faith the which leads into him " (*pistei tē eis eme*). It is clear from this, that illumination of mind preceded the reception of remission, and a right to the inheritance. He whose eyes are unopened by the gospel of the kingdom " walks in darkness ", and is obnoxious to the sentence, " he that believes not shall be condemned ". As there is but one true faith, it is also manifest that this condemnation is pronounced upon him who believes not that " one faith ", or the gospel ; and therefore styled " the faith of the gospel ". Now we have shown often that the faith of the children of Edom is not the " one faith " which the apostles preached ; nor is any other form of faith which ignores the promises covenanted to the fathers of Israel : for " faith is assurance of things hoped for, a conviction of things not seen " ; and these unseen matters of hope are the subject of the covenants of promise ; for in speaking of the death of that cloud of witnesses who had obtained renown through the possession and exercise of this faith, Paul says, " These all died in faith, not having received the promises, but saw them afar off " ; and the reason he gives for their dying without receiving, is that " God has provided some better thing for us, that they without us should not be made perfect ", or immortal.

The gospel, we have said, is the covenanted promises evangelized. To make our meaning distinct, a word or two must be said in regard to " evangelized ". This is a Greek word in an English dress, being in its own country called *evangelidzo.* This is the noun *evangelion,* with a verbal termination implying action—a putting into action the noun. Now this noun is composed of *eu,* signifying good, well ; and *angelia,* a message, from *angelō,* to narrate ; from which comes *angelos,* one sent, a message-bearer, angel. *Evangelion,* therefore, signifies *a good message,* which, when put into circulation, is *evangelized.* Now, a message to be good must be something excellent, beneficial, and to be desired by those to whom it is sent ; and because this is the fact, God has called the message, or " word he sent unto the children of Israel proclaiming peace " to them, good.

That " peace " is the subject matter of the covenants of promise ; and is the reason why we so often meet with such passages as these : " Thou shalt see the good of Jerusalem all the days of thy life. Yea, thou shalt see thy children's children, and peace upon Israel " (Psa. 128 : 5, 6), "As for such as turn aside unto their crooked ways, Jehovah shall lead them forth with the workers of iniquity ; but peace shall be upon Israel " (Psa. 125 : 5) ; " Our feet shall stand within thy gates, O Jerusalem. Pray for the peace of Jerusalem ; they shall prosper that love thee. Peace be within thy walls, and prosperity within thy palaces. For my brethren and companions' sakes (the saints) I (Messiah the Prince of Peace) will now say, Peace be within thee ! " (Psa. 122) ; " In his days shall the righteous flourish ; and abundance of peace so long as the moon endures " (Psa. 72 : 7). " He will speak peace unto his people, and to his saints ; but let them not turn again to folly. Surely his salvation is nigh them that fear him ; that glory may dwell in our land. Mercy and truth are met together ; righteousness and peace have kissed each other " (Psa. 85 : 8). " I will extend peace to Jerusalem like a river, and the glory of the Gentiles like a flowing stream " (Isa. 66 : 12).

In the song which shall be sung in the land of Judah when Jerusalem become " a strong city ", Israel sings, " O Jehovah, thou wilt ordain peace for us " (Isa. 26 : 12). Yea, " I will make with them *a covenant of peace*, and will cause the evil beasts to cease out of the land ; and they shall dwell safely in the wilderness, and sleep in the woods. And I will make them and the places round about my hill (Zion) a blessing ; and I will cause the shower to come down in its season ; there shall be showers of blessing. And the tree of the field shall yield its fruit, and the earth shall yield its increase, and they shall be safe in their land, and shall know that I (Jesus) am the Jehovah (I shall be) *when I have broken the bands of their yoke, and delivered them out of the hand of those that served themselves of them.* And THEY SHALL NO MORE BE A PREY TO THE NATIONS, neither shall the beast of the land devour them ; but they shall dwell safely, and none shall make them afraid. And I will raise up for them a PLANT FOR RENOWN, and *they shall no more be consumed with hunger in the land* ; neither bear the shame of the nations any more. Thus shall they know that I Jehovah their God am with them, and that they, the house of Israel are my people, saith Adonai Jehovah " (Ezek. 34 : 25). The Son given to Israel is styled " the Prince of Peace ", of whom it is written, " Of the increase of his government and peace there shall be no end upon the throne of David, and upon his kingdom to order and establish it with judgment and with justice from henceforth and during the age " (Isa. 9 : 7). Then, " He shall speak peace unto the nations ; and his dominion shall be from sea to sea, and from the river (Euphrates) to the ends of the earth " (Zech. 9 : 10). "And I will break the bow and the sword and the battle out of the earth, and will make Israel to lie down in safety " (Hosea 2 : 18).

Now, when the time had nearly arrived for the Prince of Peace to be born, a communication was made to Mary that she should be his mother ; and that, as Isaiah had predicted, the throne of his ancestor David should be given him by the most High, whose Son he should also be ; and that, when seated there, he should reign over the house of Jacob for the ages, and that of his kingdom there should be no end. This was announcing peace to Israel through the Son to be born. So Mary understood it ; and in the rejoicing of her spirit in God, said, " He helps his servant Israel in remembrance of mercy as he spake to our fathers, to Abraham, and to his Seed, for the age ".

That the mercy covenanted to Abraham was peace to Israel through the Messiah is also manifest from the words of the Holy Spirit spoken through the father of John the Baptizer, who said in view of the birth of the Christ, " Blessed be the Lord God of Israel ; for he visits and redeems his people, and raises up a horn of salvation for us in the house of his servant David ; as he spake by the mou 1 of his holy prophets which have been from the beginning of he age ; that we should be saved from our enemies, and fron. che hand of all that hate us ; to perform the mercy promised to our fathers, and to remember his holy covenant ; the oath which he sware to our father Abraham, that he would grant unto us, that we, *being delivered out of the hand of our enemies*, might serve him without fear in holiness and righteousness before him, all the days of our life " (Luke 1 : 68). What a beautiful comment is this upon the Abrahamic Covenant ; how forcibly it exhibits the national blessedness to come upon the hereditary seed of Abraham through the Christ. But not exclusively upon them ; but upon all other nations through him also ; for " In thee and in thy seed, shall all the nations of the earth be blessed " ; therefore it came to pass when the birth of Jesus had occurred, that his mission was proclaimed by a multitude of the heavenly host, saying, " Glory in the highest places to God, and over the earth peace, and good will among men ".

Here, then, is peace to Israel, and peace to all other nations, promised and confirmed by oath to Abraham, David, and their seed, when Christ shall sit upon David's throne as the result of " mercy and truth meeting together, and righteousness and peace embracing each other ". When Abraham rises from the dead, and becomes the patriarch, or chief father, of a believing and righteous world, the multitude of its nations will become " his seed " as well as Israel, and the saints, the kings and lords of all. This is Moses' doctrine of a future state, amplified by all the prophets. Their oracles were its depository ; and until Peter visited the house of Cornelius, these covenanted promises were supposed to be confined to Israelites alone. It was not conceived possible that men of other nations would be associated with Messiah in the government of the Jewish nation and the Gentiles. The promises of the holy covenant had not assumed the form of a message of invitation to aliens from the Commonwealth of Israel. The Jews were exclusively invited by Jesus, and by the apostles for several years after his ascension. They went about explaining the purpose of God, which was full of goodness and glory for Israel ; and inviting them to partake in it with endless life and honour. This was *evangelizing the promises*, or setting before them the hope. They were called upon to become heirs of that hope by embracing it, and becoming obedient to the commands of Jesus. It was therefore styled " the hope of their calling ", by faith in which, says an apostle, we are saved.

Understanding then that the gospel, or glad tidings, is *not* salvation of immortal souls from endless torment in material fire who believe that Jesus in flesh was God's immaculate Son and died for them ; but that it is the promises of everlasting peace and glory to the Jewish nation, and of contemporary blessedness to all other nations ; when, as one dominion, they shall exist under the government of Christ, and of his called, chosen and faithful " brethren and companions " when he shall sit and rule as a priest upon David's throne ; which promises were covenanted to Abraham, Isaac, Jacob, and David and their seed ; and confirmed by the death and resurrection of Christ ; it is these confirmed and covenanted promises *evangelized*, or circulated among men in a proclamation, in which Jews first and afterwards Gentiles *who believe said promises and recognize the claims of Jesus to be that Christ as he is described in Moses and the Prophets*, are invited to co-partnership with him in said covenanted kingdom and glory, *on condition of becoming the subjects of repentance and remission of sins in his name.* This is the Pentecostian Gospel of the Kingdom of God preached by Peter and the apostles ; the other, the salvation of immortal souls from endless torture in material fire, is the Pope's gospel—the clerical gospel of Rome, Wittenberg, and Geneva—the gospel according to Christendom, by which its intoxicated peoples are ecclesiastically policed : the gospel of Antichrist, which, admitting the divine sonship and sacrificial character of Jesus, ignores the promises, blasphemes Israel, and so " speaks great words against the most High ", who has " formed that people for himself that they may show forth his praise " (Isa. 43 : 21). Understanding, then, these things ; and that justification comes by belief and obedience, or an enlightened and obedient belief of the gospel— what intelligent man can be at a loss to perceive that they are not justified who are ignorant of, or reject the promises, when they seek, or are sung, prayed, or scared into immersion ? Belief of the gospel of Antichrist does not make water saving ; and certainly none but a Romanist, Puseyite, or baby-sprinkler, would make it saving of itself alone. What makes baptism saving, then ? For Peter says, " We are saved by baptism ". We answer according to the word, *the belief of the promises* : that is, of the gospel the apostles preached. The Baptistic, Millerite, Campbellite, Mormonite, and general paidorhantist theories of belief, are not justifying ; because they either ignore or destroy the promises. In doing this they are, as we have shown, " blasphemies ", and punishable with death. Can a man be justified by the belief of blasphemy ? Will a pious profession of love to Jesus transmute blasphemy into justifying truth ? Is the sincere belief of what the Scriptures style blasphemy less offensive to Jehovah in a modern religionist, than in an ancient Edomite ? Is it less blasphemy to say with Millerism, " God has cast away the Jews ; he will destroy the nations ; he will burn up the earth ; and we shall inherit Paradise with dominion over the beasts after the similitude of Adam " ; than to say with Edom, " The mountains of Israel are laid desolate, they are given to us to consume " ? One saying is as subversive of the truth of God, and as derogatory to His veracity, as the other. If immersed-Millerism decree the truth, Jehovah's promises, which we have set forth, will never come to pass. Hence God and Millerism are as much at enmity as God and Edom ; it is logical and scriptural therefore to place Millerism and Edom side by side against

God. We say Millerism, not simply as such ; but as representative of all Gentilisms ending in *ism*, whose theology does not teach for justification, and whose organizations do not require for admission to their fellowship, an intelligent belief and confession of the message of peace to Israel, as taught in Moses and the prophets.

Let any one read the faith of Mary, Zacharias, and Simeon, as expressed in their utterances prompted by the Holy Spirit ; and then imagine the proclamation of such gospel as sounds forth from the pulpits of the Gentiles, being made to them— a gospel which assigns the Holy Land to Edom, and consigns Israel to curse and perdition : what does he think those ancient worthies would have said ? Would not their souls have boiled over with bubbling and steaming indignation ? Would they have rejoiced that their eyes had seen such a Saviour as the Gentile character styled Jesus ? Would they have seen in him an earnest of the remembrance by Jehovah of the oath He had sworn to Abraham, and of the covenant He had made with David ? No : they would have been like our Jewish contemporaries, rejecters of Jesus, because the Gentile description of his character and mission did not accord with the Messiah as defined by Moses and the prophets. Let all, then who believe in " the exceeding great and precious promises ", and who are disposed to accept God's evangelized invitation to His kingdom and glory, which He has promised to them that obey Him—let such be honest to themselves and true to God. Let them repudiate the uncovenanted traditions of Gentilism as "blasphemies against their king ". If dipped into Baptistism, Campbellism, or Millerism, etc., let them put them off as " filthy rags "—as garments " all tattered and torn ", and " spotted with the flesh ". They are investments unbecoming the divine presence of the Nazarite King of the Jews. He invites men to walk with him in white—a white which the sectarian fullers of Edom cannot produce. " What is the chaff to the wheat, saith Jehovah ? " Some who read these lines may have been dipped into divers Gentilisms, sincerely believing they were obeying the truth ; but, if you have studied the prophets to any good purpose, you will know that the truth according to Edom is not " the truth as it is in Jesus "—your own good sense will teach you that your sincerity will not transmute the one into the other. Do you find in the Bible such a dogma as, " He that is sincere and immersed, shall be saved ? "

This is one of the gospel-nullifying principles of Edom—a mere tare sown among the wheat. Abandon it, dear friends, and consent heartily to the wholesome, unrepealed words of Adonai Jehovah, that " He who believes (the gospel or promises) and is immersed shall be saved ; but he that believes not shall be condemned ".

26

THE COMING CRISIS AND ITS RESULTS

(i) *JUDGMENT AND HOPE*

As to the approaching judgments three things may be affirmed. First, they introduce the millennium. Secondly, they are the precursors or accompaniments of Christ's second appearing. Thirdly, they are connected with a total change of dispensation. Each of these statements I hope to establish by plain and abundant testimony of scripture. It is to the first and second I would now entreat my reader's attention. The proof of the third will more naturally present itself when some other points have been considered.

Judgment has often been executed on the wicked. The deluge, the overthrow of Sodom, the destruction of the Canaanitish tribes, the destruction of Jerusalem, whether by Nebuchadnezzar, or by the Romans, the overthrow of Babylon by the Medes and Persians, as well as other similar events, each affords an instance of the execution of righteous judgment on the wicked. What is it, then, which distinguishes this grand interposition of God in judgment which is yet future from all other judgments such as have been enumerated? The distinction is in this, that the awful judgments which are fast approaching introduce the millennium; and further, *that Christ himself comes in connection with these judgments*. Let us look at the evidence of these things in scripture. But earnestly would I remind my Christian readers, that it is not the coming of Christ to earth to execute judgment which is the sum of our hope, but his descent to receive us to himself. So the subject is presented in the New Testament, however needful it may be to be forewarned of Christ's coming to execute judgment also. When he so comes, we shall come with him. Must we not have been previously gathered to him? Certainly.

No passage is more commonly or more justly quoted in proof that there is to be a millennium, than that in which Yahweh promises to His Son to give the nations for his inheritance, and the uttermost parts of the earth for his possession. But turn to Psalm 2, where this promise is recorded, and you will find that it is by the execution of terrible judgments on the wicked that it is to be made good. It is not peacefully, or by man's submission brought about by the gospel and by " grace ", that the rightful Heir takes possession of his dominions. We read of a confederacy against him : the nations rage, the people imagine a vain thing ; the kings of the earth set themselves, and the rulers take counsel together against Yahweh, and against His anointed. Their cry is, " Let us break their bonds asunder, and cast away their cords from us ". True, we learn from Acts 4 : 25-27 that this confederacy was formed in the days of Pontius Pilate, Herod, and the rulers of the Jews. But then we have intimation in the psalm that there would be a period during which the Lord would laugh at their puny rage. Not as yet interfering in judgment, He would allow them, as it were, to go to the length of their chain, but treat with utter derision their attempts to set aside His purpose, and to order the affairs of the earth after their own hearts' desire. " He that sitteth in the heavens shall laugh ; Yahweh shall have them in derision." But this period of patient endurance comes to a close. It gives place to judgment. " Then shall he speak unto them in his wrath, and vex them in his sore displeasure." God's purpose is irrevocable. Their rage and opposition cannot alter that. " Yet have I set my king upon my holy hill of Zion. I will declare the decree : Yahweh hath said unto me, Thou art my Son ; this day have I begotten thee. Ask of me, and I shall give thee the nations for thine inheritance, and the uttermost parts of the earth for thy possession." Thus far the passage is often quoted. But what follows immediately ? How are the rights of God's anointed but earth-rejected Son to be established ? " Thou shalt break them with a rod of iron ; thou shalt dash them in pieces like a potter's vessel." Could any language be employed to teach more clearly or impressively that it is by judgments on the wicked that Christ's glorious kingdom will be introduced ?

We see thus how it is God's irrevocable decree that His Son shall reign over all the earth, and how vain and puny are all man's efforts to prevent it. Turn to Psalm 96 and you will find all the earth invited to sing a new song unto Yahweh. It is in anticipation of the blessings of his reign that universal anthems are thus demanded. True, that it is by power in judgment that His reign is to be introduced and established ; and the psalm before us recognizes this. But universal blessing will attend His reign ; and hence the call for universal joy and praise. But it is not the mere execution of providential judgments which introduces this glorious period, and wakes up this universal harmony. No, the Lord comes to judge, and comes to reign. " Say among the nations, that Yahweh reigneth ; the world also shall be established that it shall not be moved : he shall judge the people righteously. Let the heavens rejoice, and let the earth be glad ; let the sea roar and the fulness thereof. Let the field be joyful, and all that is therein : then shall all the trees of the wood rejoice before Yahweh : for he cometh, for he cometh to judge the earth ; he shall judge the world with righteousness, and the people with his truth." So also at the close of Psalm 98 : " Sing unto Yahweh with the harp ; with the harp, and the voice of a psalm : with trumpets, and sound of cornet, make a joyful noise before Yahweh the King. Let the floods clap their hands : let the hills be joyful together before Yahweh the King. Let the sea roar, and the fulness thereof ; the world and they that dwell therein : for he cometh to judge the earth : with righteousness shall he judge the world, and the people with equity ". Reader, have you ever considered these passages ? It is of the judgment of the great white throne they treat. Then, the existing heaven and earth are to flee from before the face of Him who sitteth on the throne, and no place is to be found for them. Here, heaven and earth are called on to rejoice at the coming of the Lord, at His coming to judgment, as that which introduces the period of His universal reign, and of earth's blessing and delight.

Another passage beautifully depicting the happy days which are yet to dawn on this afflicted and groaning earth, is that well known one in Isaiah 11. Sweet it is (whether the language be understood literally of a change in the brute creation or figuratively of peace and concord among men) to think of the wolf dwelling with the lamb ; the leopard lying down with the kid ; the calf, the young lion, and the fatling together ; and all so gentle, that a little child shall lead them. " They shall not hurt nor destroy in all my holy mountain ; for the earth shall be full of the knowledge of Yahweh, as the waters cover the sea." Delightful prospect for this miserable world ! But how are these days of peace, and piety, and universal blessing, to be ushered in ? By the interposition of One whose lowly grace, and perfect rectitude and holiness, are so touchingly portrayed in the opening verses of the chapter. The Christian can be at no loss to say whose portrait it is with which we are furnished here. But are grace, and lowliness,

271

and perfect faithfulness, the only features presented to us ? No, we are told of his *acts* as well as of his moral excellencies— acts such as he never performed when he was here before. " But with righteousness shall he judge the poor, and reprove with equity for the meek of the earth ; and he shall smite the earth with the rod of his mouth, and with the breath of his lips shall he slay the wicked." The predictions of the millennium follow.

But if we turn to 2 Thess. 2 : 8, where the apostle seems to quote this prophecy, we find additional instruction on two points. First we find that it is Antichrist, the man of sin, that is intended by the term, " the wicked ". Both in the Hebrew of Isaiah 11, and the Greek of 2 Thess 2 the term is in the singular number, and means literally, " that wicked one ". But without insisting on this, it is enough to notice that in 2 Thess. 2 our English translators have marked that it is some one, or something, pre-eminent in evil that is intended by using a capital letter in the word " wicked ". "And then shall that Wicked be revealed, whom the Lord shall consume with the spirit (or breath) of his mouth, and shall destroy with *the brightness of his coming*." This is the other point here brought out. It is by *the brightness of his coming* that Antichrist, this wicked one, is to be destroyed. But let us examine a little more minutely the combined testimony of these connected passages.

The apostle informs the Thessalonians that the day of Christ shall not come except there come a falling away or an Apostasy first, and that man of sin be revealed. He had told them of these things when present among them, and now reminds them that they know what hindered the revelation of this man of sin. " The mystery of iniquity doth already work ", in his language ; " only he who now letteth (hindereth) shall let (hinder) till he be taken out of the way, and then shall that Wicked be revealed." The mystery of iniquity was working then, and would continue to work until, the hindrance being removed, it should issue in the revelation of the man of sin, that Wicked, " whom the Lord shall consume with the spirit of his mouth, and shall destroy with the brightness of his coming ". Thus we have the continued working and progress of evil, from its germ which existed in the apostle's day, to its maturity in this man of sin, who only meets his doom *at* the coming of the Lord, and *by* the coming of the Lord. Isaiah takes up the subject where the apostle lays it down, and shows us the blessed results of this glorious interposition, the peace, the concord, the happiness of Messiah's reign ; the earth full of the knowledge of the Lord as the waters cover the sea. The two passages together afford the most conclusive proof of all we are seeking to establish, that *the millennium is introduced by judgments on the wicked, and that those judgments attend the coming of the Lord.*

My readers will remember the quotations from Isaiah 24, as to the earth being made empty and waste, as to its being utterly broken down, and clean dissolved, and moved exceedingly. It would be well to read the whole chapter. How does it close ? What is the sequel to those overwhelming judgments which it teaches us to expect ? " Then the moon shall be confounded, and the sun ashamed, when Yahweh of hosts shall reign in Mount Zion, and in Jerusalem, and before his ancients, gloriously." The judgments commence and introduce this glorious, universal reign. I say universal : for while Zion and Jerusalem are its special earthly centre, its blessings will extend to all the earth. Thus, a few verses below the one just quoted, after having again celebrated God's interposition in judgment, making of a city an heap ; of a defenced city a ruin ; a palace of strangers to be no city ; bringing down the noise of strangers ; the prophet thus speaks of the issue, the effect of these judgments. "And in this mountain shall Yahweh of hosts make unto all people a feast of fat things, a feast of wines on the lees, of fat things full of marrow, of wine on the lees well refined. And he will destroy in this mountain the face of the covering cast over all people, and the vail that is spread over all nations " (25 : 7). Then in chapter 26 : 8, 9, the righteous are represented as saying, " Yea, in the way of thy judgments, O Yahweh, have we waited for thee ; the desire of our soul is to thy name, and to the remembrance of thee. With my soul have I desired thee in the night : yea, with my spirit within me will I seek thee early ; *for when thy judgments are in the earth, the inhabitants of the world will learn righteousness* ". Here is the definite, absolute assertion, that it is by God's judgments the inhabitants of the world will learn righteousness.

But what is the peculiar character of these judgments, that they should have such an effect ? Let my reader compare this passage with 1 Cor. 15 : 54, and he will find that these stupendous events are connected with the coming of the Lord, and the resurrection of the saints. 1 Cor. 15, it is well known, treats fully the subject of the resurrection. " For as in Adam all die, even so in Christ shall all be made alive. But every man in his own order ; Christ the firstfruits ; afterward they that are Christ's "—when ? "At his coming ". *The resurrection of the saints, then, takes place at the coming of Christ.* But what connection has this with Isaiah 25 ? We shall see immediately. The apostle declares that we shall not all sleep—that the living saints shall be changed when the departed ones are raised : " for this corruptible ", he says, " must put on incorruption, and this mortal must put on immortality. So when this corruptible shall have put on incorruption, and this mortal shall have put on immortality, then shall be brought to pass the saying that is written, Death is swallowed up in victory ". Where is this saying written ? *In only one place in scripture, and that,* Isa. 25 : 8. We have the awful judgments in chapter 24, and at the end of it, the reign of the Lord of hosts in Mount Zion. Then in chapter 25, we find that in this mountain the Lord of hosts is to make a feast unto all nations, and to remove the vail, the covering. The words quoted by the apostle immediately follow : " He will swallow up death in victory " In a word, the apostle tells us when the prophecy of Isaiah 24 and 25 will be accomplished. " *When* this corruptible shall have put on incorruption, *then* shall be brought to pass, the saying which is written (in Isa. 25), Death is swallowed up in victory." And when is this corruptible to put on incorruption ? When are the dead to be raised ? " Every man in his own order. Christ the firstfruits ; afterward they that are Christ's *at his coming.*" Could there be more decisive proof that the coming of Christ, the resurrection of the sleeping saints, and the change of those who are alive, the fearful judgments which are to destroy the wicked, and the commencement of the reign of Christ, are all indissolubly linked together ? They all are comprised in, and constitute, the grand epoch to which everything is tending, and with which nothing in the history of man, or of the world, can compare.

Another remarkable testimony to the same effect we have in Isa. 59 : 12, 15. The prophet has been lamenting in the most moving terms the deep and widespread and universal corruption which precedes this interposition of God in judgment. " For our transgressions are multiplied before thee, and our sins testify against us : for our transgressions are with us ; and as for our iniquities, we know them ; in transgressing and lying against Yahweh and departing away from our Elohim, speaking oppression and revolt, conceiving and uttering from

274

the heart words of falsehood. And judgment is turned away backward, and justice standeth afar off ; for truth is fallen in the street, and equity cannot enter. Yea, truth faileth : and he that departeth from evil maketh himself a prey : and Yahweh saw it, and it displeased him that there was no judgment." No doubt the prophet has in this passage a special eye to Israel and its moral condition. But what a picture have we here of the state of things existing at the present day ! How is it to be terminated ? The Lord is represented as interfering. In what way does He interfere ? " He put on the garments of vengeance for clothing, and was clad with zeal as a cloke. According to their deeds, accordingly he will repay, fury to his adversaries, recompence to his enemies ; to the islands he will repay recompence. So (mark, reader, this word " so ") shall they fear the name of Yahweh from the west, and his glory from the rising of the sun." Could words more accurately express, could language more emphatically announce, the very position we are seeking to establish ? What is that position ? That the approaching judgments are what will introduce the millennium. What is the testimony of the passage before us ? That all power of judgment and testimony having failed and ceased *morally* among men, the Lord will himself rise up to execute judgment *by power* ; repaying men according to their deeds, repaying recompence to the islands : thus universal is to be this interposition of God. And what is to be its effect ? " So shall they fear the name of Yahweh from the west, and his glory from the rising of the sun." From hemisphere to hemisphere is the fear of the Lord's name and glory to extend, as the result of these retributive judgments on the wicked. Had there been no other passage of scripture on the subject, we might have supposed that the testimony of this would have been completely decisive.

But does not this passage shed further light on our present subject ? Does it not afford evidence of both the truths we are seeking to establish ? Here is the answer : *"And the Redeemer shall come to Zion, and unto them that turn from transgression in Jacob, saith Yahweh "*. This also is quoted in the New Testament. Paul quotes it in Rom. 11 : 26. He has been treating of the temporary setting aside of Israel, but declares that it is only for a time : that " blindness in part is happened to Israel, until the fulness of the Gentiles be come in ; and so all Israel shall be saved : as it is written, There shall come out of Zion the deliverer, and shall turn away ungodliness from Jacob ". My readers are most likely aware that before New Testament times the Old Testament had been translated into Greek, and that from this translation, called the Septuagint, many of the quotations in the New Testament are made. This accounts for the verbal difference in many such cases as the one before us. But no one can doubt that the passage quoted by the apostle is the one in question in Isaiah 59. Nor is it possible to evade the proof afforded by the two, that it is *at His coming* the Lord renders recompense to His enemies and to the islands, so that they shall fear His name and His glory from east to west.

(ii) *A NATION BORN*

Let us now turn to Isaiah 66. There we read, amid strongest exclamations of surprise, of the earth being made to bring forth in one day, of a nation being born at once ; " for as soon ", says the prophet, " as Zion travailed, she brought forth her children ". All who love Jerusalem are called upon to rejoice with her. " For thus saith Yahweh, Behold, I will extend peace to her like a river, and the glory of the Gentiles like a flowing stream : then shall ye suck, ye shall be borne upon her sides, and be dandled upon her knees ". Who can fail to discern here the bright anticipations of millennial blessing ? But how is such blessing to be introduced ? "A voice of noise from the city, a voice from the temple, a voice of Yahweh that rendereth recompence to his enemies." Then again, " The hand of Yahweh shall be known toward his servants, and his indignation toward his enemies ". We are told that " by fire and by his sword will Yahweh plead with all flesh ; and the slain of Yahweh shall be many ". It is not that all flesh will be slain. Many, so many as to baffle description, and defy conception, will be slain ; but there will be many spared. By fire and by His sword will Yahweh thus plead with all flesh ; and what shall be the result ? " For I know their works and their thoughts : it shall come, that I will gather all nations and tongues ; and they shall come, and see my glory. And I will set a sign among them, and I will send of those that escape unto the nations, to Tarshish, Pul, and Lud, that draw the bow, to Tubal and Javan, to the isles afar off, that have not heard my fame, neither have seen my glory ; and they shall declare my glory among the Gentiles ".

276

What further ensues ? The perfect regathering of God's natural born people Israel, brought for an offering to Yahweh out of all nations to God's holy mountain Jerusalem ; " and I will also take of them for priests and for Levites, saith Yahweh ". Is this the whole ? No. "And it shall come to pass, that from one new moon to another, and from one sabbath to another, shall all flesh come to worship before me, saith Yahweh ". I enter into none of the questions which have been raised as to the precise meaning of these words. All agree that they express in one way or another the universal prevalence of true religion in the millennium. And surely the whole chapter leaves us in no doubt as to its being by overwhelming, desolating judgments, that this glorious period is to be introduced. But further ; the memorial of these judgments is in some way to remain. "And they shall go forth, and look upon the carcases of the men that have transgressed against me ; for their worm shall not die, neither shall their fire be quenched ; and they shall be an abhorring unto all flesh."

With regard to this chapter, I would only add that it also connects the judgment on the nations, and introduction of the millennium, with the coming of the Lord. " For, behold, Yahweh will come with fire, and with his chariots like a whirl-wind, to render his anger with fury, and his rebuke with flames of fire." It is then at the coming of the Lord that by fire and by His sword will He plead with all flesh, and subdue the whole world to His sway.

In Ezek. 39 : 11-16 is a passage predicting judgments so terrific, and a destruction so overwhelming, that seven months are to be occupied in burying the dead. A passage on the same subject from the previous chapter reads : " For in my jealousy and in the fire of my wrath have I spoken, Surely in that day there shall be a great shaking in the land of Israel : so that the fishes of the sea, and the fowls of the heaven, and the beasts of the field, and all creeping things that creep upon the earth, and all the men that are upon the face of the earth, shall shake at my presence, and the mountains shall be thrown down, and the steep places shall fall, and every wall shall fall to the ground. And I will call for a sword against him (that is, Gog) throughout all my mountains, saith Adonai Yahweh : every man's sword shall be against his brother. And I will plead against him with pestilence and with blood ; and I will rain upon him, and upon his bands, and upon the many people that are with him, an overflowing rain, and great hailstones, fire and brimstone ".

And what is to be the result among men of this awful interposition ? " Thus will I magnify myself, and sanctify myself : and I will be known in the eyes of many nations ; and they shall know that I am Yahweh." Then, after the fearful predictions of the next chapter we have these words : "And I will set my glory among the nations, and all the nations shall see my judgment that I have executed, and my hand that I have laid upon them ".

And though the predictions of millennial blessing which follow are restricted to Israel, they are so expressed as to show indisputably that it is the millennium that is spoken of, and that it is at the commencement of the millennium that these terrible judgments take place. The verse immediately succeeding the one last quoted, is as follows : " So the house of Israel shall know that I am Yahweh their Elohim from that day and forward ". How manifest that it is at the epoch of these terrible judgments that their national conversion takes place. " Therefore, thus saith Adonai Yahweh, Now will I bring again the captivity of Jacob, and have mercy upon the whole house of Israel, and will be jealous for my holy name ". After being thus converted and restored they are not to apostatize any more. Their blessing is to be permanent. " Then shall they know that I am Yahweh their Elohim, which caused them to be led into captivity among the nations ; but I have gathered them unto their own land, and have left none of them any more there. Neither will I hide my face any more from them : for I have poured out my Spirit upon the house of Israel, saith Adonai Yahweh ". Could there be more conclusive proof than that which the whole passage affords that the judgments of which these two chapters treat are at the commencement of the millennial period ?

If we turn to Dan. 2, what is it that follows the smiting of the image on his feet by the stone cut out without hands ? The destruction of the image is complete ; but what follows it ? What takes its place ? " Then was the iron, the clay, the brass, the silver, and the gold, broken to pieces together, and became like the chaff of the summer threshing floors ; and the wind carried them away, that no place was found for them ; and the stone that smote the image became a great mountain, and filled the whole earth." As to what the meaning of all this is, we are happily not left to our own thoughts. The prophet not only gives us the symbols, but also the interpretation of them. Still men have substituted their own imaginings and speculations for the plain words of the prophet. It is not disputed generally that the interpretation of the first part of the vision is correct. All agree that four empires or universal kingdoms are set forth : nor is there much dispute as to what kingdoms these are. Babylon, Medo-Persia, Greece, and Rome, are agreed almost on all hands to be the four empires represented by the image. But the stone is erroneously supposed by many to represent the gospel ; and that what is foretold respecting it is that it will gradually spread until the whole world, these four kingdoms included, shall, by its means, become the kingdom of Christ. But who does not see that there would thus be no destruction of the image, or of the empires which it represents ? What is foretold respecting the stone is not that contemporaneously with the existence and supremacy of the fourth empire, the stone should be slowly and gradually increasing, and as it increases, changing the character of the image, as this false interpretation suggests. No, but that at a given epoch the stone should smite the image on its feet ; that in the last days of the fourth empire a sudden blow should be given which should be fatal to the whole image ; and that then, and not until then, the stone that smote the image should become a great mountain, and fill the whole earth. "And in the days of these kings shall the Eloah of heaven set up a kingdom which shall not be abolished for ages ; and the kingdom shall not be left to other people, but it shall break in pieces and consume all these kingdoms, and it shall stand for ages." Here we have the formal declaration that it is by the overthrow and destruction of the previously existing kingdoms that the final, millennial kingdom is to be established.

Dan. 7 gives us still more full and explicit instructions. It is the same general subject, embracing many additional particulars, and the whole presented, if possible, with greater precision. Four beasts represent the same kingdoms which in chapter 2 are symbolized by the several parts of the metallic image. But the fourth is represented in a form in which it has ten horns, in the midst of which comes up another, a little one, whose rapid growth, swelling words, and valiant looks, excite the special and wondering attention of the prophet. This one continues till the thrones are set, the Ancient of days sits, the judgment is set, and the books are opened. " I beheld then ", says the prophet, " because of the voice of the great words which the horn spake ; I beheld, even till the beast was slain, and his body destroyed, and given to the burning flame."

279

And what is it that accompanies this judgment ? And what succeeds it ? " I saw in the night vision, and behold, one like the Son of man came with the clouds of heaven, and came to the Ancient of days, and they brought him near before him. And there was given him dominion and glory, and a kingdom, that all people, nations, and languages, should serve him : his dominion is an everlasting dominion, which shall not pass away, and his kingdom that which shall not be destroyed." Who that believes the Bible can resist the evidence which thus accumulates on our hands, that it is by such destroying judgments as have been considered that the millennium, or universal kingdom of Christ, is to be introduced ?

Zephaniah tells us of a great gathering of the nations ; of terrible judgments overtaking them when thus gathered ; and of millennial blessedness as that which ensues. Hear his words : " Therefore wait ye upon me, saith Yahweh, until the day that I rise up to the prey ; for my determination is to gather the nations, that I may assemble the kingdoms, to pour upon them mine indignation, even all my fierce anger ; for all the earth shall be devoured with the fire of my jealousy. For then (mark, dear reader, how God tells us when the millennium shall commence :) *then* will I turn to the people a pure language, that they may all call upon the name of Yahweh, to serve him with one consent. From beyond the rivers of Ethiopia my suppliants, even the daughter of my dispersed, shall bring mine offering " (3 : 8-10). All the rest of the chapter describes the happiness of those millennial times.

Zech. 14 I purposely pass by for the present, as it will have to be specially considered further on. In turning to the New Testament, Luke 19 may claim our first consideration. Can there be any doubt that what is there termed " the kingdom of God " is really the millennium which prophets had foretold, and which the Jewish nation were thus taught to expect ? "And as they heard these things, he added and spake a parable, because he was nigh to Jerusalem, and because they thought that the kingdom of God should immediately appear." Were they wrong, then, in expecting God's kingdom to be set up ? No, it was the expectation of its *immediate appearance* in which they were mistaken. In a certain sense it was even then among them. But it had not *appeared* : nor has it yet. Listen to the parable of our Lord. " He said therefore, A certain nobleman went into a far country to receive for himself a kingdom, and to return." There can be no mistake as to the person

THE COMING CRISIS AND ITS RESULTS

represented by the nobleman, or as to what is intended by his going into a far country. Instead of setting up the kingdom when he was here before, Christ had to be rejected by the earth, and to ascend into heaven. His servants occupy during his absence, and his citizens send after him the insulting defiance, " We will not have this man to reign over us ". What is it terminates this state of things ? "And it came to pass that when he was returned, having received the kingdom, then he commanded these servants to be called unto him." His servants are rewarded according to their works. But is this all ? No. " But those mine enemies, which would not that I should reign over them, bring hither and slay them before me." This verse we have quoted as prophetic of approaching judgment on the wicked. But what does this judgment on the wicked introduce ? *The kingdom—the kingdom in open manifestation or display.* They thought it was immediately to appear. No, says our Lord, I will tell you what must intervene. What is it that intervenes ? or rather what are the last intervening events ? *The Lord's return, and judgment on the wicked.* Our Lord was to depart ; his servants were to be held responsible to him in his absence ; he was to receive the kingdom, to return, to reward and punish his servants ; and then, last of all, his enemies were to be slain. This accomplished, what but the kingdom can remain ? The kingdom, manifested, and universally acknowledged glory : in other words, the millennium.

To pass by a number of other passages which might be adduced, what is the testimony of Rev. 11 : 14-18 ? Without at present entering into any questions as to the general interpretation of this wondrous book, suffice it to remind my reader that seal after seal having been opened, and trumpet after trumpet blown, we arrive, in the chapter before us, at an epoch of which intimation has been given in the previous chapters. Four trumpets sound their loud, shrill blast of warning and of terror ; "And I beheld ", says the prophet, " and heard an angel flying through the midst of heaven, saying with a loud voice, Woe, woe, woe, to the inhabiters of the earth, by reason of the other voices of the trumpet of the three angels, which are yet to sound " (8 : 13). Then another mighty angel is seen by the apostle, his right foot upon the sea, and his left upon the earth. His voice is as when a lion roareth ; and when he cries seven thunders utter their voices. This angel lifts his hand to heaven, and swears by him that liveth for the *aiōns* of the *aiōns* that there should be delay no longer. " But in the days of the voice of the seventh angel, when he shall sound, the mystery of God should be finished, as he hath declared the glad tidings by the prophets " (10 : 7). Such are the terms in which the last three, and especially the last, of the seven trumpets are previously announced. What, then, is the language of our chapter itself ? " The second woe is past ; and, behold, the third woe cometh quickly. And the seventh angel sounded ; and there were great voices in heaven, saying, The kingdoms of this world are become the kingdoms of our Lord, and of his Christ ; and he shall reign for the *aiōns* of the *aiōns*." Need we any further witness ? Whatever fancies men may have indulged, and however counsel may have been darkened by a multitude of words without knowledge (as, alas ! it often has been), no one dreams that this epoch has arrived, that the predictions of the verse just quoted are fulfilled. The kingdoms of this world have not yet become the kingdoms of our Lord and His Christ. When shall they become so ? When the first and the second woes trumpets have sounded, and the third woe, following quickly, and accompanying the sounding of the seventh angel, has spent itself on the guilty inhabitants of the earth ; then shall the mystery of God be finished ; then shall the many voices in heaven proclaim the transfer to our Lord and to His Christ of the sovereignty of the whole earth. But listen ! There is a second chorus. "And the four and twenty elders, which sat before God on their thrones, fell upon their faces, and worshipped God, saying, We give thee thanks, O Lord God Almighty, which art, and wast, and art to come ; because thou hast taken to thee thy great power, and hast reigned. And the nations were angry (not converted !), and thy wrath is come, and the time of the dead, that they should be judged, and that thou shouldest give reward unto thy servants the prophets, and to the saints, and them that fear thy name, small and great ; and shouldest destroy them which destroy the earth." Oh yes, it is thus the universal reign of Christ is introduced. The nations we know will be angry (see Psalm 2) ; but when the seventh angel sounds, and God takes Him His great power, and His wrath comes, and the time of the dead that they should be judged, and reward be given to the saints, while the destroyers of the earth are themselves destroyed ; when this epoch arrives, then, and not until then, shall the kingdoms of this world become the kingdoms of the Lord and of His Christ, and he shall

282

reign for ever and ever. It is by judgments, overwhelming, and yet rapidly approaching judgments, that the millennium will be ushered in.

Dan. 12 : 1, informs us, "And at that time shall Michael stand up, the great prince which standeth for the children of thy people ; and there shall be a time of trouble, such as never was since there was a nation even to that same time ; and at that time thy people shall be delivered, every one that shall be found written in the book ". Why do I quote this ? Because the passage declares that the time of trouble unequalled by any since there was a nation is when the Jews, Daniel's people, are delivered—not dispersed. Bear this in mind, my readers. The tribulation attending the deliverance of the Jews is to be such as never was till then. So says Daniel. It must be future, for the Jews are not yet delivered ; and Daniel assures us that it is then there shall be tribulation unequalled by anything till that time. " Then shall all the tribes of the earth mourn, and they shall see the Son of man coming in the clouds of heaven, with power and great glory " (Matt. 24 : 30). Ah, this is the event which is to bring the present dispensation to a close, and usher in the period of universal righteousness and peace.

Let us turn now to Zech. 14 : " Behold, the day of Yahweh cometh, and thy spoil shall be divided in the midst of thee. For I will gather all nations against Jerusalem to battle ". Here I pause. Many passages speak of a gathering of all nations. " It shall come that I will gather all nations and tongues " (Isa. 66 : 18). " For, behold, in those days, and in that time, when I shall bring again the captivity of Judah and Jerusalem, I will also gather all nations " (Joel 3 : 1, 2). " Now also many nations are gathered against thee . . . for he shall gather them as sheaves into the floor " (Micah 4 : 11, 12). " For my determination is to gather the nations " (Zeph 3 : 8). It is of the same subject the passage before us treats ! " For I will gather all nations against Jerusalem to battle ; and the city shall be taken, and the houses rifled, and the women ravished ; and half of the city shall go forth into captivity, and the residue of the people shall not be cut off from the city ". Such are the straits to which the returned Jews will be reduced in that time of unequalled tribulation of which Daniel informs us. How are they to be delivered ? " Then shall Yahweh go forth, and fight against those nations, as when he fought in the day of battle." But is this anything more than a figurative prediction of some striking providential interposition at the juncture referred to ? Read what follows : "And his feet shall stand in that day upon the Mount of Olives, which is before Jerusalem on the east ; and the Mount of Olives shall cleave in the midst thereof toward the east and toward the west, and there shall be a very great valley ; and half of the mountain shall remove toward the north, and half of it toward the south. And ye shall flee to the valley of the mountains ; for the valley of the mountains shall reach unto Azal : yea, ye shall flee, like as ye fled from before the earthquake in the days of Uzziah, king of Judah ; *and Yahweh my Eloah shall come, and all the saints with thee* ". If this does not foretell the coming of the Lord with all his saints at the period of this great gathering of all nations, where could language be found in which to clothe such a prediction ? And what follows this event ? To what is it introductory ? To a period in which, we are told, " living waters shall go out from Jerusalem " : " in summer and in winter " are they to flow. But more than this—"And Yahweh shall be king over all the earth : in that day shall there be one Yahweh, and his name one ". Here we have the whole matter. Desolating judgment on God's congregated adversaries ; the coming of the Lord, which brings this judgment ; and as the result, His peaceful reign over all the earth.

Turn now to Rev. 19 and 20. We are told previously (16 : 14) of three unclean spirits, " spirits of demons, working miracles, which go forth unto the kings of the earth and of the whole habitable, to gather them to the battle of that great day of God Almighty ". Here, in these chapters, we have the issue of this gathering. The apostle says, "And I saw heaven opened, and behold a white horse ; and he that sat upon him was called Faithful and True, and in righteousness he doth judge and make war ". We are left in no doubt as to who this is. " He was clothed with a vesture dipped in blood ; and his name is called The Word of God." Nor does he come alone. As in Zech. 14 we have read, "And Yahweh my Eloah shall come, and all the saints with thee ", so here : "And the armies which were in heaven followed him upon white horses, clothed in fine linen, white and clean ". In verse 8 we read, " for the fine linen is the righteousness of saints ". Thus he comes, attended by his saints. Woe to the wicked then ! "And out of his mouth goeth a sharp sword, that with it he should smite the nations : and he shall rule them with a rod of iron : and he treadeth the winepress of the fierceness and wrath of Almighty

God." Yes, the hardihood of God's enemies will not then protect them from His wrath. Infatuated beyond conception, they will indeed rush to the battle : but it will be to their everlasting overthrow. "And I saw the beast, and the kings of the earth, and their armies gathered together to make war against him that sat on the horse, and against his army. And the beast was taken, and with him the false prophet that wrought miracles before him . . . These both were cast alive into a lake of fire burning with brimstone." Distinguished above all others in iniquity, they will be thus awfully distinguished in their doom. And will their followers escape ? Alas, no ! "And the remnant were slain with the sword of him that sat upon the horse, which sword proceeded out of his mouth : and all the fowls were filled with their flesh." What ensues on this glorious advent of Christ and his saints, and this utter overthrow of his enemies ? Read ch. 20, and you will find Satan bound for a thousand years, and Christ reigning with his risen and glorified saints throughout that blissful period.

Here I pause. Space forbids further proof at present of what is, however, fully proved by all the scriptures which have passed under review, that it is by judgments, and by the coming of the Lord, that the millennium is ushered in. As to what it is that makes these judgments needful, we are not left ignorant. Scripture fully informs us. And there is one thing which makes study of prophecy of such immense practical importance. It is, that we shall be on earth when these judgments are executed. Our scriptural hope is to be caught up to meet the Lord in the political air, and so to come with him when he comes to execute judgment on the wicked. But we are surrounded by those principles, influences, and systems, which are ripening to that maturity of evil which mankind will reach ere those judgments come. God will judge them at the coming of Christ, when they are fully ripe. But has acquaintance with these subjects no tendency to keep us apart from such evils now ? Surely it has ; and that we might be so sanctified, or kept apart from evil, is one object God has in view in revealing these things to us.

It is not by exciting applications of prophecy to passing events that true edification is secured. The natural mind may feel the deepest interest in prophetic inquiries thus conducted ; but scripture was never designed to instruct us as to what transpires in the arena of political factions, or to occupy our souls with such subjects. " Our citizenship (*politeuma*) subsists in heavens." " Let the potsherd strive with the potsherds of the earth." It is not with such contentions that God's revelation of the future concerns itself. It forewarns us, in general terms, that wars and rumours of wars may be expected, till God shall interpose in power for the settlement of His great controversy with mankind : till, as the result of this interposition, the sceptre of universal dominion shall be wielded by the Prince of peace. But it is as to this interposition in judgment, and approaching climax of iniquity which renders it inevitable, that prophecy instructs us. And even as to this, *it is because the church will be on earth, amid the desolations of the crisis which is so rapidly approaching*, that she receives those revelations respecting it. At the coming crisis opening upon the world, the church will have been received into the royal presence, at the descent of Christ into the aerial. I do not enter here upon the proof of this. It belongs properly to a further stage of our inquiries. But I would not here withold the expression of this conviction : entreating my readers to search the scriptures for themselves. The church is instructed by prophecy as to the approaching crisis of evil and judgment, because she is to be present on earth when it arrives, and because she is now surrounded by all those active and insidious principles of evil which when ripe God will judge. The church is thus enabled morally and spiritually to judge those things now, which in their maturity of evil God will judge by the righteous retributions of His wrath. All the principles of Babylon and of the ten-horned beast are in existence and operation now. How can a Christian more effectually learn what they are, and why and how they are to be avoided, than by the prayerful study of God's prophetic awful judgments by which they will, at the coming of Christ, be destroyed ?

There are three very distinct spheres on which the judgments will fall, when the Lord cometh out of his place to punish the inhabitants of the earth for their iniquity ; Israel, the Nations, and professing Christendom. These will, indeed, be all united in the final climax of evil, and so judgment will come upon the whole. Still, as their responsibilities, and the dealings of God with them, have been and are so very distinct, each demands distinct consideration. And if we are to understand why judgment comes upon Israel we must know what Israel's calling and testimony is, and how it has failed therein. If we are to discern the grounds of God's righteous judgment upon the Gentile nations, we must be acquainted with His past and present dealings with them, and with their conduct under their special responsibilities. So also, to understand the guilt of professing Christendom, and what it is that brings judgment on the nations which are so designated, we must know what the calling of the true church is, what is its testimony, and in what respects Christendom, while assuming the place and owning the responsibilities of the church, has acted contrary thereto. These are solemn subjects of inquiry. May our hearts be prepared for them. Much that is brighter remains beyond.

27

THE SON'S POST-MILLENNIAL SUBJECTION TO THE FATHER

THE passage in which this idea is found is 1 Cor. 15. Paul affirmed that the resurrection of those " in Christ " would happen at his coming. In the next verse, he says, " Then cometh The End ". He does not say how long after Christ's coming it would be to that end. Indeed, he did not know, for " the times and seasons " were reserved by the Father in His own power, until He revealed them to Jesus Christ, " who sent and revealed by his messenger to his servant John ". This apostle, however, makes us acquainted with the truth that the end would be divided from Christ's coming in power and great glory by an interval of a thousand years, and that this long period will be occupied by the kingdom of Jehovah and of His Anointed. Though Paul could not tell the duration of this, " the Economy of the Fulness of Times ", as he styles it (Eph. 1 : 10), he records events by which the end of the economy might be known. These are, the conquest of all enemies ; the final abolition of death ; the delivering up of the kingdom to the Father by the Son ; and the Son's own subjection to God. The passage is remarkable, and deserving of quotation in full : " As in Adam all (the saints) die, even so in Christ shall (they) all be made alive. But every one in the destined order : Christ an offering of firstfruits ; next, they that are Christ's at his appearing : after that the end, when he shall have delivered over the kingdom to the God and Father : when he shall have vanquished every dominion, and every jurisdiction and power. For it is necessary that he reign until he (God) shall have put all the adversaries under his (the Son's) feet. The last enemy that shall be destroyed is death. For he hath subdued all things under his feet. But when he saith, that everything hath been put under, manifest it is, that He, having subdued the all things to him (the Son), is excepted. But when the all things shall be subdued to him (the Son) then the Son himself also shall be subordinated to Him (the Father) who has subjected the all things to him (the Son) in order that God may be the all things for all ".

To see into this matter, it must be understood that before sin entered into the world by Adam, the economy was " very good " : and God was " the all things for all " the living souls

He had made. In this state of being there was no adversary, and no death, because there was no sin, and death being absent, there was no viceregal kingdom to make war upon hostile powers, for the purpose of subduing them, and substituting the power of God instead. All was peace and harmony between God and man upon earth.

But when sin entered into the world, and death by sin, a rebellion commenced against God which has never been put down effectually from that day to this. It has ever gathered strength, and is at the present crisis more defiant of His authority than ever. But He has declared that things shall not always continue thus ; for He has sworn by His own life, saying, "*As truly as I live all the earth shall be filled with the glory of the Lord*" (Num. 14 : 21) : and therefore the Lord Jesus taught his disciples to express their heart's desire, saying, " Thy kingdom come ; and thy will be done on earth as it is in heaven ". When Jehovah's will shall thus absolutely be obeyed, " *the end* " will have arrived. The sin of the world will have been taken away ; and every curse have ceased. There will then, consequently, be no more death : and once more a state of being will obtain in which peace and harmony between God and men will exist, so that on receiving all things elaborated by the Son, He will again pronounce them " *very good* ".

This very good constitution of things terrestrial is thus indicated by John. "And I saw a New Heaven and a New Earth ; and there was no more sea. And I heard a great voice out of the heaven, saying, Behold, the tabernacle of God is with men, and he will dwell with them, and they shall be his people, and God himself shall be with them, their God. And God shall wipe away all tears from their eyes ; and there shall be no more death, neither sorrow, nor crying, neither shall there be any more pain ; for the former things are passed away. And he that sat upon the throne said, Behold, I make all things new. He that overcometh shall inherit all things ; and I will be his God, and he shall be my son " (Rev. 21 : 1-7).

Here is a state upon earth evidently pertaining to " the end" indicated by Paul, when death, the last enemy, is no more. God's tabernacle with men upon the earth is not pitched until death is destroyed. The destruction of death implies the previous suppression of sin in the world. Death's sting is sin, which causes death ; but the sting being extracted from human nature, it dies no more. Every dweller upon the earth becomes an immortal son of God, who will be with them as He is now with His only and chief begotten Son, the Lord Jesus Christ. In this post-millennial " very good " state there will be no sinners ; consequently, none separated from God, and requiring a mediator betwixt them. But in the economy of the previous thousand years, sin, sinners, and death, still exist ; hence a very different constitution of things must obtain to the succeeding arrangement in which they find no place at all. The epoch between the Millennial Economy and its successor is marked by the delivering over the Millennial kingdom to God, and it will then, in the hands of Christ and his brethren, have accomplished the work assigned to it.

The Kingdom's mission is " to break in pieces and consume all kingdoms ", and to " fill the whole earth " in ruling over all. It will be introduced into the world to put down the great rebellion against God, which is organized under the " dominions, jurisdictions, and powers ", or governments of the nations. Of course, with the means to be employed, this is not an instantaneous affair. For its full and effectual accomplishment, God has allotted a thousand years. The work to be accomplished is stupendous, but not too great for the forces of the Kingdom. All these great kingdoms, empires, and republics, are to be conquered, and their millions of armed defenders cut up and dispersed. Beside the overthrow of these rebel hosts, knowledge, righteousness, and peace, have to follow in the train of victory. The religion and law of the conqueror will be gratefully accepted by the nations as they become freed from the tyrants who oppress and brutalize them. " Of the *increase* of his government and peace there shall be no end, upon the throne of David and upon his kingdom, to order it, and to establish it with judgment and with justice from henceforth and for ever." On that throne he will reign until " the end " ; for " his kingdom shall not be destroyed, and his dominion is *unto the end* " : for he must reign until God hath put all enemies under his feet.

When the nature and constitution of the kingdom are duly considered, it will be readily perceived that it cannot, in the fitness of things continue longer than the extinction of sin, and the entire abolition of its wages, which is death and corruption. The kingdom of Christ and of God is a priestly institution; for so it is written, " the Branch shall build the Temple of Jehovah ; and he shall bear the glory, and shall sit and rule upon his throne ; and be a priest upon his throne ". The reader, I suppose, need not be informed that this prophecy is of Jehovah's Anointed in his kingdom ; and, therefore, of Jesus of Nazareth, the King of the Jews. When " the Lord God shall give him the throne of his father David " that he may sit there and " reign over the House of Jacob unto the ages ", he will be God's High Priest for the Twelve Tribes of Israel, and the nations of his dominion. This is proved by Isaiah's testimony, which reveals that " all nations shall flow unto the Lord's house " which shall be called " a house of prayer for all people ", the offerings of whose flocks and herds " shall come up with acceptance on mine altar ", saith Jehovah, " and I will glorify the house of my glory ". Then shall " many people go and say, Come ye, and let us go up to Jehovah's mountain, to the Temple of Jacob's God ; and he will teach us of his ways, and we will walk in his paths ; for out of Zion (the city where David dwells) shall go forth the law, and the Word of the Lord from Jerusalem " (Isa. 2 : 2, 3 ; 56 : 7 ; 60 : 7). Who will then be the High Priest and Teacher of Jehovah's ways, in the house of Israel's God ?—the great light to enlighten the Gentiles, and the glory of his people Israel ? There can be but one answer, and that is, " The Priest upon the throne " (Zech. 6 : 12, 13), who " shall judge among many people, and rebuke strong nations afar off ", even Christ Jesus our Lord ; who is now the High Priest of our confession, " made a High Priest after the order of Melchizedec for the Age ", but even now " a High Priest over the house of God ", " whose house are we, if we hold fast the confidence and the rejoicing of the hope firm unto the end " (Heb. 3 : 1, 6 ; 5 : 6 ; 10 : 21). Thus, what he is now doing in the presence of God for " the Heirs of the Kingdom "—making reconciliation for his household—is but the earnest of what he will do for the subjects of his dominion, when, with his reconciled ones, he shall occupy " the thrones of the house of David ".

Now, " every High Priest taken from among men is ordained for men in things pertaining to God, that he may offer both gifts and sacrifices for sins " (Heb. 5 : 1). It is clear from the testimony quoted that sin, sinners, death, and national sacrificial worship, will obtain in the world till " the end " of the thousand years beginning with the appearing of Christ in his glory. " Gifts and sacrifices ", therefore, will all that time be necessary because of sin, and being necessary, there must be a high priest to offer them for men to God in the place appointed. Now, the nature of the kingdom being Melchizedecan, or royal and priestly, its covenant, or constitution, provides that its king shall unite the two offices in his own person. This applies also to all the joint-inheritors with him in the same kingdom. Hence, they are all styled " kings and priests to God ". The kingdom is, therefore mediatorial. It stands, when established, sacerdotally between Jehovah and all who are not office-bearers and dignitaries of the kingdom. So long as this monarchy exists with a priestly constitution, " the tabernacle of God " cannot " be with men ", neither can " he dwell with them ", nor can they be " his people ". " With men " ; that is, with the entire population of the earth. He is now with Christ Jesus, dwelling in him with His fulness ; and during the thousand years, He will be with Christ's brethren, the saints, dwelling in them as in their elder brother ; but with the residue of men He will not so dwell until Christ has accomplished the work of " destroying that having the power of death, that is, the devil ", and its works, or, in other words, until he shall have " taken away the sin of the world " ; destroyed all its dominions, jurisdictions and powers ; and have extinguished death. When this is consummated there will be no obstacle preventing God's abode with men but the Melchizedec kingdom ; which must, therefore, of necessity be taken out of the way, as no longer adapted to the state of things upon the earth.

The reader will see this at a glance when he is asked, What will be the use of priests to God for men, when, because of the effectual suppression of transgression, and the extinction of sin in the flesh, there are no gifts and sacrifices to offer, no errors and ignorance to atone for ? Christ's and the saints' occupation will then be gone. It will then have expired according to the statute of limitation, which says, " Thou art a priest *for the age* after the order of Melchizedec " (Psa. 110 : 4). The word *le-olahm*, in the Hebrew text, is rendered in Paul's citation of it *eis ton aiōna* in the Greek ; which I have translated " for the age ", which is not only probably correct, but made certainly so by the scripture doctrine concerning priesthood.

The Son, then, will " deliver over the kingdom to the God and Father " of men, at the time all become His sons, because of the unsuitableness of its nature and covenant to the Ages succeeding the Millennial Age. The kingdom will not be destroyed, but only changed in its constitution, so as to adapt it to the improved and altered condition of the world. The kingdom in its Melchizedec or millennial organization is the heavens planted and the foundations of earth laid by the

Lord, when " he proclaims to Zion, Thou art my people " ; and saith, " Thy God reigneth ! " (Isa. 51 : 16 ; 52 : 7). John styles this organization in reference to that of the post-millennial ages, the former, or " first heaven and the first earth "—that constitution of Israel predicted in the sixty-fifth of Isaiah. This heaven of the kingdom is destined to be changed, so that when " the End " comes it will have " passed away " as entirely as if it had been destroyed. This constitution of the kingdom will have perished, though Christ and the Saints remain in undiminished glory and beatitude. Hence, it is written in the hundred and second Psalm, and applied to Jesus in Heb. 1 : 10, " Thou, Lord, at the beginning (*kat' archas*, at the beginning of Zion's earth and heavens) laidst the foundation of the earth ; and the heavens are the works of thine hands. They shall perish ; but thou shalt stand : yea, all of them shall wax old like a garment ; as a vesture shalt thou change them, and they shall be changed " : then Jesus creates all things new : " But thou art the same, and thy years shall have no end. The children of thy servants (Abraham, Isaac, and Jacob) shall continue, and their seed (the saints) shall be established before thee ".

Now, when the Lord Jesus has changed the whole system of things terrestrial and mundane by the Spirit of the Father, a new world will be the result, in which the constitution of society will be royal, but not priestly ; Jesus and the Saints being the Jehovah and the Elohim of the new order of things, as others were of the old, as appears from the Mosaic account of the Six Days. Jehovah, Jesus and his Elohim will have consummated the work begun by Jehovah Elohim, seven thousand years before. But though " great ", Jesus is always " the Son of the Highest ", of whom he says, " My Father is greater than I ". He is Jehovah's servant to perform an appointed work, and to establish his Father's authority in all the earth. This done, the Father no longer veils His face in a representative, but appears as sovereign in His own kingdom ; in which, however, His glorious Son is always pre-eminent, and next, but not upon, the throne. The words of Pharaoh to Joseph will express the idea I wish to convey of the Son's subordination to the Father in the Ages, that God may be the all things for all. " There is none so discreet and wise as thou. Thou shalt be over my house, and according unto thy word shall all my people be ruled : only in the throne will I be greater than thou ". The kingdom, therefore, though changed, having its priestly elements removed, continues a kingdom still—a sinless kingdom added to the universal dominion of " the Blessed and only Potentate, dwelling in unapproachable light, whom no man hath seen, nor can see : to whom be honour and power in all ages, Amen ".

Such is the exposition of Paul's saying concerning the turning over of the kingdom to the Father, as it appears to me. The kingdom is without end, but not without change. In the thousand years, it is " the kingdom of Christ and of God " ; in the after ages, " the all things " are concentred in God, " for all " the dwellers upon the earth. Mediation exists no more, since all things are reconciled, and endless peace obtains.

A DECLARATION OF WHAT THE
SCRIPTURES TEACH*

WE shall do this epitomially, and in as few words as possible.

1.—*First, then, the Scriptures reveal that the gospel was preached to Abraham.*

This is proved by what follows : " The Scripture, foreseeing that God would justify the heathen through faith, preached before the gospel unto Abraham, saying, In thee shall all the nations be blessed " (Gal. 3 : 8). Referring to this incident, Jesus said to the Jews, " Your father Abraham rejoiced to see my day ; and he saw it, and was glad " (John 8 : 56).

Upon this we may remark that all nations have never yet been blessed in Abraham ; secondly, that when all nations shall be blessed in Abraham, Messiah's Day will have been revealed ; and thirdly, that these events not having been accomplished, their fulfilment is yet a matter of hope ; hence, Abraham rejoiced in the prospect of the Future Age, then far off, but now near, because it was doubtless then revealed to him that he should sit down with his descendant, the Messiah, in the Kingdom of God (Luke 13 : 28). For Abraham, when called, went out into a country where the Kingdom is to be set up ; which country " he should after receive for an inheritance " ; " he sojourned in (this) the Land of Promise, as in a strange, or foreign country ; for he looked for a City, or State, which hath foundations, whose builder and maker (or founder and constitutor) is God (Heb. 11 : 8-10). These passages are a few of the beacon-lights which show that he looked for a State, or Kingdom, divinely established and constituted under his Descendant in the Land promised to him and to his Seed, when all nations should own his sovereignty. This he looked for as Messiah's Age ; he saw it in the eye of that " faith " which is " the assured expectation of things hoped for ; the conviction of things unseen " ; and without which " it is impossible to please God " ; " he saw it, and was glad ". This was the ancient Gospel preached to Abraham, which is still a matter of hope to all of Abraham's seed.

---

*This was written in 1847, when Dr. Thomas had reached an understanding of the Gospel. He confessed his errors and abjured them. and then, as was fitting, set out what he now believed.

THE FAITH IN THE LAST DAYS

Query : of those who preach " baptism for remission, etc.",
as the ancient Gospel, we would inquire—when the gospel was
preached to Abraham by the Lord God, did he preach to him
that Jesus was the Christ, His Son ; that he died, was buried,
and rose again, for faith ; and repentance and baptism into
the name of the Trinity for the remission of sins, in obedience
to that faith ? In the nature of things this could not have been
preached, yet he preached to him the Gospel ; and you admit
that there is but one Gospel : how do you disentangle yourselves from this difficulty ? Is it not manifest, that we have been
preaching something else than what the Lord God preached
to Abraham, and which Paul says was the Gospel ?

2.—*The same Gospel was preached to Abraham's descendants
in Egypt and in the wilderness of Egypt.*

This is proved by these testimonies. In the good news
announced by Jacob to his sons, he said, " The sceptre (the
symbol of sovereign power) shall not depart from Judah, nor
a lawgiver from between his feet, until He whose it is come :
and unto him shall the gathering of the nations be " (Gen.
49 : 10). Joseph preached the same gospel to them fifty-four
years after, saying, " God will surely visit you, and bring you
out of the land (of Egypt) unto the land he sware (or promised)
to Abraham, to Isaac, and to Jacob : and ye shall carry up my
bones " (Gen. 50 : 24, 25). None, however, of Joseph's
generation left Egypt : but by faith, Joseph, when he died,
made mention of the departing of Israel ; and gave commandment concerning his bones (Heb. 11 : 22).

The Angel of the Lord preached the Gospel to Moses at
the bush, saying, " I am the God of thy father, the God of
Abraham, the God of Isaac, and the God of Jacob . . . I have
surely seen the affliction of my people which are in Egypt,
and have heard their cry by reason of their taskmasters ; for I
know their sorrows : and I am come down to deliver them out
of the hand of the Egyptians, and to bring them up out of that
land, unto a good and large land, unto a land flowing with
milk and honey ; unto the place or country of the Canaanites,
and Hittites, and the Amorites, and the Perizzites, and the
Hivites, and the Jebusites " (Exod. 3 : 6-8). In this discourse
Jesus says, God preached to Moses the resurrection of Abraham,
Isaac and Jacob (Luke 20 : 37). What were they to rise from
the dead for ? To inherit this " good and large land flowing with
milk and honey ", promised to them in the Gospel preached to

them ; and in which they, and all their posterity, as yet, have only dwelt as pilgrims and sojourners.

By an assured expectation of the things delivered to him from his fathers, and a conviction of them then as yet unseen, " Moses, when he was come to years, refused to be called the son of Pharaoh's daughter, choosing rather to suffer affliction with the people of God than to enjoy the pleasures of sin for a season ; esteeming the reproach of (or, on account of the expectation of) the Anointed King (spoken of by Jacob when blessing Judah) greater riches than the treasures of Egypt : for he had respect unto the recompence of the reward ", which Shiloh should bring (Heb. 11 : 24). Moses, then, believed the same gospel as did Abraham, Isaac, Jacob and Joseph, and, as we shall see, preached it likewise.

" Go ", said Jehovah to him, " and gather the elders of Israel together, and say to them, The Lord God of your fathers, the God of Abraham, of Isaac, and of Jacob, appeared to me, saying, I have surely visited you, and seen that which is done to you in Egypt : and I have said (to Abraham, Gen. 15 : 13, 16), I will bring you up out of the affliction unto the land of the Canaanites . . . unto a land flowing with milk and honey " (Exod. 3 : 17). "And Aaron spake all the words which the Lord had spoken to Moses, and did the signs in the sight of the people. And the people believed : and bowed their heads, and worshipped " (Exod. 4 : 29-31). And " by faith ", yea, by this faith, which Paul defines in Heb. 11 : 1, " they passed through the Red Sea, as by dry land " (verse 29).

In Exod. 6 : 4 Jehovah saith, " I have established my covenant with Abraham, Isaac and Jacob, to give them the land of Canaan, the land of their pilgrimage, wherein they were strangers. And I have also heard the groaning of the children of Israel, whom the Egyptians keep in bondage ; and I have remembered my covenant ". From which remembrance we are to understand that the exodus from Egypt under Moses, the passage of the Jordan under Joshua, the occupation of the Land of Promise temporarily by the Twelve Tribes ; somewhat more permanently by Judah : and the events of the times of the Gentiles, which are all converging to a grand and awful crisis in the Holy Land, with all their correlates and details ; constitute the economy of means, instituted by the Almighty, through which he predetermined that the Gospel preached to Abraham should be manifested in its glorious consummation. This economy how vast ! It begins with the departing from

297

Egypt, and is accomplished in the setting up of the Kingdom of God, when the Son of Abraham shall come in power and great glory !

" Wherefore ", O Moses, " say unto the children of Israel, I am the Lord, and I will bring you out from under the burdens of the Egyptians, and I will rid you out of their bondage, and I will redeem you with a stretched out arm, and with great judgment: and I will take you to me for a people, and I will be to you a God . . . and I will bring you into the Land, concerning the which I did swear to give it to Abraham, to Isaac, and to Jacob; and I will give it to you (also) for a heritage ; I am the Lord " (verses 6, 8). This was the same gospel that the Lord God preached to their fathers. They should have that good land for an everlasting heritage when the promise should be fulfilled to the worthies enumerated by Paul in Heb. 11.

The Lord brought them into the Wilderness to prove them. But " they always erred in heart ". They were a stiff-necked and perverse generation. They despised the Gospel preached to them, and wished themselves again in Egypt. They murmured against the Lord, whose wonders they had witnessed in the Land of Ham. They were a people in whom was no faith ; so that, " the Lord sware in his wrath, They shall not enter into my rest ".

Now the Apostle saith of this generation under Moses, and of those Jews who lived in his own day, " Unto us was the Gospel preached, as well as unto them ; but the word of hearing did not profit them, not being mixed with faith in them that heard it " (Heb. 4 : 2). From which it is clear, first, that the Gospel was preached to the Israelites whose carcases fell in the Wilderness ; and secondly, that it was the same gospel that was preached to and by the apostles to their contemporaries.

3.—*The same Gospel was preached to the generation that invaded Canaan under Joshua.*

The Lord said to Joshua the son of Nun, " Be strong, and of good courage : for thou shalt bring the children of Israel into the Land which I sware unto them : and I will be with thee " (Deut. 31 : 23). At that time Moses was permitted to view the Land promised to him and his fathers, but not to enter it. He was to wait until it was made " a heavenly country" under the sovereignty of Shiloh, to whom he was afterwards introduced on the Mount of Transfiguration.

" Within three days ", said Joshua, " ye shall pass over this Jordan, to go in to possess this Land, which the Lord your

God giveth you to possess it " (Josh. 1 : 11). "And the Lord gave unto Israel all the land which he sware to give unto their fathers : and they possessed it and dwelt therein. And the Lord gave them rest round about, according to all that he sware unto their fathers " (21 : 43). But this was not the Rest promised to Abraham, Isaac, Jacob, Joseph, Moses, Rahab, Samuel, David and the Prophets ; they all hoped for the Rest to be manifested in the country lying between the Euphrates, Mediterranean, Nile, and Gulf of Persia according to the promise : this was the Gospel preached to them, whether actual residents in the Land or out of it. " These all, having obtained a good report through faith, received not the promise : God having provided some better thing (than Canaan as it was in their day) for us, that they without us should not be made perfect " (Heb. 11 : 39, 40).

The Rest in Canaan under the Mosaic Law to which Joshua introduced the nation was not the final rest which constitutes the burden of the gospel. Several hundred years after Joshua, the Holy Spirit said by David to his and all subsequent genera-tions, " If ye harden your hearts ye shall not enter into my Rest " : thus speaking of another rest in the Land of Promise differently constituted from that of Joshua. Let the reader study well Heb. 3 and 4 without referring to Word-corrupting commentators. Paul says, Joshua did not give them rest ; therefore, there remains a Sabbatism to Joshua, Caleb, etc. Where is this Rest ? In the Holy Land when it shall be constituted an heavenly country or Paradise. And remember that it is declared that no one shall enter into the rest who does not believe the truth concerning it.

4.—*This same Gospel of the Rest which was preached to Abraham is amplified throughout all the Prophets.*

Speaking of this, Paul says, " separated unto the Gospel of God, which he had promised afore by his prophets in the Holy Scriptures " (Rom. 1 : 1). Indeed, under this head, we may state summarily that all that is said about the latter day glory of the Israelites ; about the magnificence and everlasting sovereignty of David's son, of his throne, and of his kingdom ; of the future destiny of the Holy Land, of Jerusalem, and Zion ; of the benign and peaceful reign of Messiah on his father David's throne ; of his dominion over all nations ; of the glory, honour, immortality, and royal priestly dignity of his saints, etc.—all these, and much more, make up " the Gospel of God concerning his Son ".

5.—*This same Gospel was preached by John the Baptist, by Jesus, and by his Apostles, before the Day of Pentecost.*

John preached, saying, " Repent ; for the Royal Dignity of the Heavens hath come ! " " Now after John was put in prison, Jesus came into Galilee, preaching the gospel of the kingdom of God, and saying, The time is fulfilled (see Daniel) and the kingdom of God (or His Royal Dignity, or Majesty) is come : repent ye, and believe the gospel " (Mark 1 : 14). " I am sent ", said he, " to preach the kingdom of God " (Luke 4 : 43). "And he sent his twelve disciples to preach the kingdom of God, and to heal the sick. And they departed, and went through the towns, preaching the Gospel, and healing everywhere " (Luke 9 : 1, 2, 6).

From these texts it is plain that to preach the gospel was to preach about the Kingdom of God ; and vice versa, that to preach the Kingdom of God was to preach the Gospel. Did John, Jesus, and the Twelve preach for the Gospel, baptism into the Trinity for remission to those who believed Jesus was the Son of God ? No, they preached the Gospel Abraham rejoiced in ; the good things of which wrought in the hearts and minds of those who believed, dispositions and modes of thinking after the Abrahamic Type ; this was repentance because of the Kingdom of God.

6.—*The same Gospel was preached by the Twelve, and by Paul, after the Day of Pentecost.*

It would be easy to show that it was preached on every occasion recorded in the Acts. We are not now arguing, but declaring in as condensed a form as the subject will admit. We cannot now, therefore, go into minutiæ. Turn to Acts 8 : 12. Philip's discourse consisted of two general divisions ; first, " the things concerning the Kingdom of God ", and secondly, concerning " the name of Jesus Christ " : now mark, the first was the Gospel ; the second, the Mystery of the Gospel. See also Acts 19 : 8 ; 20 : 25 ; 28 : 31.

7.—*The grand principle brought to light by the preaching of the Gospel from Abraham to the Apostolic Era was—Life and incorruptibility through the Kingdom of God.*

The nature of the kingdom will manifest this. Read Daniel 2 : 44 ; 7 : 13, 14, 18, 27. Here it will be seen that the Kingdom is to be indestructible ; secondly, that it is not to be left to other people, or to pass from hand to hand ; thirdly, it is to stand for ever, that is, to be superseded by no other ; fourthly, the Saints are to take this Kingdom and possess it for ever ; fifthly, they will possess it with the Son of Man to whom, sixthly, all nations will be politically and ecclesiastically obedient.

Flesh and blood, therefore, cannot inherit this Kingdom ; for flesh and blood is destructible or corruptible. If, when God sets up this Kingdom, the administration of its affairs were committed to mortals, they could only retain it as they now do the kingdoms of the World ; but it is not to be left to successors, hence, those who are promoted to its glory, honour, peace and power, must be immortal ; so that when once appointed to office, being endowed with an incorruptible life, they can administer its affairs until it is delivered up to the Father by the Son at the expiration of a thousand years. This glory, honour, incorruptibility, life, might, majesty, peace, blessedness and dominion are attributes of this Kingdom alone ; to preach these things is to preach the Gospel through which incorruptibility and life are brought to light by Jesus Christ, the future sovereign of the world.

Such is the Gospel we now believe with our whole heart. Like Abraham, through the testimony concerning it, we " rejoice to see Messiah's Day ; and do see it, and are glad ". It is our hope ; the hope of our calling through Jesus ; " the anchor to our soul, both sure and stedfast, within the vail ". It is by this hope we are saved.

Does the reader believe the Gospel ; does he earnestly desire to partake in such a glorious inheritance as this ? Dismiss, then, " the vain and deceitful philosophy " of the pietists, dream no more of phantom " kingdoms beyond the skies " ; but be content to receive the word as a little child, and yield a willing conformity to the conditions of the Mystery of the Gospel of the Kingdom.

These are to the Jews a stumbling block and to the Greeks foolishness ; but to them which are called, both Jews and Greeks, Christ crucified, the power of God and the wisdom of God (1 Cor. 1 : 23).

1.—The first condition is that you believe that Jesus of Nazareth is the Anointed King (Christ) and Son of the Living God ;

2.—That according to the predetermination of God, he was crucified for believers' sins ; was buried ; and rose again from the dead according to the prophets and apostles ;

3.—That you be the subject of the same disposition and mode of thinking as were Abraham, etc. ;

4.—That you be immersed in the name of the Father, and of the Son, and of the Holy Spirit ; that you may become the recipient of repentance, and remission of sins, or, of an imputation of righteousness, through the name of Jesus Christ.

We cannot enter into detail. The Scriptures must be searched in relation to these conditions. We can only kindle up the beacon fires. The Word is profitable for all things. An enlightened believer being thus obedient to the faith, is baptized for the resurrection, for the Kingdom of God, and for all else the Gospel promises. He thus becomes an Heir of God, and Co-heir with Jesus of the world. He will " inherit all things ", provided—

. 5.—That he walk worthy of his high destiny, " denying himself of ungodliness, and worldly lust, and living soberly, righteously and godly in the present age : looking for that blessed hope, and the glorious appearing of the great God, our Lord and Saviour Jesus Christ ". If he do these things he will never fall.

29

WHAT WE MUST DO TO OBTAIN ETERNAL LIFE

THE Scripture not only teaches what the animal man is as a physical and a moral being, but what he may become. It shows that he has " no good thing in him " ; that he has no pre-eminence over other animals more than the perfection of his organization confers upon him ; and that therefore, he is destitute of inherent holiness, righteousness, immortality, honour and glory. He is a humbled creature, made subject to vanity, and at enmity against God and His laws.

These things being abundantly demonstrated both in the works and word of God, the future destiny of man as predicable upon the constitution of his nature, is that of an eternal cessation of his existence from the time he shall have mingled with his parent dust. This is the conclusion to which Revelation and Science will conduct every disciple of truth, who is independent of prejudice and party, and who has the courage to confess her in the face of ignorance, bigotry, and persecution . . .

The grand truth of God's word is that glory, honour, incorruptibility, and life are the reward of a character formed in harmony with the commandments delivered to man in the several dispensations of time under which they live. They are the reward of a good character ; a character which shall be pronounced by the Judge " without spot, or wrinkle, or any such thing ; but that shall be holy, and without blemish ". If glory, honour, and eternal life be worth the sacrifice of every thing on earth to obtain, then the inducement to a holy, righteous, and unblemished life in Jesus Christ is found in these, transcendently powerful. Carnal and blind are they who say that this doctrine is demoralizing ! We know no language strong enough to express the sense we entertain of the ignorance and perverseness of such cavillers. What stronger inducement to goodness and virtue could the philanthropy of God propose, than an unending, pleasurable and dignified existence in the eternal heavens ? If such a consideration will not lead men to " repentance unto life ", we are at a loss to conceive what will. " Fear ", says one of the terrorists, " will do it ! " But " cowards " have no fraternity with the heroes of the faith ; the scripture condemns them to the " Second Death ". Fear never made a genuine Christian yet ; no, nor ever will. The sons of God are freemen whom the truth has freed from all slavish fear. They love God with a " perfect love ", because they believe that He first loved them.

During the times between the Ascension and Future Advent of Jesus, the terms upon which immortality, etc., are offered to men, are contained in the gospel, and in that only. When born into the existing world, we come under the curse and a sentence of death ; or, as the Apostle saith, we are " made subject to vanity (*mataiotēs*, all that pertain to the state of good and evil and which ends in dissolution) not willingly ". It is in this sense that the world of mankind is said to be " condemned already "—" he that believeth not ", whether the faithlessness be predicated on physical or circumstantial disability matters not, all unbelievers are " condemned already " (John 3 : 18). Because of this congenital condemnation it is that we suffer evil from our birth, die and return to the ground from which we originally came ; but well would it be for multitudes if the condemnation which rests upon them did not transcend this. The sentence under which we are involuntarily born has no reference to the second death ; it subjects mortals only to present evil and to a return to the dust which is final and eternal to those who die in " time of ignorance ". Were there no other sentence than this pronounced upon mankind there would be no Second Death, which is the penalty, not of the Eden Law, but for the transgression of subsequent ones. And here I would make one remark for the reflection of our Universalist friends, namely, had there been no other sentence promulged than that in Eden, and had the word of Christ been simply and solely " all shall be saved ", then the dogma that to the extent in which all men die in Adam to the same extent shall all men be made alive in Christ, would have been true. But on the assumption that " he that believeth " means " all ", there is still a sentence of condemnation pronounced against unbelieving mortals, which restricts the " all " to a portion of mankind, and condemns the rest. " He that believeth not (the Gospel) shall be condemned."

Here then, are two sentences of condemnation, to which, if a man become obnoxious, he may be said to be doubly damned. He is condemned to the first death because he is " born of the flesh " ; and he is condemned to the second death if he believe not the Gospel ; but let the reader bear in mind that no mortal son of Adam is obnoxious to the second death because he is born of the flesh ; but, being born of the flesh involuntarily, he becomes liable to it by rejecting the Gospel of Jesus Christ. And this is the ground of the second condemnation, " that light is come into the world, and men love darkness rather than light, because their deeds are evil " (John 3 : 19).

What then do men need to be saved from ? First, from ignorance of God's way ; secondly, from moral perversion ; thirdly, from the evils of the present life, in body and estate ; and fourthly, from the dissolution of the grave. The " light " which God has revealed in the scriptures will save them from ignorance and its sequents, which are superstition, fear, bigotry, unbelief, etc. ; " repentance and remission of sins in the name of Jesus " will rectify their consciences ; and a " resurrection unto life ", or a transformation, will deliver them from " all the ills that flesh is heir to ", and restore them to a being which shall end no more.

" The wages of sin is death." Wages are paid only to those who labour : those who in their toil " sow to the flesh " will be paid for the labour they perform ; and the pay for this kind of labour is " corruption ", or " death unto death "— death ending in corruption, as the Apostle saith, " shall of the flesh reap corruption ", and of such he says in another place, " whose end is corruption " ; so that " death ", " corruption ", and " destruction " are " the wages of sin ", which every one is fairly entitled to " who loves darkness rather than light ", and refuses to accept the Gospel of Jesus Christ. We need to be delivered from our sins, and from a resurrection unto a second death and corruption, which shall be consummated in a fiery destruction, constituting the destiny of unbelievers, cowards, abominable characters, and whosoever loves and invents a lie.

What must we do to be saved from all these things ? The answer is contained in the saying of the King of Israel to his Ambassadors to the Nations : " He that believeth the Gospel, and is baptized, shall be saved " ; and, " Observe all things whatsoever I have commanded you to teach them ". What is the Gospel to be believed ? " Repentance, remission of sins and eternal life through the name of Jesus Christ." These are the glad tidings ; but upon what premises are they predicated ? Upon the testimony of Moses and the Prophets, that in the fulness of time a purification sacrifice should be manifested, styled the Messiah, " who should be cut off, but not for himself " ; who should be " a man of sorrows, and acquainted with grief " ; who should be " despised " ; one " upon whom the iniquity of all should be laid " ; who should be stricken for the transgression of Israel ; who should make his grave with the wicked and the rich man in his death ; whose dead body should not be permitted to see corruption ; who should ascend to the right hand of the Majesty in the Heavens, and who should sit there until his enemies should be subjected, and until the time of the restoration of the Jewish state and throne of David should arrive.

These glad tidings are also predicated upon the demonstration, that Jesus of Nazareth is the personage ; in other words, that Jesus is the Anointed One, the Son of the living God. This is the " foundation " of the Gospel itself, when taken abstractly from the testimony of the Prophets. Having laid this foundation, Paul preached that Jesus died for our sins, was buried, and rose again from the dead, as had been foretold concerning him in the ancient oracles of God ; where, as Jesus himself said, it is also written, that " repentance and remission of sins should be preached in his name to all nations, beginning at Jerusalem ". Does the reader, then, believe in the testimony of the Prophets and Apostles that Jesus of Nazareth is the anointed prophet, priest, king and Son of the living God ; that he was crucified for sin ; that his blood cleanses from all sin ; that he was buried ; that he rose from the dead on the third day ; that he ascended to heaven, and that he will in like manner come again to raise the dead and rule the world in righteousness—does he believe these things ? Then he believes that repentance, remission of sins, and eternal life are through the name of Jesus—he believes the Gospel.

But if thou art a believer of the Gospel, O reader, be mindful of the words of him, who will judge thee in the last day by the words of his own mouth ; he does not say simply and alone, " He that believeth the Gospel shall be saved " ; no, let heaven and earth be witness, he says, " he that believeth and is baptized shall be saved ", and at your peril, detract from the letter or spirit of the word. After reading this, if thou believest, askest thou what thou must do to obtain " repentance and remission of sins through the name of Jesus " ? For what purpose, thinkest thou, the Apostles commanded men to " be baptized into the name of the Father, Son, and Holy Spirit ", if it were not that they might obtain forgiveness of sins " through the name of Jesus " ? Your heart is purified by faith ; your state is changed by baptism. Hear the words, then, of the Apostle, and understand—" Repent, and be baptized in the name of Jesus Christ for the remission of sins ".

On the supposition that you have believed the Gospel and been baptized in the name of Jesus for remission of sins, do you now inquire what you must do to obtain the " glory, honour, incorruptibility, and life " of the Future Age ? The inquiry is appropriate and well timed ; for rest assured that you may have believed the gospel, and have most scripturally obeyed it, but unless you hold fast your begun confidence unshaken to the end ; unless you persevere in well doing, you had better never have known the truth. " Save yourselves ", says Jesus, " by your perseverance " ; to which Paul, by whose gospel you will be judged, adds, " God will render to every man according to his deeds : to them who by patient continuance in well doing, seek for glory, and honour, and incorruptibility ; eternal life ". Can you continue in well doing unless you begin to do well ? Can you " seek for " a thing, which you pretend to know you already possess ? No. " God only hath immortality " —with Him is " the fountain of life " ; and all the intelligences of His boundless dominion who may have this as a quality of their being, have derived it from Him as a recompence for their faithful obedience in a previous state. Are you not ambitious of the glory, honour, and tranquil dignity of these celestials ? Would you not be ravished with delight in the possession of an angelic nature, an undefiled and incorruptible inheritance, and an eternal relation to all worlds ? Strive then, that you may be " accounted worthy to attain to that Age " through " a resurrection from among the dead ", when you shall " die no more ", and " be equal to the angels of God " (Luke 20 : 36).

In conclusion : " The wise shall inherit glory, but shame shall be the promotion of fools ". Reader, be wise ; for " wisdom is the principal thing ; therefore, get wisdom ", seeing that he is happy who findeth it. Dost thou inquire what there is extant through which you may become wise ? Hear the Apostle, what saith he ? " The Holy Scriptures are able to make thee wise unto salvation through faith which is in Christ Jesus " ; and these writings teach that " the fear of the Lord is the beginning of wisdom ". Dost thou fear Him with that religious veneration which knows no torment ? Dost thou fear, or venerate Him, because thou lovest Him for His abounding goodness to the children of men ? Then

you possess the element of that wisdom, which, though foolishness with men, is " more precious than rubies " in the sight of
God ; and incomparably more valuable than all the things
you can possibly desire. " Length of days is in her right hand,
and on her left hand riches and honour. Her ways are ways
of pleasantness, and all her paths are peace. She is a tree of
life to them that lay hold upon her ; and happy is every one
that retaineth her." Be wise, then, I repeat, if you would
" shine as the brightness of the firmament " in the Future
Age ; apply your heart unto wisdom, for, in this, " the time
of the End," " the wise shall understand " " the things of the
Spirit of God ".

30

DR. THOMAS ADDRESSES HIS READERS

THE time is short, and the days are few and evil. A voice has resounded through the world, calling your attention to the fact that the dispensation of the times under which we Gentiles live is fulfilled. Whether it be consummated immediately, or within the lifetime, at most, of the generation now existing, is a question which at present we intend neither to discuss nor determine ; but from the events which we see transpiring in relation to the ecclesiastical and secular affairs of men, collated with the things noted in the Scriptures of truth, we are satisfied that the time which remains is brief, and that our eternal well-being demands that we not only believe that he will come, but that we *prepare to meet the Lord.*

Eighteen centuries have rolled away like a vapour since the banks of the Jordan resounded with the proclamation, " Prepare ye the way of Yahweh, and make his paths straight ! " This was *the voice* of the Elijah whose appearance was predicted by Malachi, crying in the wilderness of Judea ; whose mission was of God, who sent him to revive the fathers' dispositions in their descendants (Luke 1 : 17), and to bring back the disobedient to the wisdom of just persons ; and thus, *to make ready a people prepared for the Lord.* To carry this into effect, John, the son of Zacharias, commonly called the Baptist, and by the prophets *Elijah*, because he came in the spirit and power of Elias, made his appearance in the fifteenth year of the reign of Tiberius Caesar. The grand purpose of his mission was " to make ready a people prepared " for the reception of the Lord Messiah at his first coming. This he accomplished by traversing " all the country about Jordan ", announcing " the baptism of repentance for the remission of sins ", in consequence of which multitudes flocked to him from Jerusalem and other cities, " and were all baptized by him in the river Jordan, confessing their sins " (Mark 1 : 5).

This is the manner in which that " burning and shining light " prepared Messiah's way ; and made ready " a people " to receive him, giving them the knowledge of salvation by the remission of their sins. Now, ponder well, we pray you, this question ; *if such a preparation were necessary to make ready a people prepared to receive the Messiah at his first coming, is not a preparation equally demanded by which to make ready a people prepared to receive him at his second appearing ?* This is our firm conviction, and, believing assuredly that " the day of Christ " is at hand, we address you all, without distinction of name, party or denomination, in the words of sacred text :

> " Come out of Babylon, my people,
>   That ye be not partakers of her sins,
>   And that ye receive not of her plagues.
>   For the sins have followed her into the heaven,
>   And God hath remembered her iniquities."

Say not to yourselves, we are Protestants, and therefore not in Babylon. Babylon is a system of things made up of every departure from the positive institutions and practices of the New Testament. Original Christianity, which is as pure in the sacred writings as when first delivered to the Jewish nation by the Apostles, recognizes only " one Lord, one Faith, one Baptism, one Body, one Spirit, one Hope, and one God and Father of all ", but if you lift up your eyes, and contemplate the aspect of the ecclesiastical world, you will behold lords many ; faiths, or gospels, without number ; baptisms seven ; as many bodies as there are sects ; spirits of all kinds but " the Spirit of Christ " ; and more fears than hopes. The present religious system of " Christendom ", in whole or in part, can nowhere be found in the scriptures, except as " the Apostasy ", which they declare would arise, and cover the face of the nations as with a veil of " strong delusion ". The morality of the social system is vicious, giving countenance to all unrighteousness, viciousness and malice ; and judging from what comes out of their mouths, the hearts of all kinds of religionists are full of envy, deceit and malignity ; being whisperers, backbiters, slanderers, haters of truly good men, despiteful, proud boasters, volatile, and so forth ; being lovers of trifling more than lovers of God. Upon such, His law pronounces death.

This being the obvious condition of the world, is it prepared to receive Messiah ? The Scripture says that " the unrighteous shall not inherit the kingdom of God ". Now when he appears, it is to introduce that kingdom in all its glory ; therefore, the " unwashed, unsanctified, and unjustified " will have no share in his dominion, for it is such only whose characters are defined in the Book of Eternal Life, who will partake in the honours of the Age to come.

Do you inquire what you must do, that you may inherit eternal life ? That you may be prepared for him at his coming ? We answer that the scriptures teach that we must return to first principles : to those institutions which are sanctioned by the apostolic writings. We must obtain " the knowledge of salvation by the remission of sins ". This is the first step ; for having before proved that by practice as well as nature, all are under sentence of death, it behoves us first to be released from sin, that, in the act of release, we may pass from the sentence of death to that of life. The instant, therefore, that a man obtains remission of his sins, he acquires in that act a right and title to eternal life.

Do you inquire what you must do to obtain this right and title to eternal life in the remission of sins ? Permit us to quote a few passages from the New Testament in reply to this question. First, then, it is written in Mark 16 : 15, 16 : " He that believeth (the gospel) and is baptized shall be saved " (from his sins) ; again, in Acts 2 : 38 : " Repent, and be baptized every one of you upon the name of Jesus Christ, for the remission of sins " ; verse 41, " Then they that gladly received his word were baptized " ; again, in chapter 3 : 19 : " Repent and be converted, that your sins may be blotted out " ; again, chapter 8 : 12 : " When the Samaritans believed Philip preaching the things concerning the kingdom of God and the name of Jesus Christ, they were baptized, both men and women " ; again, chapter 8 : 38 : "And Philip and the Ethiopian went down both into the water, and he (Philip) baptized him " ; again in chapter 10 : 43 : " To Jesus give all the prophets witness, that through his name whosoever believeth into him shall receive remission of sins ". And Peter said, " Can any man forbid water that these should not be baptized ? " None objecting, " he commanded them to be baptized in the name of the Lord " ; again, in chapter 13 : 38 : " Through this man is preached to you the forgiveness of sins ; and by him all that believe are justified from all things, from which ye could not be justified by the law of Moses " ; again, in chapter 18 : 8 : " Many of the Corinthians, hearing, believed, and were baptized " ; and again, lastly, in chapter 22 : 16 : "Arise, Saul, and be baptized, and wash away thy sins, calling upon the name of the Lord ". Why should we darken counsel by appending comments to these simple and emphatic replications ; we will only add the reply of Jesus to the young rich man, who demanded of him, " Good master, what good thing shall I do, that I may have eternal life ? " Jesus said, " If thou wilt enter into life, keep the commandments " ; these are contained in the passages we have quoted, and in the " all things " which Jesus commanded his Apostles to teach those who were baptized in his name.

If you inquire, Is this all that is to be done to acquire a right and title to eternal life ? We answer, it is. But you will observe that to obtain a right and title to an estate is not the same thing as to obtain possession of it ; a right and title may be acquired, but under certain conditions it may be forfeited. No one can enter the Kingdom of God, or possess life eternal, without first obtaining a right and title ; though vast numbers, it is to be feared, who have acquired a right and title, will forfeit them ; and consequently never realize any share in the glory and renown of the future age. You will perceive, therefore, that in order to enjoy or possess the things to which we obtain a title by obeying the Gospel, we must also patiently continue in well-doing till the Lord comes, be that event sooner or later ; in other words, the interval between believing the Gospel and being baptized, and our departure hence, must be occupied in forming our characters after the model of Jesus ; " who is the exact representation of the character of God ", and therefore, the very best after which we can aspire. Character and not opinions will be the test of our admission into the Kingdom of God ; let us form, then, such a character as we have delineated in the Lamb's Book of Life—the New Testament ; and be assured, whether our names be repudiated by our contemporaries, or ourselves persecuted to the deprivation of the means of subsistence, we shall be invested with incorruptible life, and crowned with glory and honour in the future age.

The character we are required to form that we may realize the " one hope of our calling " must be inspirited by the truth ; that is, the law of the Lord must dwell in us, with the courageous determination to obey it, or live in conformity to it, and to contend earnestly for it, at all hazards. God must be in all our thoughts ; and our actions must be shaped with a view to His approbation alone. How will this or that be approved by our Father in Heaven, and not what will the people or their leaders say, should be the only question permitted to stand up between our conceptions and the practice of them. In short, " the grace of God that bringeth salvation " teaches us that " denying ungodliness and worldly lusts, we should live soberly, righteously, and godly, in the present world ; looking for that blessed hope, even the glorious appearing of the great God and our Saviour Jesus Christ ; who gave himself for us, that he might redeem us from all iniquity, and purify unto himself a peculiar people, zealous of good works " ; it charges " them that are rich in this world that they be not high-minded, nor trust in uncertain riches, but in the living God, who giveth us richly all things to enjoy ; that they do good, that they be rich in good works, ready to distribute, willing to communicate, laying up in store for themselves a good foundation against the time to come, that they may lay hold on Eternal Life ". Such are the things which constitute the character of the man whose religion is pure and undefiled, and who will be accepted when the Day Star shall illume the world.

When the ancients had obeyed the Gospel, they did not insulate themselves ; on the contrary, attracted to a common centre by the love of the truth, they associated themselves together into communities, that they might continue in all the things enjoined upon them by the Apostles. They met together every first day of the week, termed the Lord's day, because he rose from the dead upon that day. Being assembled, they sang his praise, celebrated his death, supplicated his favour, exhorted one another to love good works, and a patient continuance in well-doing ; they searched the Scripture, and in proportion to the strength of their affection for the common truth, so they were knit and compacted together in the bonds of love and brotherhood in Christ. Their hope was one. They earnestly desired the appearing of Jesus Christ, because they expected then to be raised from the dead ; or, if at his coming, to be transformed into the similitude of his glory. Their love was perfect ; and they loved one another in the ratio of their love to God, who first loved them ; there was no fear in their love, " for perfect love casteth out fear " ; and, unlike the worldly-minded and false-hearted religionists of this Laodicean age, as they conceived in their hearts, so with their tongues did they the truth express. In those days of primitive simplicity in the faith, they did not worship God by a proxy, whom they hired at so much per annum to preach the traditions of men ; nor did they masquerade, or " trip it on the light fantastic toe ", like an opera *danseuse* ; but they walked as becometh saints, ennobled by the truth, and destined for the good society of the Messiah's age.

In the Scripture of truth God has set out our destiny before us in the most intelligible terms. He pronounces us *sinners by nature and practice* ; and because sinners, corruptible and mortal " in body, soul and spirit, the whole person " ; as it is written, *the wages of sin is death.* This life is probationary. We are placed here to prove ourselves worthy of the destiny we may choose. " The gracious gift of God is eternal life through Jesus Christ the Lord." Which will you ? Life and Death are set before you ; will you strike for freedom from the law of sin ; or choose ye rather to fret out the " few and evil days " which may remain to you as the bondslaves of this perishing state and " die accursed " ? God invites you to reconciliation ; " Come unto me ", says Jesus, " all ye that are weary and heavy laden, and I will give you rest ". Have you no ambition beyond the mean and grovelling aspirations of this animal life ? Are the glories of personal decoration with silks and velvets, and gold, and precious stones, the choicest brilliants after which you sigh ? Is the honour which comes from vain and foolish man, corruptible and defiled in all his parts, your highest aspiration ? Is the immortality of fame with future generations the most renowned for which you long ? Fellow mortals ! Of what value are baubles such as these to tenants of the tomb ? Are the particles of dust which once rejoiced in the glory and renown of a Nebuchadnezzar, a Cyrus, an Alexander, a Caesar, or a Napoleon, more happy or estimable than those of a Lazarus ? All these things perished in the using, and now are equally valueless to all, both of high and low degree.

Being destitute of all true riches and good things by nature, our benevolent Creator has offered us " glory, honour, incorruptibility, and eternal life ", with an " inheritance which is incorruptible, undefiled, and that shall never fade away ". He invites us in the Gospel to become heirs of these things ; and, by our future conduct, to prove ourselves worthy to possess them. Would you not be arrayed in splendour which will excel the glory of the Sun ? Would you not be exalted to the dignity of associate kings with the glorious monarch of the Future Age ? Would you not be invested with an incorruptible life, that you may eternally enjoy " the inheritance in the light " which is to be revealed at the appearing of the " bright and morning star " ? Let, then, the dispositions of the ancient Christians be revived in us, their descendants ; and let us forsake our disobedience, and return to the wisdom of just persons ; and thus the Truth will make of us " a people prepared for the Lord ".

Forget the things which are behind, and press forward to the things which are before. Though you may belong to the straitest sect of popular religion, and in all good fame with its officials, " come out from it " and obey the Gospel for remission of sins, and a right to the promised kingdom. Romanism and Protestantism are forms only of " the Apostasy " from original Christianity. There is but one true and genuine religion ; all others are counterfeits. You can only be " accounted worthy " to attain to the resurrection of the just by a right and title derived from that religion. The Old and New Testaments are the only documents in which it is found pure and undefiled by the traditions of men. If you would become Mohammedans, you must study the Koran, that you might learn in what Mohammedanism consisted ; even so, if you would become Christians, you must study the religion of the Christian Scriptures in these oracles, which alone contain it. The motive, then, presented to you, by which you may be induced to " count all things but loss ", is the excellency of the things to be brought to you at the coming of the Lord. If you invest yourselves with the wedding garment, in the way the scriptures direct, and we have endeavoured to point it out in this well-intentioned address, you will be honoured to " sit down with Abraham ", the Prophets, Jesus and his Apostles, " in the Kingdom of God " ; but if the cares of this world and the deceitfulness of riches should unhappily lead you to put away these things from you and to " judge yourselves unworthy of eternal life ", there is but one thing for you ; as it is written, " the Lord Jesus shall be revealed from heaven with his mighty angels in flaming fire ; taking vengeance on them that know not God, and that obey not the gospel of our Lord Jesus Christ ; who shall be punished with everlasting destruction from the presence of the Lord, and from the glory of his power, when he shall come to be glorified in his saints, and to be admired by all them that believe " (2 Thess. 1 : 8). But that it may be your part to eschew the evil coming upon the world, and to lay hold on the hope set before you in the gospel, is the sincere and humble prayer of yours, in all philanthropy and benevolence,

JOHN THOMAS.

Love, practical benevolence, towards mankind.

desire to do good